The Essential Anne Wilkinson

The Essential Anne Wilkinson

selected by Ingrid Ruthig

The Porcupine's Quill

Library and Archives Canada Cataloguing in Publication

Wilkinson, Anne, 1910–1961
[Poems. Selections]
The essential Anne Wilkinson / selected by Ingrid Ruthig.

(Essential poets series ; 11)
Includes bibliographical references.
ISBN 978-0-88984-376-9 (pbk)

I. Ruthig, Ingrid, 1961–, editor II. Title.
III. Series: Essential poets (Erin, Ont.) ; 11

PS8545.I42A6 2014 C811'.54 C2014-905187-5

Copyright © The Estate of Anne Wilkinson, 2014.
1 2 3 • 16 15 14

Published by The Porcupine's Quill, 68 Main Street, PO Box 160, Erin, Ontario N0B 1T0. http://porcupinesquill.ca

All rights reserved. No reproduction without prior written permission of the publisher except brief passages in reviews. Requests for photocopying or other reprographic copying must be directed to Access Copyright.

Represented in Canada by Canadian Manda.
Trade orders are available from University of Toronto Press.

We acknowledge the support of the Ontario Arts Council and the Canada Council for the Arts for our publishing program. The financial support of the Government of Canada through the Canada Book Fund is also gratefully acknowledged.

Canada
Ontario
Ontario Media Development Corporation
Canada Council for the Arts Conseil des Arts du Canada
ONTARIO ARTS COUNCIL
CONSEIL DES ARTS DE L'ONTARIO

Table of Contents

Foreword

In December 1953, in her private journal, Anne Wilkinson speculated that poetry is 'a means by which certain temperaments adjust to being alive,' with 'words as a ritual for those incapable of prayer.' It reveals a good deal about the drive behind her own writing, that language provided a way of coming to terms with living in a world still very much bound by tradition, colonial ties and the privileged Canadian establishment into which she was born.

Wilkinson's close-knit family, British expats turned New World pioneers in the 1830s, had an illustrious history. By the early twentieth century, the Oslers had succeeded in attaining estates, knighthoods and a solid footing in politics and the upper echelons of Edwardian society. Although stiff values had begun to loosen, a woman's sense of self-worth and fulfilment remained confined to family, friends, and perfection in home life. To entertain any expectation of solitude, to produce art or pursue a literary career, was to entertain censure and disappointment. So, despite her unconventional education and sensitive disposition, Wilkinson, born in 1910, could not quite shed the fact that she was a product, even a reflection, of that world.

In the 1940s and 1950s, when Wilkinson wrote and published, Canadian poets were few and far between. Although still largely informed by British poets such as Dylan Thomas — to whose work Wilkinson's was, at one time, compared — the writing they produced was increasingly influenced by the surge of modernism in America and, in particular, by the work of W.B. Yeats, D.H. Lawrence, T.S. Eliot, and Ezra Pound. Canadian publishing opportunities in literary journals and with book publishers were limited, even more so for the handful of women writing poetry. Gaining the support of male peers was no small consideration in seeking recognition for them.

Given this narrow field of literary and gender-biased prospects, Wilkinson's own efforts were hardly destined to be, or be thought, groundbreaking. In fact, she believed her voice, in order to be heard, needed to blend in: 'I work to rid myself of a too marked individuality. I do not credit "originality" or "individuality" as virtues. In my case they count almost as disabilities. Certainly one must have one's own voice but it should be capable of merging with the larger voice of men (man?). Mine is too insistently me.' She was not a graduate of a university where professorial luminaries like Northrop Frye held influential court, and she did not belong to any particular established literary group such as the Montreal Group of modernists. Yet, as a woman writer whose first book did not appear until she was forty, and who published only two collections of poems before her death at age fifty, she nevertheless established a reputation as a highly regarded, anthologized, mid-twentieth-century, modernist poet. Frye, Earle Birney, Dorothy Livesay, Alan Crawley and others praised her work, and A.J.M. Smith introduced and edited her posthumously published *Collected Poems*.

The powerful polarities affecting her life are not only evident in her poems, but also in her private journal writings. In these she could be extremely critical, and entries often reveal her frustrations: 'Started work on several poems simultaneously about two weeks ago. The pattern is irritatingly familiar. The first heaven flowing rush—this is it! A week later the desolation of knowing that this not only is not "it", but is atrocious, has no relation, except for the odd line, to poetry. Then the slow laborious reworking.' She also notes, 'Have a sudden sense of impatience with the great bulk of contemporary writing of the so-called "serious" type. It (the moderns) is already academic and o so solemn. Those who attempt the simple are thin to the vanishing point. But the greater number, in poetry, are obscure, tortuous and torturing. They give the impression of poets flaying themselves into feeling; paraplegic poets cutting off their legs and begging the pain to come. I'm sick of all these harrowed little fellows dropping their guts on paper!' Self-deprecating, she adds, 'I've been a prime offender but fortunately am little read,' then goes on to log recent news of her children and social visits with family and friends. Later she writes, 'Continual contact with people exhausts my energies and leaves no power or patience for anything else.'

Wilkinson's ingrained sense of family tradition, home and nature, however, fed her creative energies. While the marital and material confines of Toronto taxed her, she found solace and rejuvenation at the Osler family's Roches Point estate on Lake Simcoe. 'Toronto is hot and parched and my ears are homesick for the sound of water and a brick house seems a prison.'

She was keenly aware that 'Woman's position in the world, even in the modern world, is remarkably inelastic. If she acquires an interest, cultivates a talent outside husband, children and house, she automatically is subject to the qualms of divided loyalties.' Torn between domestic duties and a desire to become part of the larger world of poetry, she believed '[t]o write a good poem is to achieve a kind of brotherhood with all the poets of all the ages who have written good poems, [...] with all men and women who are lit with the love of their craft. There is a high craft of being a wife and a mother but I do not seem to have the feel of it.'

In all her writings it is clear that her preoccupations and the tensions they imposed took a toll on her psyche. She doubted, second-guessed, demanded and criticized while fully acknowledging the double-edged sword of her 'desire to publish and the sense of horror at self exposure.' She grappled with her sense of isolation and of failure as a writer, as well as wife and mother. As she strove to interrelate the bonds of family and home with those of the universal, of memory, life, death and Nature, she often despaired. The realities of womanhood could not easily be reconciled with the demands of the poetic self.

Her poems can be direct in approach, incisive and unflinching in depiction of subject—'High as fear / The tightrope, / Thin as silk the string / My feet are walking walking / Since my mother cried / And the doctor cut the cord / And stranded me here' (untitled poem). Occasionally, lines flare with political and social satire—'Thermapane the windows yawn / On unexecutive underpants / Waving amputations at / Nylons in a neighbour's lot' ('Notes on Suburbia'). At other times they verge on the hermetic or mythical—'Skies in Asia catch / On uptilted wings of temples / In the Near East the talk is of stables' ('Poem in Three Parts'). However, her work ethic, as documented in the poem 'Lens', her attention to reinvention and to craft (to literary tradition and form, as well as to language's rhythm and music) remain at the core of each piece.

Critic Robert Lecker postulated that the long version of Wilkinson's poem 'Letter to My Children' reveals her poetic: 'Touch everything available / To consciousness.' For her, it was imperative to capture by way of the senses 'the quick and the dead', that is, the actual living moment, as well as tradition, memory and death. The key to achieving this was to avoid those things that limit experience or threaten a fully engaged life and to maintain a child's unrestrained sense of the elemental, of innocence and wonder. In 'Four Corners of My World', her prose piece about her childhood, she expressed in this way the difference of perspective between children and adults: 'Their [adults'] greatest offence was in regard to Time, [...] whereas we, with a more philosophical concept of the clock, knew that Time, in their sense, did not exist. [...] Slowly but certainly the enemy won, and thereby robbed us of immortality.'

She was also consumed with seeking balance amid social pressures and gender politics in an era that did not easily recognize or accommodate female self-expression. Although she stated that her poet's voice needed to divest itself of the female in order to be heard, her woman's perspective infuses the work, and does so with a singular quality.

This selection of poems, to my mind, best illustrates the essence of Wilkinson's work — the voice, wit, ear, language, sensibility, preoccupations, craft, and poetic range that fuse to identify the work as her own. They show us the places her poems inhabit, and ring with the traditions of language and literature. Allusion, music, structure, image, meaning, symbolism and inventive wordplay resonate and refashion familiar traditional forms such as lullabies, nursery rhymes, carols, fables and puns. Throughout, her toughness and honesty, as well as her belief in a freedom to be and to create, surface alongside the elemental and universal, the mythopoetic, metaphoric and metaphysical.

Although Wilkinson's output was cut short by her early death, her work remains relevant as a record of human experience, and continues to reward both engagement and close reading. Remarkably, her poetic voice seldom seems removed by time. Instead, in the way its language marks the universal, it reaches beyond 'the dead' and maintains a connection with the quickened present.

If words are the ritual of a writer who, by her own admission, was 'constantly in love with life and always on the brink of despair', the poems they shape suggest she was also capable of prayer.

I am grateful to Simon Dardick and Carmine Starnino for their support of this project, and to Véhicule Press, publisher of *Heresies: The Complete Poems of Anne Wilkinson*, for permission to reprint these poems. I am also indebted to Dean Irvine, editor of *Heresies*, and Joan Coldwell, editor of *The Tightrope Walker — Autobiographical Writings of Anne Wilkinson*, whose careful work provided both foundation and touchstone.

— Ingrid Ruthig

Summer Acres

I

These acres breathe my family,
Holiday with seventy summers' history.
My blood lives here,
Sunned and veined three generations red
Before my bones were formed.

My eyes are wired to the willow
That wept for my father,
My heart is boughed by the cedar
That covers with green limbs the bones of my children,
My hands are white with a daisy, sired
By the self same flower my grandfather loved;

My ears are tied to the tattle of water
That echoes the vows of ancestral lovers,
My skin is washed by a lather of waves
That bathed the blond bodies of uncles and aunts
And curled on the long flaxen hair of my mother;

My feet step soft on descendants of grass
That was barely brushed
By the wary boots of a hummingbird woman,
The Great Great Grandmother
Of my mid-century children.

II

September born, reared in the sunset hour,
I was the child of old men heavy with honour;
I mourned the half mast time of their death and sorrowed
A season for leaves, shaking their scarlet flags
From green virility of trees.

As ears spring cartilaged from skulls
So my ears spring from the sound of water
And the whine of autumn in the family tree.
How tired, how tall grow the trees
Where the trees and the family are temples
Whose columns will tumble, leaf over root to their ruin.

Here, in my body's home my heart dyes red
The last hard maple in their acres.
Where birch and elm and willow turn,
Gently bred, to gold against the conifers,
I hail my fathers, sing their blood to the leaf.

The Up and the Down of It

As I came down
I met a man
Going up a narrow stair.
He wore a beard and hairy
Had the gall
To swear his name was God.
'Well met,' I answered, modest,
Lowering my catholic
Appetite of eyes,
'Alone, without a witness
I'll confess: I'm Mrs. Bloom,
The loitering Moon Goddess.'
He blushed, beard, gall and all
A heavenly red
And squeezed against the wall, afraid,
And I a simple witch
With only the silky power
To stroke the bat
That flaps the shutters in his belfry.
I mumboed a humble spell
I'd learned on earth from men
On burning terms with hell
Then let God pass.
Ascending on the right
He reached his tower.
I, two steps at a time,
Jumped my way to grass.

Theme and Variation

This is the noisy silence of a tree
The rustle in the fern is the noise of fear
A twig is a nerve; it snaps the heart to pounding.

This is the swollen silence under the sea;
The hush and push of pressure soundless, sounding,
Drowning the human splash, the man-made tear.

This is the spiral'd silence in a cave
Where silence echoes itself; it echoes a jest
As a shell forever uncoils the thread of a wave.

This is the silence of love, and though the ear part
It cannot hear, it will not hear the rest,
The pause between compulsions of the heart.

After Reading Kafka

Here at my door I swing between obsessions:
Hall by day, corridor by night.
I am obsessed with exits, bound
To qualify the latitude of light,
To mourn the quantity of shadow
Beaked and flocked in flight across the meadow,

Spreading eagles on the stubble in the hall.
The hall is my terrain. I pace
Its length from where I am to who I'll be
When the sun falls from the sill;
It falls away from the window,
Window wedged in the narrowing ends of the wall;

I walk it every day, love summer months
When air and time and I are white with searching;
I name its flora, feed its fawn,
My eye is on the storm across the ceiling;
Leaking drains spread a cloud, streaks
Of hail crack and flake the paint in drifts
About the floor. I stare

Until an ounce of light and two of space
Trace a stain to the bearded face of God.
Pity him, a King, dependent now
On my erratic eye to right his halo;
He begs my eye to stay,
Begs my tongue call holy holy holy;
I yawn and as I turn he fades away.

The down-rays focus on the baseboard, spot
The dirt, the crunched and crunching cockroach, in
And on the wood in warts.
Though I remember in my head
This house where I was born, my feet forget
And pound the alleys, bruise their soles in byways
Leading nowhere from the hallowed hallway
And eyes forget their little blink of time,
The wasting of the worn thin planes of day
Flying lower, closer to the ground.

And yet, in June when time is light and big
I've come so near the end of it, if I'd a stick
I could have held the blind;
Before my last lid fell
I saw beyond the heel of Caliban to Ariel.

Light is my Love! I dallied, lost
The white years in a wink.
Do flora deera fawn breathe on?
Can they outwit the dark?
I shield a traitor
Am betrayed by the off-beat of a tock-sick heart.

Reassemble, join the scattered stems,
Fumble for an ankle in the black,
Put back the flesh; send broken feelers
Out to spy along the wall — Signal
If you touch an opening in the line to home!

Delicate as ears, fingers fest
(Walls are seeping)
Weeping blisters cry out from their tips,
Cry up up up the arm to the sky in my head;
I scold but still the blisters rise,
Hang glutinous in streamers from my eyes.

Can the wounded walk the voyage back?
Feel their door distinct from a hundred doors?
A key is cut for cunning
Is not strength to try a hundred locks.

(Did Noah save obsessions, two by two
Or did the green sea suck
At hall and corridor, deposit coral
Where the drowning drift from hide to seek?)

I tear my foot (a nail was detoured in the sun
An hour ago) but if it bleeds
I do not know, I cannot see in the dark;
The stream may be red or white or the old flood
Forcing twin obsessions into the sea
Or up the traffic'd gangplank to the ark.

The storm is gone from the ceiling;
God is not there;
I cannot comfort him, say 'let beards be'
Or smile and shave him when I cannot see.

Half-way home or where?
Fingers burn as brassy knobs rebuke them;
The key is grown, is heavy and
The python, patient, waits, across the corridor;
He does not hurry me;
We struggle, never touching skin to scale;
The end is at my door
My own two hands move docile to my throat
I choke, I splutter 'Hands!' I call them off;
I chide them, whine 'You trespass, Hands, take care!'
But they are deaf
Or death is shouting and they do not hear.

To a Psycho-Neurotic

You are each man's plight, distorted;
Therefore we cannot bear with you
Or the image of our near defeat
Written in black and white and pain
Across your face.
We stuff our ears against the wolf
That howls for thee and me.
We jolly you and say the sky is blue
And flowers are sweet and morning dew
A tonic for what ails the world and you.
But underneath we breathe
Your soul'd predicament;
We know the torture-chamber of the will
That 'will not',
The blanket that wraps 'do',
In 'do not',
We know the pressure of persisting
Will-rot.
We love and hate you; being us
You're doubly vulnerable—
Once in yourself, once in our lusty bluff.

Accept this truth:

You are no stranger in this rare assembly
Where the gods clutch bleeding heads
When the audience sleeps;
At worst you house an abdicated king
Who tossed away his crown.

Before you settle in despair
Listen, I pray you listen
To our voices; they are weak
But audible.

(We do not offer you child's comfort)

Two conditions of man are fixed:
The quick and the dead.
Beware the drowsy twilight bait
That lures a man from home
And traps him, traitor
In a stranger's camp.
Throw in your widow's mite,
Defend the quick,
Their victory is here and now
And will not shrink
Though they concede the ultimate defeat.

Lullaby

You'd sleep? Then come, I'll tell you where to go—
As angel or as eagle to a cloud;
Float, barely bruised, new-born, with lulla lulla
Rock-a-bye, white is the gull as the star
Is white and the snow.

But if I smother,
Breathe a feather
As a shroud?

Too soft? I know another place for sleep—
Love, shed your skin and throw your bones on sand;
The waves rest curled; they break with lulla lulla
Rock-a-bye, white is the foam as the fleece
Is white on the lamb.

But sand—the pain
From one small grain
Has drenched my eye.

You cry? A king! Awake to guide the dream!
In sleep the crown's awash, unwound the grief—
Come, cradle on your feet, with lulla lulla
Rock-a-bye, white is the dawn and the spray
Is white on the reef.

I was born a boy, and a maiden, a plant and a bird,
and a darting fish in the sea
— Empedocles

I live in only one of innumerable rooms
When I damp the fire with purposeful breath,
Stare at ash, sharpen
My pencil on stone at a cold hearth

Or flick the dust on good white genesis of paper,
Flocking the air with rhymes for death, soft
As the fluff of sleep or witched by broom-
Sticks, rough with rattle tall tales of bones.

Yet always I huff out the flame with breath as live
And green as Irish grass, recalling the gills
Of my youth when I was a miner
Deep in the hills of the sea.

I was a poet then. Boldly I carried my light
Through all the pressure of black water.
My blood was cold with fire for I swam
In the glimmer of a self-ignited lantern.

And I was born a boy for I bore a boy
And walked with him in the proud
And nervous satrapy of man —
Though who can hide the accent of a mother tongue?

And I was a maiden all forlorn
A long long time ago.
But the time for maidens is said to be brief
And I do not remember it otherwise —

A time of bells, with the crystal
Tinkle of grief
To indicate the supersonic moment
Pitched an octave higher than the heart's belief.

And I was born a plant. My lettuce life
Was sunny as the leaf is green.
I linger still in daymares of my flowering era—
If I blazed no light, I caught and held its sheen,

Tangled the moon in man, submissive in my flora.
For mine is a commonwealth of blood, red
And sluiced with recollection. Portage
From the sea is in the salt of my sweat,

My roots are running with the juice of stems
When pale for home they grope for a touch of earth.
Boy and maiden meander through the dendrous veins
Of everyone under the sun

But who has been a bird?
Featherless our pilots know their mammoth stretch
Pinned precarious to naked skin.
What child, from white verandah steps

Heaving his gravity with angel faith
Has not cried his tears on concrete
And on concrete learned
His kind has no primeval right to wings?

Empedocles presumed Olympic Sire;
Out of a Goddess by a God.
Beside him put his peer,
The man who stands, knowing he swam in mud.

Lens

I

The poet's daily chore
Is my long duty;
To keep and cherish my good lens
For love and war
And wasps about the lilies
And mutiny within.

My woman's eye is weak
And veiled with milk;
My working eye is muscled
With a curious tension,
Stretched and open
As the eyes of children;
Trusting in its vision
Even should it see
The holy holy spirit gambol
Counterheadwise,
Lithe and warm as any animal.

My woman's iris circles
A blind pupil;
The poet's eye is crystal,
Polished to accept the negative,
The contradictions in a proof
And the accidental
Candour of the shadows;

The shutter, oiled and smooth
Clicks on the grace of heroes
Or on some bestial act
When lit with radiance
The afterwords the actors speak
Give depths to violence,

Or if the bull is great
And the matador
And the sword
Itself the metaphor.

II

In my dark room the years
Lie in solution,
Develop film by film.
Slow at first and dim
Their shadows bite
On the fine white pulp of paper.

An early snap of fire
Licking the arms of air
I hold against the light, compare
The details with a prehistoric view
Of land and sea
And cradles of mud that rocked
The wet and sloth of infancy.

A stripe of tiger, curled
And sleeping on the ribs of reason
Prints as clear
As Eve and Adam, pearled
With sweat, staring at an apple core;

And death, in black and white
Or politic in green and Easter film,
Lands on steely points, a dancer
Disciplined to the foolscap stage,
The property of poets
Who command his robes, expose
His moving likeness on the page.

In June and Gentle Oven

In June and gentle oven
Summer kingdoms simmer
As they come
And flower and leaf and love
Release
Their sweetest juice.

No wind at all
On the wide green world
Where fields go stroll-
Ing by
And in and out
An adder of a stream
Parts the daisies
On a small Ontario farm.

And where, in curve of meadow,
Lovers, touching, lie,
A church of grass stands up
And walls them, holy, in.

Fabulous the insects
Stud the air
Or walk on running water,
Klee-drawn saints
And bright as angels are.

Honeysuckle here
Is more than bees can bear
And time turns pale
And stops to catch its breath
And lovers slip their flesh

And light as pollen
Play on treble water
Till bodies reappear
And a shower of sun
To dry their languor.

Then two in one the lovers lie
And peel the skin of summer
With their teeth
And suck its marrow from a kiss
So charged with grace
The tongue, all knowing
Holds the sap of June
Aloof from seasons, flowing.

The Red and the Green

Here, where summer slips
Its sovereigns through my fingers
I put on my body and go forth
To seek my blood.

I walk the hollow subway
Of the ear; its tunnel
Clean of blare
Echoes the lost red syllable.

Free from cramp and chap of winter
Skin is minstrel, sings
Tall tales and shady
Of the kings of Nemi Wood.

I walk an ancient path
Wearing my warmth and singing
The notes of a Druid song
In the ear of Jack-in-the-Green.

But the quest turns round, the goal,
My human red centre
Goes whey in the wind,
Mislaid in the curd and why of memory.

Confused, I gather rosemary
And stitch the leaves
To green hearts on my sleeve;
My new green arteries

Fly streamers from the maypole of my arms,
From head to toe
My blood sings green,
From every heart a green amnesia rings.

Topsoil to the Wind

We have mislaid ourselves, purposely
As a child mislays a burden;
As if in miracle of treason
Pastures willingly
Threw topsoil to the wind.

We gnaw the forked and brittle
Bone of wish and call it food,
Party every hour to murder
At the altar of our adulthood.

In aisles between the graves we waste
The landed fish, our flesh.
Our hearts, unrisen, yield a heavy bread.

Carol

I was a lover of turkey and holly
But my true love was the Christmas tree
We hung our hearts from a green green bough
And merry swung the mistletoe

We decked the tree with a silver apple
And a golden pear,
A partridge and a cockle shell
And a fair maiden

No rose can tell the fumes of myrrh
That filled the forest of our day
Till fruit and shell and maid fell down
And the partridge flew away

Now I swing from a brittle twig
For the green bough of my true love hid
A laily worm. Around my neck
The hangman ties the holly.

Little Men Slip into Death

Little men slip into death
As the diver slides into water
With only a ripple
To tell where he's hidden.

Big muscles struggle harder in the grave.
The earth is slow to settle on their bones,
Erupting into mounds or sprouting flowers
Or giving birth to stones.

And how to stand a tombstone
With the ground not quiet yet,
And what to say, what not to say
When moss is rooted and the stone is set?

Daily the Drum

If we had a keen vision and feeling ... it would be like
hearing the grass grow and the squirrel's heart beat, and
we should die of that roar which lies on the other side of silence.
—George Eliot

I

Daily the drum is burst
It is not only or foremost
The din of squirrel hearts
Or the spangled noise of grass
These are simple sounds
Like bird love,
Not the sounds we die of.

II

On the other side of silence
I can hear the bones
Of bold and trembling girls
Clacking castanets
In dance of fire and fear

And who is deaf enough
When young men cry
And hailstones break the panes
That glaze the lovers' eye,
Or terror's tin scream rises,
Not from a throat
But from the key that locks
The sickness in the mouth?

The service at our graves
Comes clear, and bells,
But who can hear
The hidden grinding mirth
When etiquette conceals
The date and nature of our death?

And every hour a child's
Black coal of trouble
Picks at the poet's ear
Sharper than any other,
For child and poet wind
A one-day clock. 'NOW,'
It strikes, 'NOW is forever.'

These are the sounds that murder.

Boys and Girls

Boys and girls come out to play
In air, in water;
All together duck, dive, somersault,
Push the waves about as if they owned
A cool blue liquid fortune;

Then, mysteriously,
For no one gives a signal,
They climb the ladder, throw
Their spongy selves on silver dock.
The pale boards darken round their bodies
Where the water runs.

The plumpness on the girls is new
And not yet of them;
Awkwardly as the farmer's boy
His Sunday suit
They wear a flounce of hips,
The prickling breasts.
Their minds have gone away to sleep
In a far country;
Nothing IS, except to tease
And nurse them into women.
They do not speak to boys unless to jeer,
And sit apart,
But out of the corners of their eyes
They look at them incessantly.

Boys are proud, groin
A phoenix, fire and ash
And new-found agony;
Minds are here, not stars away
And fine nerves sing
Like wire stretched from pole to pole
In a prairie wind;
Nowhere are they cradled

In a warmth of fat
So they must tremble, boast,
Insult the lolling maidens,
Girls they hate
Whose bodies swim in their veins,
Whom somehow they must touch.

Mysteriously, again,
For no one gives a signal,
It's water time.
Pink girls rise and run, sticky
As foam candy at a fair,
Shriek and mimic fear
When the crowing boys push
Into the quivering lake
The girls they'll kiss next year.

Poem in Three Parts

I

Those behind me
Those about me
Millions crowding to come after me
Look over my shoulder.

Together we consider
The merit of stone
(I hold a stone in my hand for all to see)
A geologist tells the time it has endured
Endurance, a virtue in itself, we say,
Makes its own monument.

We pause, resent
The little span
A miser's rule
Inched out for man

But blood consoles us
Can be squeezed from us
Not from stone.

Saying this fools no one
A sudden bluster of words
Claims for human seed
A special dispensation
Foxes and flowers and other worthies
All excluded.

Immediately sixteen creeds
Cry out to be defended—
A state of emergency exists;
Flying buttresses
Revolving domes, a spire extended
By the spirit of
A new and startling growth of thorns

Skies in Asia catch
On uptilted wings of temples
In the Near East the talk is of stables.

II

Above-below the din
A few quiet men
Observe the cell's fragility

How Monday's child
Makes Tuesday's vegetable
And Wednesday petrifies
The leaf to mineral
While Friday sparks the whole in fire
And Sunday's elements disperse
And rise in air.

III

The stone in my hand
IS my hand
And stamped with tracings of
A once greenblooded frond,
Is here, is gone, will come,
Was fire, and green, and water,
Will be wind.

To a Sleep Addict

Turn your compass from
The point of sleep.
Let the fixed pole wait.
Why hurry the traveller home?

The track is short so beat
The racing blood
For when its foaming dries
No whip can make you bleed.

The linen that covers us
At last, is cold and worms
Are hatched in shadows
Of our human arms.

Speak now

For we must hold our peace
When resurrection springs
From the crook of an ulna
And slithers through the grass.

Where Cliffs, Reflected, Cower

Where cliffs, reflected, cower
I see the image of a stranger
In a sheltered pool.

He clings to crumbling
Ledge and the clatter
Of three pebbles, loosed and tumbling,

Drowns the edgy grief
Of fingernails and the torn quick
Pleading for his life.

I hear him sigh. Fatigue lets go
And up he comes, though he comes crashing down
Where hawks are crowned, and kingly

Feed on the delicate ways of flesh
Then sharpen jaded beaks
On a jag of bone.

Below the clouds but far
Above his head the hawks are lagging.

I would cry my heart around
And stretch it to a wide red net
To catch the falling stranger in.

I'd hold him still and stunned
But safe from vultures and the titter
Of small birds

Waiting for his thud
Of matter on the ground.

But my red boasted net
Is less than air, the mesh
Too weak with words

To bear his weight
Or frighten off the plunge
Of preying birds.

Shorn of grace
I stare at the mocking pool
And throw a stone

To break the image of his fall
And my cold face
And the white gull bearing our souls away.

Nature Be Damned

I

Pray where would lamb and lion be
If they lay down in amity?
Could lamb then nibble living grass?
Lamb and lion both must starve;
For none may live if all do love.

II

I go a new dry way, permit no weather
Here, on undertaker's false green sod
Where I sit down beneath my false tin tree.
There's too much danger in a cloud,
In wood or field, or close to moving water.
With my black blood — who can tell?
The dart of one mosquito might be fatal;

Or in the flitting dusk a bat
Might carry away my destiny,
Hang it upside down from a rafter
In a barn unknown to me.

I hide my skin within the barren city
Where artificial moons pull no man's tide,
And so escape my green love till the day
Vine breaks through brick and strangles me.

III

I was witch and I could be
Bird or leaf
Or branch and bark of tree.

In rain and two by two my powers left me;
Instead of curling down as root and worm
My feet walked on the surface of the earth,
And I remember a day of evil sun
When forty green leaves withered on my arm.

And so I damn the font where I was blessed,
Am unbeliever; was deluded lover; never
Bird or leaf or branch and bark of tree.
Each, separate as curds from whey,
Has signature to prove identity.

And yet we're kin in appetite;
Tree, bird in the tree and I.
We feed on dung, a fly, a lamb
And burst with seed
Of tree, of bird, of man,
Till tree is bare
And bird and I are bone
And feaster is reborn
The feast, and feasted on.

IV

I took my watch beside the rose;
I saw the worm move in;
And by the tail I yanked him out
And stamped him dead, for who would choose
To leave alive a sin?

The pale rose died of grief. My heel
Had killed its darling foe,
Worm that cuddles in the heart
To ravish it. If worm not tell
How should rose its fairness know?

V

Once a year in the smoking bush
A little west of where I sit
I burn my winter caul to a green ash.
This is an annual festival,
Nothing to stun or startle;
A coming together — water and sun
In summer's first communion.

Today again I burned my winter caul
Though senses nodded, dulled by ritual.

One hundred singing orioles
And five old angels wakened me;
Morning sky rained butterflies
And simple fish, bass and perch,
Leapt from the lake in salutation.
St. Francis, drunk among the daisies,
Opened his ecstatic eye.

Then roused from this reality I saw
Nothing, anywhere, but snow.

A Sorrow of Stones[1]

I. SONG

In this graveyard, hedged, they lie,
A lady and her gardener.

On windless nights they rise and see,
Across the hedge, the high corn grow,
And appled moons on apple boughs
And petit pois all in a row;

Never bleeding heart or lily,
Or the pink, black-centred poppy;
Gone the wind's anemone.[2]
More than sun and rain they sought,

Not by rain and sun alone—
Petals pocked with brown and blight
Died of love one summer night;
In the rosebed, tree of stone.

II. STONECUTTERS

i

He works methodically, slow,
Chips at stone; grave hands, grave mouth;
And this his solitude: each blow
Breaks the skull and dugs of myth.
Stone in hymn endures, and yet
Stone is subject to his flint.

Plumb he cuts and fits the rock
Of ages to a garden walk;
Or dates it, stands it upright on
Grassy roof-top of a tomb.

ii

Down to pebble, now, or chalk,
Stone by daily weather worn.
Dwindles rock to grain of sand,
Waits the coming of new land
When promised bubble breaks earth's rind
With hurricane of granite wind.

III. PENELOPE

The turf she strokes above his head
She spins into his hair and beard;
Her fingers sieve the soil and rush
With quickening of their common flesh;
Stone becomes (her hand on stone)
Sweet and pact of marrow bone.

And thus the gay grave-loving nun
Whose lenient Lord has bidden her
This fitting habit, husband, wear,
Sits beneath the spreading sun
And pays no heed, cuckoo, cuckoo,
To bird or man, so she be true.

IV. WHEN A BODY BREAKS

i

When a body breaks or is
Cast off from its hemisphere
Something grave has gone amiss.
Danger, danger, everywhere.

Moon broke loose, or was she thrown
Altar high that none dare doubt
Her powers, now more potent grown,
As Helen's have, with chant and rhyming?
No man puts to sea without
Her tides' consent; and at her waning
Virgins pale, and bribe with moon-blood
Goddess of their maidenhead
Whose light can stone or warp a womb
Or send the lovers mad.

ii

It happened on a Tuesday, noon
(A body breaks or is cast off),
And being neither moon nor Helen
I fell down a well,
Commonplace abyss,
Black and waterless,
And in the falling turned to stone.

I shot through earth; now am come
Right back where I started from
In outer space,
Our point of genesis.
A tunnel travelled indicates
Some kind of birth, a milky way,
But not to me; my mouth
Is stone and sucks on meteors.

Twinkle twinkle how I wonder
What I'm falling from up yonder.
Virtue? Vice? Abstract nouns?
If vice, it is my sloth, my own,
My slug in hiding under a stone
But not under me anymore

For I am on all sides exposed
And falling down,
On through graveyards where the dead
Stars lie cold, their glitter gone.

I hail white Jupiter.
God-white Jupiter, I call,
But he is king and need not stare
At stone, except in monuments.
Venus combs her copper hair
As I come plunging by,
And Mercury, the slippery one,
Talks to redfaced Mars,
But none of them talk to me. O
Try another tongue, cry *Marduk*
Ishtar Nebo Nergal.
They pay me no heed as I drop,
No more than Sin and Shamash.

It is other than I had imagined. I thought
To travel behind two plumed white horses,
I thought to lie like cream in a long black hearse.
I had not calculated on this
Fall without end.

---

1. Country saying for a graveyard.

2. Anemones are also called windflowers.

Variations on a Theme

A man needs only to be turned round once with
his eyes shut in this world to be lost.
— Thoreau

I

There is always a first flinging
Of the blood about in circles,
A falling down, a sickness ringing

In the ear, a swivelling eye
Uprooting tree whose tendrils flower
On sagging skin of sky.

Green blades cut, they spin so fast.
Round and round, a child on grass
Whose name in anagram is lost.

II

I turned round once; I shut my eyes;
I opened them on truth or lies.
And this is what I saw though
Cannot say: or false or true.

From arteries in graves, columns
Rose to soil the sky, and down
Their fluted sides the overflow
Slid to earth, unrolled and spread
On stalk and stone its plushy red.

Trees had shed their limbs, become
Mobile marble guards. Secret
Their manoeuvres in this land;
And while they marched a mad dog's tooth,
Rabid violet, tore half my hand.

The wind blew from the south
Before I turned, but here a north
Wind blew, and I was lost. It blew
A milch cow dry, a new moon down;
Then higher roared until it blew
Seven fuses of the sun.

III

We shut our eyes and turned once round
And were up borne by our down fall.
Such life was in us on the ground
That while we moved, earth ceased to roll,
And oceans lagged, and all the flames
Except our fire, and we were lost
In province that no settler names.

IV

I shut my eyes and turned once round;
I opened them on alien air;
Sea had shrunk to farmer's pond
And sky was pink and distance near.
A forest and its nights were now
Woodpile for an old man's fire;
And where above me one black crow
Had cawed my spring, two dirty doves
Sang daintily. I stoned the birds
But no stone hit, for of white gloves
My hands were made; I stole a stick
To break the sky; it did not crack;
I could not curse—though I was lost,
Had trespassed on some stranger's dream
Where swan forswears his lust,
The gull his scream.

V

I shut my eyes and turned twice round;
Once for death, once for love.
I fell down twice upon the ground
But what I saw I cannot prove.

Death turned me first. When he had done
Black rings moved about the sun;
Love turned me next. I fell to rest
In quicksand, and was quickly lost.

Death turned me first, will twirl me last
And throw me down beneath the grass
And strip me of this stuff, this dress
I am, although its form be lost.

Untitled

High as fear
The tightrope,
Thin as silk the string
My feet are walking walking
Since my mother cried
And the doctor cut the cord
And stranded me here.

Numberless as clowns
Are my beginnings —
Teeter, crazily totter,
Windmills for arms;
The long street breathless
And I more breathless than windows,
Waiting.

But I am two times born
And when a new moon cuts the night
Or full moons froth with my
And witches' milk

I walk the tightrope
Free and easy as an angel,
Toes as certain of their line of silk
As the sturdy ones
Whose feet are curled with earth.

Letter to My Children

I guided you by rote—
Nipple to spoon, from spoon
To knife and fork,
And many a weak maternal morning
Bored the breakfast hour
With 'manners make the man',
And cleanliness I blessed
But shunned its neighbour,
Puzzled all my days
By the 'I' in godliness.

Before you turn
And bear your faultless teeth at me
Accept a useless gift, apology,
Admit I churched you in the rites
Of trivia
And burned the family incense
At a false god's altar.

If we could start again,
You, new begotten, I
A clean stick peeled
Of twenty paper layers of years
I'd tell you only what you know
Yet scarcely know you know,
Teach one commandment,
'Mind the senses and the soul
Will take care of itself,
Being five times blessed.'

With winter here my age
Must play with miracles.
So if I grant you wishes three
Scoff and say I owe you five,
Five full and fathomed senses,
Precision instruments

To chart the wayward course
Through rock and moss and riddles
Hard or soft as ether, airy
Airy quite contrary
Where will the next wind blow?

With sense alive you're wiser
Than the man who ploughs the profit
From his field,
For you, a child, still touch
Taste, smell out heaven and hell
When lying hidden
In the waves of wheat his acres yield.

I'd set your heart by relativity,
With space for slow and fast,
Set five alarms to wake and catch
The shadowless noon
Before it moves to after.

And luminous by thy dial
To read the pale
Gold numerals of dawn
Thin on the face of the midnight watch.

Your kingdom comes with senses
Schooled to top professionals;
The ear, a master bred on dissonance
Of urban sound
Will mark the drop in pitch of towns
Adrift in fog
And the lowering of evening song
When the strut is gone
From the tenor birds;

You'll shiver but you'll hear
The sharp white nails of the moon
Scratch the slate of midnight water;
Your ear will share
The loneliness of curlews crying,
Record the laugh of loons
On the delicate grooves of madness.

Before you tar with age
Swing to hot percussion jazz
Of insects, dance
To carnal charivari
Broadcast from distended throats of frogs.

And when the windy autumn blows
Hoist antennae, gather
The blazing brass of your being
To compass the ocean's scale
And crescendos
Surfed from a sea in storm.

When waves go limp come home,
Push the water in your bath and echo
On a porcelain reef
The older swell and foam;
Adjust, as seamen do on land, to gales
Blustered from a gutted shell
On a parlour mantel.

Uncage the tiger in your eye
And tawny, night and day
Stalk the landscape for the contour
Of a fern or arm,
Gorge on pigment squeezed
From barley fields
Or part the strawberry leaves

That hungry eyes may water
On the fruit and feast of colour;

Let eager pupils measure
Girth and bravado of bulldozer;
Watch the flex of iron muscle
When giant shovels
Grind their jaws and roar,
'Like Samson I can lift a ton
Of terra in my teeth.'

Speed your vision till it follows
Power and plumb of a bullet's line
From gun to heart,
Slow your eye with patience, see
The bud relax-
Ing as the petals yawn apart.

Touch everything available
To consciousness,
Birch and bark of cedar, tables
Worn to silk by women
Rubbing their restlessness
To polished wood;
Shut your eyes and feel a way
To linen and lover, marvel
At aluminum, cold in the sun
And at the thermossed fire
And chill of stone.

Touch worms and warts
In gratitude for shudders, stroke
The soft white bulge of peonies
And trace their crimson veins
Back to the milky memory of mothers;
Sharpen wit where nerve ends

Lace the skin of fingers —
Their tips will clock the pulse
Beat of a leaf—
And when by some enormous morning grief
You are undone
Feel the warm salt water
Where your eyes swim, green
With childhood
In the last sea vestiges of home.

And with a scholar's nose
Catalogue the flowers
Fighting for precedence in June,
Learn the lesson
Stinked at you from skunk or drain
And from pot pourri of
Department stores inhale
The current substitutes for love;

Smell the vigour
Packed in snow at noon and metal
In the air
When stars show up for duty
On the dim lit wards of winter
And breath is everywhere white with veils
And the vows of nuns.

Taste a thesis on your tongue,
Honey, lemon, spring sprung water
Loaded with geology.
Skin and flush of peaches, red
Tomatoes picked and bitten in the sun
All gush the juice and seed of summer
To the learned mouth.

And sense how prehistoric fathers
Weigh our modern cells with jungle genes
When huge our appetite for lean
And fat of meat
Sets saliva dreaming of the kill
A million years behind the nearest hill.

In milk and curd of cheese
Guess the whey and whyfore
Of our interval need of peace;
For bread and wine
Let wisdom on your tongue
Pause to conceive a fivefold grace.

'Sleep well' — I wonder why
We harp on sleep, our certainty.
I'd turn the message inside out
And have you listen
With immaculate ear
To what the bells of matin say,
'Wake well, my child,
Don't lie on your nose,
Today is a holy day.'

Notes on Suburbia

I. A BETTER HOME FOR THE EXECUTIVE TYPE

In treeless fields, row on row
Burgeons the ranch-style bungalow.
Thermapane the windows yawn
On unexecutive underpants
Waving amputations at
Nylons in a neighbour's lot.

II. WHAT WE HAVE DONE TO BE SAVED

Faith has come to earth again
With Tide and Bendix and a Ready-mix
Mix-master, easily converted
The (m)ad-men say (turn
Dial no. 10)
To pie in the sky or the moon's
Cool cure for sunburn.

Electric shock opens doors,
Eliminates the footprints
On the tile of floors;
Children genuflect
As TV trucks roll by
With preachers spreading news of colour
In a bright hereafter.

Babies born in this Utopia
Press their belly buttons,
Howl to God the navel's out of order
When walls of flesh won't open,
Dance or sing or dry the diaper.

Mothers need not slap or sigh,
Tear their hair or hope to die;
Mother pulls a lever, then
Dinner waddles in,
Quick frozen, pressure cooked and pressure eaten.

'For what we are about to receive'
Said the dog—
Said the cat, 'Let me be thankful.'

III. ON THE SEVENTH DAY

In six days man made this Suburbia.
On the seventh day he rested, bumper to bumper,
His chassis headed for a privy, Pisa
In the depths of darkest Canada.

Roches Point

This land rings,
In stone of its houses,
In cedar and sod,
The myths of my kin.
The long lake knows our bones;
Skin and scar and mole, sings
Them like a lover, truly.

Here eternity lit
On sunburned shoulders
Till seven cat-black summers
Stalked each other and us,
And for our terror
Deadly nightshade
Flowered in our wood.

The body still goes back
For of necessity
It makes strange journeys.
I, my being,
Shut the door against return
And in the attic pack
One hundred summers,
Seven burning wounds,
A root of deadly nightshade
And the silky waters
Where our epochs drowned.

About Anne Wilkinson

Anne Cochran Wilkinson (née Gibbons) was born on September 21, 1910 at Craigleigh, the Toronto home of her maternal grandfather, the banker and politician Sir Edmund Boyd Osler. As a member of this prominent Canadian family and as the second child of Mary Osler and George Gibbons, a lawyer from London, Ontario, Wilkinson spent her early years in privileged society. The family travelled widely, over the years visiting England, Bermuda, California, Italy, France and Egypt. Yet, she later revealed the 'four corners of my world' were the various family homes in London, Toronto, California and her Grandfather Osler's country estate at Roches Point on Lake Simcoe.

Wilkinson's education was unconventional and somewhat erratic, with a leaning to the progressive. She was instructed informally at home, through governesses, and for a brief time in a nursery school employing the Italian Montessori method, which was established and equipped by her mother in their London, Ontario house. Wilkinson, her elder brother Alan, younger sister Betty, and 'six children of family friends participated in what may well have been the first nursery school in Canada.' Later she also attended several private schools.

In 1919, when she was nine, her father died of multiple sclerosis, and her mother returned with the three children to Toronto and Craigleigh. Within five years, her grandfather had also passed away, and the Gibbons family revisited California. Her mother remarried in 1926.

Wilkinson published her first poem at age fourteen in the *Singing Youth* anthology, while boarding at the progressive Edgewood School in Connecticut. She then passed the College Board examinations, but declined the offer of a place at Pennsylvania's Swarthmore College. Instead, she attended a finishing school in Paris and travelled with family members to Italy and Egypt. Of this time Wilkinson, who had become engaged to two suitors, wrote 'we visited strange lands because of unsuitable attachments, or too many.'

Family continued to provide a level of stability after the loss of her father, but it also bound her to, and with, tradition and social expectation. In July 1932 in The Lodge's garden on the estate at Roches Point, she married the pediatric surgeon Dr. Frederick Robert Wilkinson. The newlyweds moved to London, England and lived there for a year, while he completed postgraduate medical training. They returned to Canada when he contracted tuberculosis of the lungs, and after his recovery in a Gravenhurst, Ontario sanatorium, the couple moved again, in 1934, to New York City in order to further his career.

From 1935 onward, family life engulfed Wilkinson. She gave birth to four children — only two of whom survived infancy; sons Jeremy and Alan — and adopted a daughter, Heather. In 1939, they returned to Toronto, where her husband became a surgeon at the Hospital for Sick Children.

She had published several poems in literary journals by 1946, despite demands of family, marriage difficulties and having developed rheumatoid arthritis.

Between the publication in 1951 of her first collection of poems, *Counterpoint to Sleep,* (First Statement Press, Montreal) and her second book, *The Hangman Ties the Holly* (Macmillan, Toronto, 1955), Wilkinson became seriously ill with pericarditis, and was also divorced from her husband. Not long after, in early 1956, her mother, with whom she'd always had a close relationship, died of multiple sclerosis, just as her father had. Wilkinson was unable to write anything for more than a year.

She saw herself as an outsider to the Canadian writing community, yet she was highly regarded as a modernist poet by her peers, and her work was sought after, supported and praised. Her poems were broadcast on CBC Radio's *Anthology,* and recorded on the album *Six Toronto Poets,* alongside the works of W. W. E. Ross, Raymond Souster, Margaret Avison, James Reaney and Jay MacPherson. She attended the Canadian Writers' Conference at Queen's University in Kingston; gave readings abroad; published a history of the Osler family (*Lions in the Way,* Macmillan, Toronto, 1956); became a founding editor and patron of the literary quarterly *The Tamarack Review* and published a modern fairy tale for children, *Swann and Daphne* (Oxford University Press, Toronto, 1960). Anthologized in *The Oxford Book of Canadian Verse,* her poems were also celebrated by artist/filmmaker Joyce Wieland, composer Oskar Morawetz and author Michael Ondaatje.

In 1959 Wilkinson underwent an operation to remove a cancerous lung. However, her health continued to deteriorate, and she died at Toronto General Hospital in her fifty-first year, on May 10, 1961. Her autobiographical essay 'Four Corners of My World' was posthumously published, with a memorial tribute, in *The Tamarack Review* later that same year.

Anne Wilkinson: A Bibliography

POETRY

The Hangman Ties the Holly (Macmillan, 1955)
Counterpoint to Sleep (First Statement Press, 1951)

PROSE

Swann and Daphne (a children's story, Oxford University Press, 1960)
Lions in the Way: A Discursive History of the Oslers (Macmillan, 1956)

EDITED COLLECTIONS & OTHER WORKS

Heresies: The Complete Poems of Anne Wilkinson (1924–1961)
(ed. Dean Irvine, Véhicule Press, 2003)
The Tightrope Walker: Autobiographical Writings of Anne Wilkinson
(ed. Joan Coldwell, University of Toronto Press, 1992)
The Poetry of Anne Wilkinson and a Prose Memoir
(ed. Joan Coldwell, Exile Editions, 1990)
Elegy: Voice and Piano (Oskar Morawetz, words by Anne Wilkinson, Aeneas Music, 1989)
The Collected Poems of Anne Wilkinson and a Prose Memoir
(ed. A.J.M. Smith, Macmillan, 1968)

Mentor and Muse

Mentor and MUSE

Essays from Poets to Poets

EDITED BY BLAS FALCONER,
BETH MARTINELLI, AND
HELENA MESA

Southern Illinois University Press
Carbondale

Copyright © 2010 by the Board of Trustees,
Southern Illinois University
All rights reserved
Printed in the United States of America

19 18 17 16 5 4 3 2

Library of Congress Cataloging-in-Publication Data
Falconer, Blas.
Mentor and muse : essays from poets to poets / edited by Blas Falconer, Beth Martinelli, and Helena Mesa.
p. cm.
Includes bibliographical references.
ISBN-13: 978-0-8093-2989-2 (pbk. : alk. paper)
ISBN-10: 0-8093-2989-1 (pbk. : alk. paper)
ISBN-13: 978-0-8093-8587-4 (e-book)
ISBN-10: 0-8093-8587-2 (e-book)
1. Poetry—History and criticism. 2. Poetics.
I. Martinelli, Beth, 1970– II. Mesa, Helena, 1972–
III. Title.
PN1136.F335 2010
808.1—dc22 2010000274

The paper used in this publication meets the minimum requirements of American National Standard for Information Sciences—Permanence of Paper for Printed Library Materials, ANSI Z 39.48-1992. ♾

CONTENTS

Introduction

There's a painting that Diego Rivera completed when he was thirteen years old—an obvious imitation of Monet's *Water Lilies*. Rivera's work is often associated with folk art, or with depictions of historical events and political themes. Although he is not typically considered to be a technically sophisticated painter, a scan of his juvenilia reveals other strikingly precise imitations of iconic work from various and wildly different artistic movements. Clearly, Rivera should be reconsidered. He made deliberate choices in his murals of industry and in his later paintings of rural life, in the primitive rendering of a hand or the angular lines in a body or the impressionistic brushstrokes in a bundle of flowers. Imagine how Rivera had begun, learning from the great masters, learning multiple methods to render a landscape, a still life, a human figure; from there, he discovered how best to paint his subject. He discovered his own style.

The idea that art itself can be the artist's best teacher is one of the initial sources of inspiration for this book. One would only need to read Homer and Virgil and Dante, the letters between William Wordsworth and Samuel Taylor Coleridge or Marianne Moore and Elizabeth Bishop, to recognize the long tradition of poets mentoring and inspiring poets. But the lines of influence, in a modern world, might be difficult to identify. Thus, we started our project with an open call and then later invited poets—friends, teachers, strangers whose work and approach we admired—past, present and future mentors to us all, to consider the poems that most influenced and inspired them. Our hope was to see the lines of influence within their work and, in the process, to see how they came to understand different elements of poetry. Their responses explore pace and punctuation, repetition and myth, voice, audience, and form, among other subjects. The poets then present writing prompts as well as example poems, challenging readers to discover their own insights into various literary principles.

Many of the writers here consider how one particular poem has influenced and informed their understanding of poetry. For example, in

"Recording Mortal Sight: The Drama of Prosody," Phillis Levin addresses the elasticity of blank verse by looking at a poem by Anthony Hecht, while Lisa D. Chávez turns to Jim Daniels's "How" to identify the possibilities of narrative in her own poems. Several poets also remind us that mentorship often comes from sources far outside the written world. David Keplinger looks to a city and its ancient architecture, and also to his own early theater training, as he contemplates ways to both muffle and unveil emotion in his poems. Kevin Prufer likewise finds answers to the problem of prosody in the darkness of a movie theater as he views Stanley Kubrick's classic *A Clockwork Orange*. Prufer then applies this new understanding of the potentially discordant relationships between music and meaning to the unmistakable and ever-enduring musical score of Emily Dickinson. On another note, Stephen Dunn teaches us to learn from—and mentor—ourselves, to return to our poems not as writers but as readers.

Wallace Stevens states that some write poetry "because one is impelled to do so by personal sensibility and also because one grows tired of the monotony of one's imagination, say, and sets out to find variety."[1] Drawing upon the work of others, a host of different traditions, experiences, and sensibilities, our poets (and essayists) introduce new ideas and approaches to writing poems, from formal verse to political verse, even re-envisioning concepts we take for granted, such as metaphor, reconsidered in "Lookalikes" by Stanley Plumly. They also demand that the readers expand what they know, not only to stretch the imagination but to do so with flair and craft and understanding. Deirdre O'Connor, for example, contemplates the uncanny in a lyric poem, and her writing prompt challenges readers to lose themselves, to allow the poem (and the poet) to unravel.

Section one asks readers to broaden their understanding of figurative language, image, setting, narrative, persona, and lyricism. The anthology begins with Patricia Clark's "Double Vision: The Tactic of Indirection in the Lyric Poem," which not only responds to the surrounding world but also asks the poet to create "tension through details and specifics" in a lyric poem. Stanley Plumly, Claire Kageyama-Ramakrishnan, and Victoria Chang all consider transformation through discussion of figurative language and the image, laying the foundation for Jeff Hardin's and Lisa Chávez's discussion of narrative elements. Of course, each of these writers demonstrates the rich complexities and nuances of familiar poetic elements.

For example, Shara McCallum asks the reader to move inward and, through the reinvention of myths and persona, to confront the self, and Mira Rosenthal demands that readers both dislocate and de-familiarize themselves via translation in order to heighten one's relationship to language.

While section one's essays suggest that the poet should push beyond basic poetic elements, section two asks the apprentice poet to contemplate form and structure. The essays explore blank verse, anaphora, repetition, punctuation, and white space, as well as dramatic monologue, argumentation, and collaborative writing; however, each essay inherently discusses an element beyond prosody or structure. For example, Michael Theune's essay builds upon William Butler Yeats's notion of poetry making a quarrel with the self: he asks the reader to move outward and quarrel with others. Joelle Biele's study of Christopher Smart's use of anaphora offers her a new way to order experiences and also an instrument for building humor or irony. The section ends with two essays that ask the poet to approach revision through form. In turning to terza rima and syllabics, respectively, Diane Thiel and Michael Waters suggest that structure can guide the poet to the finished draft.

Finally, the third section synthesizes what writers pondered and practiced in sections one and two by broaching the daunting subjects of voice and revision, audience, and identity. For example, Nancy Eimers offers suggestions for how to maintain one's sensibility, stance, style, signature, or "handwriting"; Angela Sorby asks us to think about the audience for our poems and the expectations for how a poet *should* write; and Maria Melendez considers the role of cultural identity in defining one's voice. Meanwhile, William Olsen encourages the writer to break with strategies set forth by one's own poem, and Kevin Prufer suggests adopting a music in opposition to the poem's tone; in doing so, both Olsen and Prufer dare the writer to challenge expectations, both the reader's and the writer's.

Together, these essays escort readers through the unexpected realms of poetry—its lyricism, its narrative, its arguments. Moreover, they demonstrate subtle and intimate relationships that continue today between writers. In reading these essays, one can witness the often private dialogue taking place as it's taking place, as one writer learns from reading the work of another. This last exchange occurs silently, unconsciously, in the simple enjoyment of another's words.

We are indebted to the Center of Excellence for the Creative Arts at Austin Peay State University for its generous support. We would also like to thank those who assisted us at various stages in the editing process, especially Stephanie Dugger, Julie Bush, and Kathleen Kageff. Finally, we are grateful to Bridget Brown for her guidance and encouragement from the very beginning.

Note

1. Wallace Stevens, "The Irrational Element in Poetry," in *The Poet's Work: 29 Poets on the Origin and Practice of Their Art*, ed. Reginald Gibbons (Chicago: University of Chicago Press, 1979), 48–58.

ONE

Double Vision: The Tactic of Indirection in the Lyric Poem

Patricia Clark

No doubt I'm not alone in remembering a comment by former U.S. poet laureate Robert Pinsky, perhaps on one of the evenings he appeared on Jim Lehrer's *NewsHour*, concerning political poems or poems penned in response to war and a particular evil. He said usually the best such poems were written—I'm paraphrasing here—"long before the event happened." I was tantalized by his comment even as its essential correctness struck me. Of course, one expected him to say "long *after* the event took place," shades of William Wordsworth and "the spontaneous overflow of powerful feelings."[1] The idea that a poem written long before the event could "respond" to the event better than one closer to its time intrigued me. Now it is spring in Grand Rapids, Michigan—and the more I mull over Pinsky's comment, the more it points to what I think is an essential part of lyric poems, and that is the use of indirection. By illustration and discussion, then, I offer two poems to consider.

One of my own poems, first. It's titled "Riverside Ghazal" and it appears in my second book of poems, *My Father on a Bicycle*. I use this poem as an example because readers and audiences at readings have often, mistakenly, assumed that the poem was written in response to the September 11, 2001, attacks in the United States. Here is the poem, in full:

> Most watery of all the trees, these willows
> stand in water. Ice pools around the ankles of willows.
>
> A tree's name should reveal its nature.
> *Salix babylonica*: the first word is for willow.
>
> Doesn't it sound stretchy and pliable?
> *Babylonica* is for the weeping part of willow.

From a quotation in Psalms: by the rivers of Babylon
we wept. The people hung harps on willows.

The weight gave them a bent, permanent shape.
A girl flings her hair down, a young willow.

A golden color, like a shout, all the length
of the fronds. They light up the willow.

Nearby on the concrete ramp, an ice-filled boat
waits for the sun to unmoor it, sail it past the willows.

In the season of thaw, this ice giving way.
By the rivers of America, we wept these willows.[2]

When I try to locate, now, the reasons that a reader might assume this poem is about September 11, I look first to the poem's last line. That the poem is ostensibly about willows, about something seen along a river—perhaps in one of many large and medium-sized cities all across our country, from Missoula, Montana, to Pittsburgh and Chicago—is not lost as the poem concludes but heightened and made symbolic. Yes, there are earlier references to weeping, but that comes both from the poem's mood and from the image of the willows. The idea of a people in mourning, the people of Babylon, is probably what caused me to write—and I do remember quite precisely the surprise of the word coming out from my pen—the word "America." It isn't a word I have used in other poems. It was pre–September 11, even pre-2001. Other sad elements had worked their way into the urban landscape that I saw before me. The poem spoke, in indirection, to a soul-weariness all across our land.

The second poem for illustration is Stanley Plumly's "Lapsed Meadow." The poem is organic, not people-filled, though people are mentioned, especially the people of Ohio, and farmers, along with "plows and pasture." A reader arrives at the poem's ending to find, surprisingly, a dedication there: *for James Wright*. In truth, organic or not, "Lapsed Meadow" is an elegy and an especially brilliant one, I feel, in its tight adherence not to address or allude to the elegized person (Wright) but to stay, instead, focused on the ostensible subject: a lapsed meadow and a solitary apple tree in its midst. Nevertheless, an elegiac tone permeates the poem, and the reader senses this long before noticing the dedication.

The figure of the apple tree is the objective correlative that works the poem's magic. Reading the poem over, I notice again Plumly's skill. The poem, in miniature, imitates what the poet does: appears to focus on something but instead veering, returning, elegizing something else. The poem is called "Lapsed Meadow," after all, yet the poem can't leave the tree alone, returning to it in conclusion as the writer must. The tree stands by itself alone in a field, forgotten and ignored, pugilistic almost in how it is "bare-knuckled" (sure, the pruned branches end in a knuckle but also a foreshadowing personification) and—James Wright's own word (if ever a poet can *own* a word)—"blossoming."

The apple tree is a low-growing one and thus is taken over by the meadow it should rightly tower above. A democratic tree, then, so low indeed that the meadow rises up to join it: "by fall it looked / like brush among burdock and hawkweed." The people of Ohio seem to want their nature to have its use, or usefulness; when it runs wild, as it does in this meadow, they call it "a waste of nature." A waste, the poet indicates, only for some. He, by contrast, finds some wisdom: "And true, / you could lose yourself / in the mind of the thing." This is no waste, then, but verdancy, and room to roam and think, what a poem knows is the opposite of waste. The heart of the matter is that the lapsed meadow sounds a lot like poetry—something not valued highly by the commercial world but extremely valuable to those who care, who revel in its roominess.

The poem comes to celebrate the apple tree, the meadow, and, by inference, James Wright for sheer persistence, and the poem's epiphanic conclusion states it well:

> But I call it crazy
>
> the way that apple,
> in the middle of a field, dug in, part of the year
> bare-knuckled, part of the year
> blossoming.

The indirection of Plumly's poem is of a different type than in the previous poem. Plumly's poem signals elegy first with its tone but then with the dedication. Without the dedication, the epiphany would remain, I think, but appear to celebrate holding on and persistence, not a particular person. Two kinds, then: one, indirection by virtue of preceding its reference, and second, indirection by *not addressing* the elegiac subject at all. In both cases, I would credit the writer moving beyond the "triggering subject" (to use Richard Hugo's term) for the surprising insight of their separate conclusions.[3]

I imagine that there are many groupings of types of indirection—and it would be instructive to have student writers locate some themselves. There is irony in pointing young writers along the road to indirection as they—hopefully—begin to figure out what some of their own poems are about, after struggling to tell the detail well and accurately. Now, throw them a curve and ask them to write about X by looking at Y. Paradoxical, isn't it? Yes, and no. Sometimes the direct glance isn't the way to find the object: the deer in the woods, the song sparrow among the branches, the earring dropped in the grass. Blur your eyes a bit, and bam, the thing shows right up.

Though the complexities and rewards of this lyrical tactic may seem obvious, let me offer a few notes of reinforcement as well as encouragement. First, any attempts made by a writer to look around, closely, at the world at large will have tremendous payoffs in his or her writing. Certainly the texture of one's writing is affected. Another concrete reward is that tension is added in one's writing by this kind of double-seeing. When the narrative itself may be lacking in tension, the indirect view of another landscape is a way of adding tension through details and specifics. The complexity of this type of seeing often accurately duplicates how we see the world anyway—this simply highlights it somewhat. How often have you realized that the dark day you have just lived through, or the "monsters" you saw today as you rode the bus to work, were there precisely because you had had a monstrous night at home and now viewed the world through that lens?

Finally, the more one studies the world around one or looks at art, history, or architecture and writes about these subjects, the more one's vocabulary and vision of the world have to grow. A wonderful side effect of indirect writing is a burgeoning vocabulary rich with botanical terms, architectural elements, or painterly details and colors. Let's celebrate growth.

WRITING PROMPT

Free write first: locate an incident involving strong feeling (perhaps a significant loss or a long-ago anger, joy, or incident that still calls forth a wealth of mixed feelings) and write out the details of what happened, using as many sensory and particular details as possible.

Write Stanley Plumly's poem in longhand. Be watchful while you write out the sentences and words of others. What do you notice? What do the details suggest beyond the visual? What mood is starting to be created? Where do hints of feeling for James Wright emerge in a poem ostensibly about a tree and a lapsed meadow?

Now: make a visit to a local art museum or gallery. Or, lacking such opportunities, turn to a postcard of a work of art or a landscape recently visited. Then, on a later writing day, go on to describe the art or landscape, thinking about the above-mentioned incident but refusing to refer to it.

LAPSED MEADOW / *Stanley Plumly*

Wild has its skills.
The apple grew so close to the ground
it seemed the whole tree
was thicket, crab and root—

by fall it looked
like brush among burdock and hawkweed;
looked as if brush had been piled,
for burning, at the center.

At the edges, blurred,
like failed fence, the hawthorns, by
comparison, seemed planted.
Everywhere else there was broom

grass and timothy
and wood fern and sometimes a sapling,
sometimes a run of hazel. In Ohio,
some people call it

a farmer's field, all fireweed
and thistle, a waste of nature. And true,
you could lose yourself
in the mind of the thing,

especially summer, in the full
sun or later, after rain and the smell
of rain—you could lose
yourself, waist- or head-high,

branch by leaf by branch.
There could be color, the kind that opens
and the kind that closes up,
one for each part

of the light; there might
be fruit, green or grounded—it was always
skin-tight, small and hard.
There would be goldenrod

still young or yellowing
in season, and wind enough to seed a countryside
of plows and pasture.
But I call it crazy

the way that apple,
in the middle of a field, dug in, part of the year
bare-knuckled, part of the year
blossoming.[4]

for James Wright

Notes

1. William Wordsworth, "From Preface to Lyrical Ballads," in *The Norton Anthology of English Literature*, 7th ed., vol. 2, ed. M. H. Abrams (New York: W. W. Norton, 1999), 242.

2. Patricia Clark, *My Father on a Bicycle* (East Lansing: Michigan State University Press, 2005), 24.

3. Richard Hugo, *The Triggering Town: Lectures and Essays on Poetry and Writing* (New York: W. W. Norton, 1979), 11.

4. Stanley Plumly, *Summer Celestial* (New York: Ecco Press, 1983), 14–15.

Lookalikes

Stanley Plumly

You might call this a descriptive report, which means that its signal ambition is to paraphrase the content—that is, the contents—of a poem entitled "Simile," a poem that appears in a new collection called *Old Heart*. I'm certain, in the space available, that I'll not have enough room to say all that might be said: not because my poem as a text is infinitely inexhaustible (a redundancy?) but because all texts—at least as understood by postmodernism—are apparently inexhaustible subjects, objects, and window glass darkly.

I'm trying to limit myself by use of the term "descriptive"—or what is visible and touchable as opposed to what is not. In a way that transcends issues of "isms" and interpretations, I'm looking to present the imagination of the literal in a more personal sense: how the mind and heart in good time acquire such matters as experience, information, knowledge, wisdom, gravity, guilt, fear, anger, loss, longing, and so on down the litany—acquire and attach these invisible things to visible things in order to make metaphor. Make *from*, as I've often said, not *up*. It's this personal, idiosyncratic, individual text of the assembly of who we are that is the truly inexhaustible in poetry.

SIMILE

This heart I found at lowtide this morning,
accurate to a fault, hand-sized, heart-shaped,
with the thick weight of a heart, a perfect
piece of limestone cut by hand by the sea
who knows how long, brought up from the bottom
again and again, split like our own hearts,
nicked from the top half down, as if in another
life it had been real, stone atrium, stone sorrow,
stone ventricles, stone arteries and veins.

And these glittering halves of oyster shells
I picked this afternoon, like the stones
worn into shape, swirled, half-eaten-out, still
oiled and pearly-wet, with edges sharp enough
to clean a fish. Imagine that the oysters
have survived, like the eyes of the otherworldly
or symbols of some sexual potency, look-alikes
for testicles or a woman's soft insides,
as we drink them down by swallowing them whole. . . .

In the doctrine of signatures things become
themselves as something else, as we are who
we are word of mouth. Then I found a bird,
a kind of gull, eaten by the fish and other birds,
one missing wing, one eye, the rest of it
so rendered past resemblance you throw it back,
into the void, the chaos it came from,
yet the moment it goes under it's a memory,
a metaphor, we say, for what we can't quite

name, tip of the tongue, whistle in the bone,
death in its variety, its part-by-piece detail.
Like the skull washed up one lost-and-found
new year, fallen from the ocean sky,
dead off the moon, something to conjure with,
now set on the desk on the bony back of its head,
neither human nor animal but brilliant white
brain-coral, pitted, scalloped, furrowed
at the brow, its stone, teardrop-shaped face

a mask for mourning. Unlike the shapely clouds,
changeable, emotional, a skein of moving mare's
tails, a skimmer's broken wing, cumulonimbus
palaces where once-and-future beings act out
their human longing. I went down to the sea,
the source of life, it was filled to overflowing.
The blue horizon line, however many miles,
parted nothing more than air from bluer water,
though it was poetry to say what it looked like.[1]

The "doctrine of signatures" is an ancient medical concept updated through the practice of medieval and romantic medicine and corrupted in modern times into something like a quid pro quo of resemblances, in which, for example, a walnut cracked open looks like the cerebral cortex, suggesting—literalizing, actually—that eating walnuts will make you smarter. And what do oysters resemble? Hence their fabled powers as an aphrodisiac. Such "signs" from nature derive originally, it's thought, from the Hippocratic method of reading real signs of illness and applying medicinal herbs. Language, as another kind of signing, has its history lodged in similar transformations of metaphor and simile.

Resemblances are our masks for meaning, even the way in which words themselves are masks. What interests me, always, is the source of the mask, the thing that resembles another thing, the way an image resembles the idea of it. This poem "Simile" is based on objects I actually found at the beach at different times—washed up, as it were. "Washed up" in every sense, since each had the wear and tear of the timeworn or time-torn. Including the broken, breaking shapes of clouds moving from land to sea or the other way around. I "found" in each of these objects, these things, a correspondence in my own literal experience—resemblances, figures of connection. What else is there for the contemplative mind except making connections—the actual to the thing it is like? Metaphor, thus, perceptual first of all, conceptual, perhaps, later. The image becomes, in its own good time, an idea: the image, at that point, being an idea with a body. Poetry is what we say something is in all its "is-ness" because that something becomes, at the same time, something else.

Note

1. Stanley Plumly, *Old Heart* (New York: W. W. Norton, 2007), 39–40.

Beauty and Its Opposite Conceit

Claire Kageyama-Ramakrishnan

Dante had Beatrice; Petrarch coveted the fair, chaste, and unattainable Laura; and Shakespeare bred difference into the life of his Dark Lady. As Beauty's opposite, his darkly complected beloved, with wiry strands of black hair, epitomized the antithesis of qualities Laura possessed. The Dark Lady became, as some critics have suggested, a reinvention of idealized Renaissance conceits. While the point is nothing new, the poems seemed *new* to me then, when I first read them. During my first semester in college, I discovered Shakespeare's use of conceits, or Petrarchan inversions. To this day, I still hold deep affection for Sonnet 127 and Sonnet 130, poems that speak more to me now, as a poet in my late thirties, writing my own poems and working through themes of affectation and affliction, beauty and the Protean attainment of it. Shakespeare taught me to use hyperbole, oxymoron, metaphor, influence, and paradox. But more important, he convinced me of the Dark Lady's beauty, of an aesthetic to weave into the fabric of my own writing.

Sonnet 127 invokes a history of illegitimacy and adoption and attempted erasure. Nature conceived the face of natural beauty; human beings took hold and distorted it, so that natural became unnatural. The face of Nature evolved for a time as masquerade and artifice, a bastardized version of ill-effected beauty, when Elizabethan-style makeup and accessories hid the beloved, making it impossible to distinguish between the beloved's natural and made-up features:

> In the old age black was not counted fair,
> Or if it were, it bore not beauty's name.
> But now is black beauty's successive heir,
> And beauty slandered with a bastard shame;
> For since each hand hath put on nature's pow'r
> Fairing the foul with art's false borrowed face,

Sweet beauty hath no name, no holy bow'r,
But is profaned, if not lives in disgrace.

Historically, a dark lady wasn't ideal, neither equated nor associated with the aesthetics of beauty. Her lineage was one of omission (her emergence starting with Sir Philip Sidney's dark-eyed Stella). The old way of looking at beauty succumbs completely to a different possibility with the debuting of the dark Shakespearean beloved and a speaker who channels our gaze, with iambs and rhyme, to the lady's blackened hair and eyes, darker bosom, questionable ethos: a tanner and blacker beloved, neither chaste nor free of bodily odors and earthy accoutrements. The turn away from blonde beloved is merely suggested, never explicit, with the succession of the darker "heir" finalized in the last quatrain:

Therefore my mistress' eyes are raven black,
Her eyes so suited, and they mourners seem
At such who, not born fair, no beauty lack,
Sland'ring creation with a false esteem.

The sonnet ends with closure and acceptance of the changed standard in the couplet:

Yet so they mourn becoming of their woe,
That every tongue says beauty should look so.[1]

The consensus ("they") agrees with the oxymoron: the blacker beauty, though she *is* beautiful to the speaker, is homely. The relinquishment of the previous "fair" beauty leads to suggestions of bereavement and complicity to embrace the paradigm shift.

The adoption of the dark beloved at the end of Sonnet 127 has primed her to be anything but ideal in Sonnet 130. Once more, the Dark Lady is the antithesis of graceful, refined, gracious, melodious, and lithe. She possesses neither Greek symmetry nor balanced architecture nor Aristotelian beauty of utility.[2] She is quite the opposite of the Petrarchan beloved or the ones that other English sonneteers exalted and exaggerated in their poems. She resembles all that the other beloveds are not:

My mistress' eyes are nothing like the sun—
Coral is far more red than her lips' red—
If snow be white, why then her breasts are dun—

If hairs be wires, black wires grow on her head:
I have seen roses damasked, red and white,
But no such roses see I in her cheeks,
And in some perfumes is there more delight
Than in the breath that from my mistress reeks.
I love to hear her speak, yet well I know
That music hath a far more pleasing sound.
I grant I never saw a goddess go;
My mistress, when she walks, treads on the ground.
  And yet by heav'n, I think my love as rare
  As any she belied with false compare.[3]

Neither dreamy and ethereal, nor gorgeously bejeweled with sapphire or emerald eyes, without hair falling in scintillating tendrils, the Dark Lady has arrived. The absence of a Petrarchan prototype means the blonde goddess has surrendered her velvet gown and relinquished her pearlescent teeth, rosy cheeks, and voluptuous, cherry-skinned lips. Into the closet she goes with her much sought-after wig.

And in my own work, the Dark Lady has turned into "The Denver Lady":

I remember the Denver Lady well.
She sewed me
a cushion out of terry cloth
and autumn-colored yarn.

I remember her hair—
Damascus-steel bun,
her beauty
beneath her cage of bones.

I remember a blue spot on
her face, her wrinkled cheeks smoothed
when she smiled her
ginger-stained teeth.

She sang to me one night,
Go ne ne, go ne ne.
When she turned senile,
she still had lids,

lavender like mother-of-pearl.
The Denver Lady
is the woman standing
in the middle of Sawtelle

clutching a twisted maple stick,
a purple chrysanthemum
tucked in the waist
of her butterfly kimono.

She doesn't remember
the child I was.
She doesn't know
the woman I've become.[4]

Neither young nor beautiful in the standard Western sense, nor "black," the aged beloved is Issei, or a Japanese immigrant, situated in West Los Angeles. A caregiver, possibly a grandmother, great-aunt, or friend who is like a grandmother, the Denver Lady has "lavender" epicanthic lids and "ginger-stained teeth" rotting and falling out. Her flaws are markers the child remembers her by, with repetitive phrasing ("I remember . . ."). The child's voice merges with the adult's, and the result is a more mature individual who knows grief because she has felt it. Matrilineal and maternal legacy are both unrequited love, Beauty and its opposite. The child's affection for the woman cannot be reciprocated. The old woman who once cared for the child has succumbed to old age, senility, the disease of Alzheimer's. Despite this, the child turned adult still recognizes the Denver Lady's remarkable interior and exterior beauty. What's more, she knows the Denver Lady doesn't possess the kind of beauty that society warmly embraces. The Denver Lady was never the epitome of what society considered beautiful. The Dark Lady–turned–Denver Lady is now a woman of color whose tan and wrinkled skin bears "a blue spot," gradations of discoloration, hair that reminds the speaker of the wavy patterns of Damascus steel. Then again, wasn't the Dark Lady always a woman of color, a muse who inspired us to create our own fictions?[5]

WRITING PROMPT

It's time we all stepped out of the closet, in this age of lasers, hair extensions, Restylane, virtual reality, and digital enhancement. It's time to seize the natural beauty in our lives. Here I invite poets to observe and explore their natural surroundings. Write a poem of any size and length. Consider the following question: What do you find beautiful in your life that others don't? To start, you might look closely at a tree, insect, animal, or landscape. Or you might consider how a person you know is beautiful in an unusual and unexpected way. In the early stages of writing rough drafts, you can jot down images of what you encounter with your eyes and imagination. For instance, Shakespeare's speaker tells us how the Dark Lady looks, smells, sounds, and walks. In my own poem, my speaker celebrates the Denver Lady's flawed facial features, suggesting through a series of stanzas why the old woman is worth remembering. Whatever you choose to write about, you should convince your reader that what you are describing is beautiful to you although it may be ugly to someone else.

Notes

1. Sonnet 127, *Shakespeare's Sonnets*, ed. Stephen Booth (New Haven: Yale University Press, 1977), 110.

2. I am indebted to Denea Stewart-Shaheed for drawing my attention to the Greek perspective of beauty.

3. Sonnet 130, *Shakespeare's Sonnets*, 112.

4. Claire Kageyama-Ramakrishnan, "The Denver Lady," *Shadow Mountain: Poems* (New York: Four Way Books, 2008), 15–16.

5. My English 1302 students, especially Reginald LeDoux, felt that the Dark Lady was black—a black person with black hair—despite Stephen Booth's note that Shakespeare used black to describe her "brunette" hair. In his notes to Sonnet 127, Booth writes, "[T]he speaker's relationship is to a brunette, who is, therefore, not 'fair' in that she is not blonde, and who is also not 'fair' in that she is morally foul" (*Shakespeare's Sonnets*, 434).

The Arresting and Fluxing Image

Victoria Chang

In the poem "Portrait with Commentary," Tomas Tranströmer, a Swedish poet and psychologist, calls a newspaper "that big dirty butterfly."[1] Tranströmer's image is both stunning and memorable. In another poem, "About History," he likens anonymity to an unexpected image: "anonymous as grains of rice."[2] While reading Tranströmer's poems, one is immediately and continuously struck by such images. In "The Half-Finished Heaven," a lake "is a window into the earth."[3] In "Vermeer," gold studs in a chair "flew in with incredible speed / and stopped abruptly / as if they had never been anything other than stillness."[4] In "Storm," constellations are described as "far above the oak / stamping in their stalls."[5] In "Lament," the "moths settle on the windowpane: / small pale telegrams from the world."[6] In "Early May Stanzas," he observes "[i]n the silent pools, midge larvae—their dancing furious question marks."[7] And although seemingly impossible, there are many more images as startling as these.

At the most obvious level, Tranströmer's images are arresting because they are oftentimes surprising. But surprising images alone would not make Tranströmer's poems truly memorable; rather, the manner in which he transforms images is what renders his poems both memorable and appealing. His poems are particularly powerful because his images are always in flux—they both stretch and morph and at times have tremendous velocity. But the morphing and movement of images also serves a greater purpose—to function as the medium or channel that Tranströmer uses within his poems to travel across conventional boundaries of time, space, the self, and consciousness. Tranströmer, like many poets, is a seeing poet, one who hones in on the image, but unlike many poets, his eyes and mind never rest too long on any particular image. When he observes, he always sees beyond what's immediately in front of him, from the seemingly banal to the infinite. Tranströmer's way of seeing, through a mobile image, stretches his poems beyond our immediate canvas of the knowable world into the mysterious and the unknown.

In "Along the Radius," themes of individual insignificance and the unknown appear readily. The title itself raises a series of mysterious questions—what radius, who or what is along the radius, and what is happening along the radius? The poem is divided into three sections where the first section provides the context, the second section articulates the speaker's stretching and wandering mind, and the final section returns to the thoughts relayed in the first section, but something has changed.

In the first section, Tranströmer establishes the physical setting and introduces the first-person speaker:

> The ice-bound river is blazing with sun
> here is the world's roof
> silence.
>
> I'm sitting on an upturned boat on the bank
> swallowing the drug of silence
> spinning gently.

These first two stanzas appear deceptively motionless and silent; in fact, "silence" occurs twice—once in each stanza. But upon closer investigation, the "ice-bound" river is "blazing with sun" and the speaker is "spinning gently." Even in the first section of the poem, things are already beginning to spin, stretch, and change. And not only has the "ice-bound river" naturally morphed already from a previously flowing body of unfrozen water, but in the second line, the river stretches beyond its frozen tundra to instantaneously become "the world's roof." Such rapid changes allow Tranströmer's images to grow beyond their respective selves.

In the second section of the poem, the images exhibit their most bendable moments.

> A wheel spreads out endlessly, turns.
> Here is the center, almost
> still.
>
> Further out, perceptible movement: the steps in the snow
> the writing which shuffles along
> the facades.

It's as if the speaker is resting at the center of a metaphorical wheel. The trope of a wheel seems like a disjunctive leap from the first section, but it can be seen as an alteration of "silence / spinning gently" in the prior stanza; instead of silence spinning, we now have a "wheel" that spins. But this wheel "spreads out endlessly," and instead of the first-person speaker who sits on an upturned boat on the bank, the speaker in the form of "I" disappears from the poem and becomes a less self-conscious, less self-absorbed observer. Even the self has changed; even the self has a roving eye that can roam from interiority to exteriority.

As the wheel keeps getting larger and larger, it expands at its outer edges beyond space, time, the known self, and consciousness. Initially, the image of the wheel stretches into the more physically tangible and conventional images such as "the steps in the snow," "the writing which shuffles along / the facades"—which, although unspecific, could be any literal writing (letters, graffiti, and the like)—or "the rumbling traffic on the highways," which is a very specific and literal image of cars and trucks motoring along on freeways. But as the wheel becomes more amorphous, odd images begin to appear—"the silent traffic / of ghosts," for example. Suddenly, the poem has shifted from tangible, conventional, and mostly physically imaginable images to less tangible images or the shadows of images—the unseen. The poem's images stretch even further, and in fact, in this second section, Tranströmer uses the literal phrase "further out" three times. The "silent traffic / of ghosts" stretches to "the tragic masks in the headwind / in the whine of speed," and the headwind extends further to

> the rush
>
> where the last words of love evaporate—
> the drips that creep
> on the steel wings—

Note the appearance and increase of dashes as the poem continues its widening, as if the words themselves need hooks to fasten themselves to each other as they begin to lose contact with the tangible. In the second half of the second section, there are five dashes alone. Tranströmer even returns to earlier images such as the "steel wings" that echo the "rumbling traffic" or the metal automobiles on the highway. But now, the automobiles have become a new image or a plane with steel wings. And the plane isn't any ordinary plane—it's a plane flown by a kamikaze pilot who is likely dead:

> where the last words of love evaporate—
> the drips that creep
> on the steel wings—
>
> profiles that cry out—the suspended headphones
> chatter at each other—
> kamikaze!

The pilot is never physically embodied, but his existence is simply implied by the chattering headphones that no longer have ears attached to them. Similarly, the people targeted by the kamikaze plane and pilot are bodiless. They are "profiles that cry out." By the time the reader confronts the kamikaze pilot and plane, the poem's images have stretched drastically: from the "ice-bound river" and the wheel that began the second section to a bodiless plane.

But for all of Tranströmer's desires to avoid stasis, he is a poet who seems to resist permanent change; he resists what he seems to be cultivating. His speakers live within this contradiction, and thus his poems often evoke a sense of flux. In "Along the Radius," the poem returns to where it began, but the speakers or the landscape is transformed. In the third section of the poem, we return to the "ice-bound river," but the river now "glitters and is silent." In the first section, the river is "blazing with sun / here is the world's roof / silence." The adjustments are seemingly minor, but they are significant. The new river is silent, whereas the old river was merely a part of silence. The new river acts—it "glitters," whereas the old river "is blazing" with something instead of simply "blazes." There's transformation here, in natural spirit and in Tranströmer's language.

Beyond the morphing of the river, silence gains control and power in the final section of the poem. In the first section, the speaker is "swallowing the drug of silence," but in the final section, silence "paints over" the sound of the speaker's footsteps in the snow: "My steps were explosions in the ground / that the silence paints over / paints over." Silence becomes larger than humans and diminishes the significance of humans.

The classical view of the image was one where an image represented the actual object being described—art as imitative. The modernists viewed the image differently. Their image had iconographic value that went beyond the actual thing itself. In the contemporary world, we think of an image as derived in some way from Ezra Pound's famous dictum, "An 'Image' is that which presents an intellectual and emotional complex in an instant of time."[8] Pound's "intellectual and emotional complex" implies that both mind and body/soul can coexist in an image and in the greater poem. But the device of image in Tranströmer's poems often expands upon Pound's model. Image, in many of his poems, is reassessed and repackaged into other images or more pliable versions of the original image, all in greater service to Tranströmer's distortions (whether of time, space, the self, or consciousness).

One of the definitions of the image in *The New Princeton Encyclopedia of Poetry and Poetics* states that an image is "a psychological event in the reader's mind."[9] This seems to represent how images live within Tranströmer's poems, for here, the image is equated with the mind—an amorphous, complicated, and living body. Here, the image goes beyond the act of recording objects in order to service some emotional and dramatic effect.

Tranströmer's pliable and psychological images engage the speakers and the reader along a journey through a dark forest without any obvious or apparent exit. As Tranströmer's passengers, we have arrived somewhere that is simultaneously specific and universal. Along the way, our imaginations have been flexed, and we are somehow knowingly and unknowingly changed in the end.

WRITING PROMPTS

1. THE ARRESTING IMAGE

Think of five "things" or objects and write them down. These things can be natural, such as birds, or artificial, such as a child's ball.

Think of Tranströmer's images, such as a lake as "a window into the earth" or a newspaper as a "big dirty butterfly." Try to use figurative language in the way that Tranströmer does by likening your objects to something completely unusual. The more you allow your imagination to work, the better. Visualize your chosen objects and let your mind roam. The goal is to stray as far away from the original object as possible.

Next, take your phrase and add human emotion, feeling, and/or intellect. The goal is to make the image transcend the description of the actual object itself. Let the poem become dependent on some emotional drama: allow the poem to have dramatic effects or narrative elements.

Another option is to take an existing poem and populate the poem with these new, arresting images. Take weaker images and try to work in these new images for surprising effects.

2. THE MOVING IMAGE

Start with one image and describe it in your notebook. Make this image have more classical roots, meaning, simply describe the image. But still describe it in an interesting and unusual way.

From this first description, make the image move or morph as Tranströmer's images change and transform. Go anywhere you want.

Keep leaping as Tranströmer does to different places until you feel like ending the poem. Go back and look at what you have written and edit out lines, phrases, or images so that your leaps are even more surprising.

ALONG THE RADIUS / *Tomas Tranströmer*

1

The ice-bound river is blazing with sun
here is the world's roof
silence.

I'm sitting on an upturned boat on the bank
swallowing the drug of silence
spinning gently.

2

A wheel spreads out endlessly, turns.
Here is the center, almost
still.

Further out, perceptible movement: the steps in the snow
the writing which shuffles along
the facades.

The rumbling traffic on the highways
and the silent traffic
of ghosts.

And further out: the tragic masks in the headwind
in the whine of speed—further out:
the rush

where the last words of love evaporate—
the drips that creep
on the steel wings—

profiles that cry out—the suspended headphones
chatter at each other—
kamikaze!

3
The ice-bound river glitters and is silent.
The shadows lie deep
and voiceless.

My steps were explosions in the ground
that the silence paints over
paints over.[10]

SEVEN REASONS FOR DIVORCE / *Victoria Chang*

—During the Shang Dynasty (1765–1123 B.C.)

DISOBEDIENCE (TO IN-LAWS)
I am the girl who wakes within an ocean,
making winter melon soup for my mother-in-law,
whose taste buds rise like thorns.

JEALOUSY
Your new maid returns to your room again.
I am in the kitchen, chopping pork into a guillotine
of red river. The stew smells like your boiling heart.

DISEASE
I am thinning, unable to hold even a hairpin up.
My body pocked like a Fabergé egg.
My face in the mirror has a hole in it.
Why won't it grow back?

ADULTERY

He built a hurricane for me. You had the same chance
to hunt in me. Idiot. How you missed my heart
in its throbbing coat, I will never know.

STEALING

Yes, I ate them. The red bean, a roiling surf
on my tongue turned to mud
only because you found out.

BARENESS

Something is thundering in my body.
You can hear it in the soil, bulbs breaking out into a cathedral.

TALKING TOO MUCH

I still mean what I did not say.[11]

Notes

1. Tomas Tranströmer, *The Great Enigma: New Collected Poems,* trans. Robin Fulton (New York: New Directions, 2006), 71.

2. Ibid., 80.

3. Ibid., 66.

4. Ibid., 190.

5. Ibid., 4.

6. Ibid., 64.

7. Ibid., 184.

8. *Literary Essays of Ezra Pound,* ed. T. S. Eliot (New York: New Directions, 1935), 3–4.

9. *The New Princeton Encyclopedia of Poetry and Poetics,* 3rd ed., s.v. "Image."

10. Tranströmer, *Great Enigma,* 118–19.

11. Victoria Chang, *Circle* (Carbondale: Southern Illinois University Press, 2005), 9–10.

Gallant with Delight: A Use of Setting

Jeff Hardin

Philip St. Clair's "Water" still stands as one of my favorite poems, with all the sentimental affection one has for a first love. In fact, I have a framed broadside hanging above the desk in my office. I read the poem practically daily:

> Early evening on the river: a moon
> Launched from a stump on the other side
> Begins an angular flight
> To the dark. A small boat, riding
>
> Dangerously low on sluggish water,
> Whines against the current. In the stern
> A man bends over an outboard, frail
> At full-throttle, close to a stall.
>
> Tilted, riding a wooden seat
> Over the middle thwart, a small boy
> Watches the trees on shore. For him
> The illusion of speed
>
> Is incomplete: he turns to his father,
> Wanting him to go faster. In the prow
> The family dog, alert, elevated
> Over the others, looks straight ahead—
>
> Free of the backyard chain, tail
> Rapping the boat at each new smell,
> He braves a vanishing horizon
> Mouth open, gallant with delight.[1]

I admire the poem's faithfulness to how setting—its available range of images—contains already the basic elements that often drive a poem: tension, metaphoric/symbolic resonance, and meaning. Such a simple formula, if we wish to call it a formula, yet the truth remains that even a formula—a sonnet, for instance—often produces unpredictable sounds, images, and insights. An attention to setting grounds a poem both literally and figuratively—with echoes of the physical and the spiritual—and if the poet is faithful to describe clearly the literal, then chances are very good that the figurative will be discovered and made clear as well.

Seeing St. Clair's principal nouns placed beside each other—water, moon, boat, man, boy, dog—gave me hope then, as it does now, that a poem can arise out of the simplest things and can still become magical, instructive, and mystery-filled. Notice, for instance, how his naming of these items propels the poem's arc—its own "angular flight"—through the stanzas. Notice, in particular, the evocation of time and place in the opening line, the fragmentary stillness preceding the colon. Notice how something as simple as a colon both stops and extends the *felt* experience of time so that when we encounter the moon, it seems launched not only from the stump, not only from the stillness, but also from the poem's syntax. Which came first, though? The syntax? The image/perception? Or the place, the setting? I vote for setting, for paying attention to what is there in the landscape, and for trusting that the poem's movement through time and place—as well as through emotion, tone, imagery, diction, theme, and the like—is a matter of the poet's attentiveness to what is already there.

Critic Willard Spiegelman tells us that description is a way of "add[ing] a new item to the totality of available reality."[2] In other words, each new description, while showing us *what already is*, also shows us *what is possible* since, before the description, our conception of the world didn't quite exist in the same way. For example, Jim Simmerman's short poem "Low-ku" states simply,

> Look: a picket fence
> is just a lot of little
> crosses holding hands.[3]

I find it hard to see a picket fence now without remembering his words. What is possible to see (or think about)—both literally and metaphorically—has increased for me, after reading this poem. And that fact is one of the pleasures of description, for description reveals what is worth remembering and carrying onward. Scott Russell Sanders says that we read stories (and I would add poems, plays, and essays) in order to educate our desires, in order to give us an image of what we might aspire to become.[4] Poet Joseph Brodsky goes as far as to say that every new aesthetic reality makes our ethical reality more precise.[5] What are these writers telling us if not that description has a moral component? If we look at St. Clair's poem, we might ask ourselves what desires, attitudes, beliefs, assumptions, and/or values we are being educated toward. We might wonder what his use of setting adds to our engagement with and understanding of the poem.

For one, we note that the water is "sluggish" across which the boat rides "[d]angerously low." Some might call the use of "sluggish" a matter of word choice, of diction, but we might also be mindful that this word choice can be traced back to the writer's attempt simply to describe the scene. That its use has figurative importance to the purpose of the poem is a by-product, a reward, of first attempting to describe the moment. Many will say that description can never be accurate since ultimately it is a matter of interpretation, of subjectivity, and I agree, but only to a degree. Can we agree to start with what is there in the landscape—a wheelbarrow, rainwater, and chickens, for instance—and then give subjectivity freedom to interpret to its heart's contentment? If we're looking at a wheelbarrow, rainwater, and chickens, I doubt that we'll get into an argument about how one or the other of us has subjectively foisted that chicken onto the scene.

"Water" provides us with three views of the world, and herein, it seems, the poem makes its argument and increases our "available stock of reality." First, we can be like the father, concerned with the work of the moment, worrying over the frail motor. What occupies his mind is obviously important and necessary, but it prevents him from sharing the moment with his son. His sight is directed not out but down, toward the concern of the motor. In other words, he isn't "free." Second, we can be like the son, watching and wanting to go faster. What he expects does not match the moment. He looks at the trees and at his father, both with dissatisfaction. He isn't "free" either. Third, we can be like the dog. Only the dog is free. Only the dog looks straight ahead. Only the dog is "gallant with delight." What the father, son, and dog look at—motor, trees, horizon—was always there in the setting, though. Attention to these details brings us the figurative importance of each, the new reality toward which we might aspire.

I grew up alongside the Tennessee River, and the images out of St. Clair's poem could very well be what I saw on any given day. The problem, though, is that I didn't know back then that I was witnessing poetry. Poetry was Wordsworth, Coleridge, and Shelley. Poetry was Shakespeare's sonnets about love. Poetry was Grecian urns, when my world was drunken adults sitting around a campfire telling stories into the early morning hours, waiting on a barbecued hog to get done. In other words, poetry had nothing to do with my world, with my setting. Poems like "Water" teach me that poems don't have to come entirely out of the fabrications of the mind—they can come out of what I look at every day. The first poem I ever published twenty years ago was about throwing a hatchet at a tree, something my friend Albert and I did on the banks of Horse Creek. Twenty years later, I published a poem about floating that same creek with Albert, "fishing poles in hand, a Maxwell House can of red worms / dug up from a place we kept a secret past the barn." Even now that ordinary phrase we used so many times—"a Maxwell House can of red worms"—sings like nothing else I know. Albert's been dead almost a decade now, an accident with a gun, but I like to think that inside the poem I wrote for him, he looks around and recognizes the creek bed and cottonwoods, the perch and bass and catfish. He would say, "I know this world. This is my world."

It was my world too, the one we shared for a while. It was a poem.

WRITING PROMPT

Make a brief list of places to which you feel a strong connection, places that you remember in detail. Maybe you once witnessed something going on in this place—men sitting around a campfire; a young child backing slowly toward the edge of a wooden bridge; an old couple dancing in their back yard; a truck trying to cross a shallow creek—whatever suits your powers of observation. After choosing a setting that you remember in detail, make a separate list of nouns, simply naming the things that inhabit the place. Give yourself time to see what might otherwise go unnoticed. Think of yourself as an archivist, entrusted with items of immense value. Just as St. Clair's poem relies on a series of nouns—water, moon, boat, man, boy, dog—choose from your own list of nouns in order to build touchstones into your poem, as few or as many as your poem seems willing to accommodate. Also, if possible, just as St. Clair's poem has a principal action—a boat going down a river—allow your poem to be guided by a central action or context. Doing so will provide your poem with a ready-made arc, a beginning leading toward an end, a problem heading toward a solution, a conflict working toward a resolution. Attempt to describe what the setting provides, trusting that its "available stock of reality" will lead not only to a felt experience of the place but also to an insight about what the things in that place could teach you, about what these things could represent about being there, and about being.

ALWAYS UPSTREAM OR DOWNSTREAM / *Jeff Hardin*

We'd push out in an old canoe to float Horse Creek,
fishing poles in hand, a Maxwell House can of red worms
dug up from a place we kept a secret past the barn.
Maybe we had all day—who knows—and maybe a day
meant nothing to us, for all of eternity belonged
to the wind on our faces and the slip-slap sound
of the paddle seeking cool and dark-green, still pools
thick with bream and bass and slick-bellied catfish.
Someone had told us catfish were mythic creatures
that could rise up to walk on water and up the slick banks
to perch themselves in cottonwoods; and maybe they could,
but we never saw them, always upstream or downstream
and never quite lonely enough in our hearts. Albert,
who was not my brother by blood but whose memory
on earth I'll fight you for, would take his rod and reel,
bait the hook with such a gentleness, a patience—
he made a music of it, a visionary music
in praise of fish hid out beneath decaying logs
or sunning themselves in shallows. Such iridescence,
olive and yellow—such craft of dorsal fin and gills.
And the two of us stalled in the middle of nowhere,
the only two people in the history of the world
who would ever see these fish! His cast was flawless,
smooth, almost silent, a balletic motion despite the limbs
we had to navigate. The world believed its wars
and greed, believed its clocks and fame and arguments
of history, while silence seemed to push at us
from every side, until the boat bumped the creek bed.

Even now the bliss of that surprise, the memory of it,
the climbing out to drag and tug, to hear the grit
of an existence that sometimes must be hauled
from one dry place to deeper water. Men grow old
to learn a young boy's trust of everything that is;
but Albert won't grow old, just young and younger,
forever tying flies, biting off the excess string,
trailing his hand in the coolest water of earth;
and I'll grow old and older, the wide world filling up
with loss of all we ever saw and marveled at
there on that creek from which long summers go on drinking.[6]

Notes

1. Philip St. Clair, "Water," *Zone 3* 2.2 (Spring 1987): cover.

2. Willard Spiegelman, *How Poets See the World: The Art of Description in Contemporary Poetry* (Oxford: Oxford University Press, 2005), 4.

3. Jim Simmerman, "Low-ku," *Prairie Schooner* 75.3 (Fall 2001): 86.

4. Scott Russell Sanders, "The Power of Stories," in *The Force of Spirit* (Boston: Beacon Press, 2001), 91.

5. Joseph Brodsky, *On Grief and Reason: Essays*, trans. Barry Rubin (New York: Farrar, Straus and Giroux, 1995), 44–58.

6. Jeff Hardin, "Always Upstream or Downstream," *Florida Review* 32.1 (Spring 2007): 94–95.

Not Metaphor but Magic: The "How" and Why of Narrative Poetry

Lisa D. Chávez

My grandmother told me stories. I wish I could say that these were the stuff of great tradition: family stories handed down orally for generations. They were not. They were stories from the Little Golden Books, often sanitized versions of fairy tales, and, to be more accurate, my grandmother read them to me. Until she taught me how to read—which happened before I entered kindergarten. I don't remember her lessons, but I do remember getting to pick out a new book at the store each week. The ones I chose were invariably about talking animals, and I loved these stories because they were not my experience—they were a way for me to experience the world as I thought it should be. My earliest memories are of stories—of reading or being read to and, later, of trying to write my own stories, trying to place myself in a world beyond my own.

When I was in kindergarten, I told everyone about the pony that I kept at my grandparents' house. Understand that there was no pony. My grandparents' house was small, on the corner of a busy street in southern California, and while we did have some unusual animals living with us—a duck named Petunia, a sparrow named Tucker and other birds—there certainly was no pony in the small backyard. At school, no one questioned me, but finally, when I related one too many unlikely pony adventures, the teacher asked me if I was "telling stories." I nodded, until I saw her frown. I was five years old, and it was the first time that I'd had to question the separation between my imagination and real life. I understood quite well that I didn't have a real pony, but I also knew that telling stories created another world. I thought my teacher remarkably unimaginative—didn't stories come alive for her, too? For me, stories were not metaphor but magic.

The point of stories, that oldest human magic, is that they are both true and not. In the world as it is, Sethe may not "really" be haunted by the ghost of her daughter Beloved, but she is in the context of the novel, and in the "real" world, it is quite possible that a woman can be haunted both by the loss of her child and by the terrible scars of slavery. Thus, Toni Morrison's novel is both true and fictional, and it is this combination of truth and fiction that makes literature compelling.

My early education in literature was fairly traditional. Often, the lyric—elusive and elliptic as it can be—simply baffled me. As an undergraduate, I had no idea what Keats was saying in "Ode to a Nightingale" (though my already poetic mind clung to lines like "Fled is that music: Do I wake or sleep"), but I immediately fell in love with "La Belle Dame Sans Merci" and "The Eve of Saint Agnes."[1] They told stories. Still, I remained under the impression that poetry was primarily "difficult" and hard to understand—that I might end up repeating a line over and over again, but the meaning of the poem would remain elusive. I became convinced that the narrative poems I'd read were just flukes, and these early classes hardly sparked my interest in poetry.

And it wasn't until I got into my first undergraduate poetry class with Alaskan poet John Morgan (who has been known to write a narrative poem or two) that I finally read contemporary poetry and realized that people still wrote "story poems" and that I could do it too. My interest shifted from fiction to poetry immediately.

My early influences were poets I read (including many Native American poets, especially Louise Erdrich, Linda Hogan, and Joy Harjo) and poets I later worked with: Norman Dubie, Ai, Alberto Ríos. It is no surprise, then, that my earliest poems emulated them: I wrote dramatic monologues and other narrative poems, often very short-lined until Tito Rios taught me to understand the use and tension of the line. I had no understanding of form: I didn't know how to use stanzas for effect, and often my poems were one long block of text. Since then, I've learned that the narrative poem is remarkably flexible.

Some of the narrative poets I loved, such as Sharon Olds, rarely employed regular stanzas, and, in fact, a quick glance through her early books will show that sometimes she dispensed with any stanza breaks at all. Some poets are able to stretch the stories they tell over an elegant trellis of stanzas, letting the form dictate the breaks. And other poets, even the great formalist Robert Frost, tend to use stanza breaks in narrative poetry much as a prose writer would use paragraph breaks. (In Frost's "Home Burial," he begins a new stanza each time the character speaking changes, just as a fiction writer begins a new paragraph with each new speaker.) I often tell students that the quatrain is particularly well suited for the narrative poem: there is something solid about those four lines, especially if they begin to approach—often unconsciously—iambic pentameter. The quatrain is unobtrusive, and often people will completely miss the "form" of the poem when it is employed, and yet it structures the narrative in a way that suggests an orderly movement from one part of the story to the next. Of course, the quatrain is also the traditional ballad form, and perhaps this is why it feels so well suited to narrative poetry.

Not that the poet always wants to tell a story in an orderly fashion. One of the things that fascinates me is the way stanza and line length can add a kind of tension to a story beyond the tension inherent in the narrative. I believe poetry has an advantage over short stories in this way—not only can writers use the narrative to create tension, but they also have the tool of line length or stanza to make that tension more or less pronounced, as they see fit. A poet can work with the form—for example, using stanzas in an unobtrusive way—or they can work against the form, by forcing stanza breaks against the story the poem is telling, thereby creating more tension and a sense of uneasiness in the face of what looks ordered. A famous example of this is Theodore Roethke's "My Papa's Waltz": the quatrains of the poem both echo the beat of the dance and also demonstrate a sense of order because of the regular stanza length. Yet the scene and subject of the poem is anything but ordered—instead, we witness a drunken romp.

Most often, contemporary poets seem to dispense with regular stanzas when writing narrative poetry. And that's not a bad thing. Sometimes one long stream of text is just what we need. Or we can break the stanzas as if they were paragraphs, indicating a new topic or shift in the narrative. And though what we create is certainly a poem rather than a short story (unless it falls into the murky ground of prose poem versus flash fiction), the genre distinctions are not always as distinct as we have been led to believe.

One of the forms I find compelling is the list poem, especially because most of the list poems I really enjoy tend to tell stories. While I've read successful list poems that do not have a clear narrative—Joy Harjo's "She Had Some Horses," Raymond Carver's "The Car"—I tend to prefer the ones that do, if you consider, as I do, the creation of a character a type of story. While such poems undoubtedly draw on fictional techniques, especially the oft-repeated "show, don't tell" directive, they also use devices more often attributed to poetry. Consider a poem by one of my favorite poets, Jim Daniels.

The poem "How" is a list of things that run through the head of a truck driver who has "at least four more hours of driving" as he considers his failing marriage and the fact that he "still loved his wife no matter." The poem is not formally structured; it has no set stanza form, but it does have a fairly regular line length, one that falls very roughly into iambic pentameter. The controlling format of the poem is repetition, the continued use of the phrase "and how." Daniels is clever not to overuse this—while a repeated phrase can become as rhythmic as a chant, that quality distracts from a narrative if overused (think of the way children repeat a word over and over until it loses meaning—this can be valuable in prayer or chant or even in a lyric poem when the attention focuses on language and image, but it distracts from the forward movement and tension inherent in narrative). The first use of "how" is in the title, of course, and the title is also the first word of the poem, which begins with the trucker's proposal to his wife at a train crossing. Using the techniques of both poetry and fiction, Daniels foreshadows what will happen in the story by telling us that the man proposed as his future wife "sat behind him on his Harley / but she didn't hear him." While they do marry, this issue of not hearing one another is important in this poem that ends as the character picks up his CB and asks *"Hey, hey, anybody out there?"*

What happens in between is a stream-of-consciousness list of regrets that run through the truck driver's head as he drives his truck. We learn about his affair, and his wife's, and we learn that his wife is leaving him. We learn about how much he loves his children and that he has quit drugs, "even pot," and wishes he'd gone to college. In this list of events from the character's life, we get moments of humor:

> and how he'd been safety boy of the year
> when he was ten years old and how that's
> the last time he got an award for anything
> and how he knew he was feeling sorry
> for himself but couldn't help it

This is a particularly skillful moment in terms of character development. The inclusion of the truck driver's last award is quite sentimental, and if the poet had left it to stand on its own, readers would rightly reject it. Instead, he includes this detail and then undercuts it by having the character tell us that he knows he is being pathetic but is indulging himself anyway. It's an interesting moment in the poem because we see that the character is wallowing in self-pity but is also smart enough to recognize it. Thus Daniels has developed a complex character, much as a fiction writer might build a character. He gets away with what verges on sentimentality because of the use of a kind of "first person third person"—it is the character who feels sorry for himself, not the poet. Daniels also uses specific detail (listed events) to *show* us what the truck driver is like, and he creates a character who is not one-dimensional. This is where the conventions of narrative transcend the somewhat artificial genre distinctions we try to impose on literature: for a story to work, regardless of genre, it must have a compelling, complex character and a forward movement fueled by the character's conflicts and desires. Certainly this is what we see in "How."

This poem is not a dramatic monologue, but it does draw on some of the traditions of the dramatic monologue in that we have a character who is not the author speaking (thinking, in this case), the character is shown in a clear setting (driving his truck at night), and he is thinking back over his life in a moment of crisis (when his marriage is on the verge of disintegration). And as all poetry must, "How" includes specific detail and imagery.

Young poets often make the same mistake in dramatic monologues that they do in the larger subset of narrative poetry: they get so involved in telling the story that they forget about lyrical language and imagery. While a dramatic monologue is a bit tricky in that the poet must always walk a careful line between sticking to images that seem reasonable for speech and not omitting images altogether, the narrative poet has more freedom. Still, images must fit the subject at hand, and they should move the narrative forward or tell us more about the character.

In "How," Daniels is always aware of this balance. While the poet plays with the colloquial phrases his truck driver would actually use ("tooth for tooth stick in the eye"), he also includes moments of lyricism ("his family crumbling into pebbles, then fine dust"), and later, as the character contemplates his guilt over his own affair, he notes that the wife has "brought / the guilt back now and it still worked / how it still dug and bulldozed."

These images are not overwrought flights of fancy, and they seem believable for the working-class character. Thus, we are not thrown out of the poem to contemplate the poet's ingenuity; rather, we continue our suspension of disbelief, continue to believe in this character.

I spoke earlier of how a poet can use form to work with or against the tension inherent in the narrative. "How" cultivates narrative tension in its conflict: we wonder if the truck driver's wife will leave him. In the second stanza, Daniels's character thinks about

> how driving the truck lately
> he wanted not to slow down
> on some exit ramp, keep barreling on
> till he was dead.

Though this threat is not acted on in the poem, it is sufficiently compelling to make a reader continue to follow the story. However, this poem does not rely strictly on narrative to keep its momentum. A careful reader will note that something happens formally in this piece: because the title is also the first word of "How," the poem appears to begin with the uncapitalized word "he." While this use of the lowercase at the outset of the poem hints at the character's own lack of self-worth, it does something more: it indicates that the poem begins in medias res, and in (almost) midsentence. The stanza breaks mimic paragraphs by indicating shifts in thought or topic, and each begins with "and how." The repeated phrase occurs more frequently as the poem continues (twice in the second stanza compared to ten times in the final stanza). In addition, there is no capitalization, and the poem itself has no end punctuation until the final line. "How" is one long, breathless sentence that begins fairly calmly and gets progressively more breathless as the character's emotions build. The poem offers a beautiful mélange of poetic devices—repetition, imagery, specific detail, and careful use of form—as it continues to push a narrative to its climax.

And now, another story, or more accurately, an anecdote, since this has no real narrative line. I remember well the first time I read T. S. Eliot's "Tradition and the Individual Talent" as an undergraduate. One of the things I was most struck by were these oft-quoted lines: "Poetry . . . is not the expression of personality, but an escape from personality."[2] I found those lines troubling and fascinating, particularly because I was of an age when my personality, emotions, and identity seemed all-important. I wanted to argue the point, but I also felt that I understood the need to escape personality—or at least my own—because it resonated so well with how I viewed stories. When I was a little girl, buying my weekly Little Golden Books, I wasn't looking for something about me, or even for something about the world I lived in. I was looking to slip into another world, another mind. As a young adult, I probably was misreading Eliot—perhaps instead of art as an "extinction of personality," I sought only to surrender my own. And I still do that. While now I look for both what is very different from me and what is close to my own experience, what I love best about story is that moment when I am gone, when I'm wholly in the head of the character, whether that be a character in a three-hundred-page novel or in a two-page poem. I want to be transported. I want to really feel the ordinary—yet entirely individual—pain of Daniels's forty-year-old trucker who thinks he's wasted his life. I want to be him, if only for the time it takes to read the poem. That is what story does. It is both truth and fiction, and it lets us live other lives. And when we write narrative poetry, we are drawing on one of the oldest human traditions, the telling of tales that transform.

WRITING PROMPT

Think about the way objects and belongings can show us what a person is like, the way specific things can tell us a story.

You can do this exercise in several ways. You could think about what you tend to carry with you and begin by emptying your backpack, purse, or even wallet onto a desk and making a list of everything you have with you when you leave the house. Or you could list everything that is in a familiar place: a bedroom or an office or even a car. First, simply list, and make the list as specific as possible: not a pen, but a red pen grooved with teeth marks from when I chewed on it while trying to write a love letter. Don't forget to use imagistic language: a pen gnawed like dog's bone. Take ten to fifteen minutes to do this.

You may find the beginnings of a narrative already in place, and now your task is to turn that list into a poem. Imagine a speaker who has collected all these things, and add and subtract real (or imaginary) things that add to the speaker's character. Play with the order of the list so that narrative tension builds through the objects themselves. For example, the first things in the list may seem innocuous, even random, but as the list continues, we begin to see a connection between the objects, and as they take on more weight, we learn more about the speaker of the poem, who he or she is in that particular moment, and what these objects mean to him or her. Let your imagination take you where it wants to go. Remember, you don't need to be bound by your list. Go ahead—take the character you've created out of seemingly random details—go ahead and tell us a story.

HOW / *Jim Daniels*

he proposed to her at a train crossing
as she sat behind him on his Harley
but she didn't hear him above the train's
roar and he bumped his helmet against hers
when he turned to repeat the question
shouting it, indisputable after months of hedging
and how he turned forward again
waiting till she said yes and how
he wanted to kiss her but the train was gone
so he revved up and crossed the bumpy tracks

and how his wife was leaving him now after
fifteen years and how he'd messed up bad
a few years back with another woman and how she kept
throwing that in his face again now suddenly
because this time it was her
her in love with someone else
tooth for tooth stick in the eye
and how driving the truck lately
he wanted not to slow down
on some exit ramp, keep barreling on
till he was dead and this was over

and how his older boy suspected something
and what could he ever say to him,
his family crumbling into pebbles, then fine dust
and how he couldn't breathe without choking
and how they were the only couple
still married among their high school friends
and how shocked everyone would be and how he gave her

diamond earrings for their anniversary last month
and how she cried knowing it was no use
and how on the road in the truck he imagined her
with the other faceless man and how, strangely,
he could sleep now, the insomnia gone
how sleep was his escape and how he daydreamed
about the peace of sleep, about how he wished
he'd never given up the guitar
and how he'd been safety boy of the year
when he was ten years old and how that's
the last time he got an award for anything
and how he knew he was feeling sorry
for himself but couldn't help it

and how he'd given up all drugs
even pot because he wanted something
to be clear and how he'd stayed with his wife
broken off his affair, a final choice
and how relieved he was not to have the guilt
scraping at his insides but how she'd brought
the guilt back now and it still worked
how it still dug and bulldozed

and how he wished he'd tried college
fifteen years ago instead of marrying,
but how he still loved his wife no matter,
and how he'd always loved driving, her hands
on his waist on the back of the bike
and how he'd cured his restless heart
but now she'd caught it and it wasn't going away
and how riding his Harley it just seemed light
and empty, the breeze stinging his face
the helmet too tight

and how he loved his kids
and took them fishing though one got seasick
and how he cradled the sick one's damp head
as he bent over the side of the boat

gentle and how he wanted someone to cradle his head
just like that and how he wished he could vomit up
all the badness and be done with it
and how he was disappointing his parents
one more time and how he was looking for a new job
because business was bad and how he was 40 years old
and the skin on his face was tightening
into creases and how his beard was sprinkled with grey
and how tired he was and just wanted to sleep
but he had at least four more hours of driving
and how he picked up his CB and pressed the microphone
and said *Hey, hey, anybody out there?*[3]

IN AN ANGRY SEASON / *Lisa D. Chávez*

They've gone to witness the river's mad
descent into spring. The heave and thunder
as the ice shakes itself from the shore,
the way the frozen slabs—pachyderm gray
and similarly sized—shear one into
another as the Yukon shudders awake.
From a hawk's height the pipeline bridge
mocks the river's riot and churn. Perched
there, they watch—then his pale hand
turns her tawny face to his and
they kiss, roar of loosed ice echoing.
They are both just nineteen.

And now they sit, hands clutching brown
bottles, in a one-room cabin turned
tavern. A wooden counter, scabbed over
with men's names. A Naugahyde couch,
slouching by the door. One man at the bar,
face flat in a puddle of beer.
His phlegmy snores. The room choked
with smoke. The one they call Dirty Dave
is telling a story: "We picked up this squaw

hitching her way into town. Weren't no room
in the cab, so she crawled in back. I went after her.
I said, whatever you hear, boys,
don't stop this truck." Laughter. He grins,
gap-toothed and mean. Leers at the girl.
"I like it when they fight." She shivers.
Twists at a strand of her black hair.
Her boyfriend draws her closer.
Six men—they've been drinking
all winter. One girl. One nervous
boyfriend. A mining camp a hundred miles
or more from the town. And Dave stares
at the girl. "What do you think of that?"

And she thinks: There is so much evil
in this world. And she thinks of her hand,
squeezing the bottle till it breaks, scraping
this man's face to bone with the shards.
And she thinks of the river, how in some
angry seasons it could not be contained—
bridges snapped like thread, whole villages
devoured by the Yukon's flood and fury.
And she hears the river shift and growl.[4]

Notes

1. John Keats, "Ode to a Nightingale," in *English Romantic Writers*, 2nd ed., ed. David Perkins (New York: Harcourt Brace College Publishers, 1995), 1252.

2. T. S. Eliot, "Tradition and the Individual Talent and Reflections on Contemporary Poetry," in *Poetry in Theory: An Anthology 1900–2000*, ed. Jon Cook (Malden, Mass.: Blackwell Publishing, 2004), 102.

3. Jim Daniels, *Blessing the House* (Pittsburgh: University of Pittsburgh Press, 1997), 34–36.

4. Lisa D. Chávez, *In an Angry Season* (Tucson: University of Arizona Press, 2001), 89.

Myth, Persona, and the Personal

Shara McCallum

In eighth grade, my English class studied Greek mythology. Trying to interest a roomful of disaffected adolescents, our teacher staged a *Jeopardy!* game around the subject. I'm not someone who easily recalls facts under pressure, so I was surprised to find myself of value to the team. The Greek gods and goddesses we'd been learning about, with their virtues and flaws, were vivid in my teenage imagination, reminiscent of most of the adults I knew. It came as little surprise to me that Aphrodite was beautiful but also filled with jealousy and rage; that Demeter, devastated by the loss of her child and blinded by grief, ruined everything in her path; or that head god Zeus presided over the universe while debasing himself, assuming animal form to have sex with the human women he desired.

As a college junior years later, I took my first creative writing workshop and was introduced to the world of contemporary poetry. Before that class, I'd read Yeats's "Leda and the Swan" in a modernism course; in another, I'd studied Milton's *Paradise Lost*. Throughout my education, I had been schooled in the belief that "great literature" was built on the foundation of Greco-Roman and Judeo-Christian myths, yet until I took a poetry workshop, it didn't dawn on me that living poets might still have something to say about these stories.

Perhaps more than any other contemporary poet, Louise Glück has spent a career rewriting Greek myths. In her poems, these stories have provided a way into, through, and out of the themes that are her core concerns as an artist: mother-daughter and other familial relationships; thwarted or destructive forms of romantic love; marriage and divorce; and the individual's struggle with an indifferent or unreachable God. Over the course of her career, she has sustained a lyric-dramatic voice that both contains and exposes her obsessions, ones—given the recurrence of subject matter and point of view—that appear to stem from her own experience.

What myth has afforded Glück is access to archetypes, providing a broader context for the seemingly personal utterances of many of her poems.

Assuming personae, as Glück has often done in adopting the voices of various mythic characters, has been another means for her to expand and deepen the subjectivity of her work. The speaker of a poem is always a persona since the voice on the page is never identical to the writer's voice off the page, even when the material is strictly autobiographical, but I distinguish between the kind of first-person perspective wedded to the lyric poem and the kind we encounter in what has come to be called the "persona poem." The latter comes out of the tradition of the dramatic monologue. In the case of the persona poem, the speaker is not overtly an aspect of the poet but rather serves as a mask for the poet.

Louise Glück's poem "Pomegranate" is an example of how the poet's retelling of myth and use of persona come together. Delivered from the point of view of Persephone, daughter of the goddess Demeter, the poem recounts this famous mother-daughter saga, but its success resides in its many departures from the story's usual unfolding. Contrary to Hades' characterization in traditional versions, Glück's Hades is a sympathetic figure, a lover who helps Persephone to see her mother's "true" nature. Through his encouragement, the poem implies that Persephone will free herself from the clutches of an all-consuming mother (perhaps only to fall into his). Unlike Demeter's typical casting as Mother Earth, Glück presents her as self-serving, one who "parades" her grief "over our heads" and demands that she remain the center of attention. "Consider she is in her element," Hades says, with more than a trace of sarcasm, "the trees turning to her, whole / villages going under." "Pomegranate" suggests that if you are going to rewrite a myth, you need to do something different, in part to justify repeating a tale that has been rehashed countless times.

Beyond Glück's novel take on Persephone's story, "Pomegranate" is a rich poem to consider in terms of its use of persona. Speaking as Persephone in the poem, Glück uses persona as a deflecting device that yet hints at her own stake in the matter. Surveying the early books of poems by Glück, we see that the daughter's voice comes up again and again and that images of a distant or destructive mother are manifold. Taken together, these recurrent motifs imply that Glück's life is behind the version of the story we receive in "Pomegranate."

That poetry might still reveal and speak out of the details of the writer's life is not a particularly popular idea in the wake of the confessional movement of mid-twentieth-century American poetry. Partly a response to confessionalism's excesses, among other reasons, the current literary climate exhibits abundant skepticism toward and at times outright disdain for poems that emerge from a writer's own experience. To argue, as I would, that autobiographical poems are resonant in good measure *because* of their personal relationship to the writer is to risk being regarded as sentimental or narcissistic.

Beneath the many eloquent diatribes against autobiography lies, I think, a fundamental disbelief in the authenticity and ultimate meaning and value of individual human experience. A number of contemporary writers, queasy about using their life as source material for their art, perform acrobatic feats to prevent autobiographical details, or anything resembling a sincere voice recounting an actual life, from entering their work. When we consider the history of poetry, going to such lengths to avoid meeting oneself in a poem seems a strange practice. The tone of urgency found in poems that emanate from the writer's life—the feeling we have as readers that the poet has something personally at risk—dominates many of the poems we most admire. Poems steeped in personal experience arrive out of vastly different aesthetic positions, written by poets from diverse backgrounds, eras, and societies. John Keats's "Ode to a Nightingale," Langston Hughes's "The Negro Speaks of Rivers," and Paul Celan's "Fugue of Deaths" are just three examples.

Many contemporary poets who mistrust the use of personal material end up writing poems as an exercise in either extinguishing the "self" or in drawing attention to the self as a "construct." This characteristic of a large slice of contemporary American poetry is perhaps a coincidental feature or direct result of our "postmodern moment." However postmodernism and modernism before it are implicated in what has arguably become a strong movement in poetry, what troubles me is the relationship between questions raised about the nature of the "self" and the result: a seemingly inexhaustible supply of poems distinguished by a voice that must doggedly demonstrate allegiance to irony, skepticism, self-consciousness, fragmentation, and detachment. The failing of such poems, for me, is rooted in the prevailing assumption that there is no poet-speaker who can be naturalized in and by the poem.

In stark contrast to poems that dismantle or sidestep the concept of an authentic speaker, Glück's work is grounded in an aesthetic that insists upon its primacy. Her body of work derives much of its power from the distilled emotional and psychological essence of the voice, the persona, we encounter in her poems. Often she achieves this most in poems like "Pomegranate," which posits a connection between the lyric, authorial self (Glück) and the dramatic speaker of the poem, in this case Persephone. "Pomegranate" gives us the pleasure of a familiar story, subverted, enriched, and ultimately remade by Glück's voice and the aspects of her life that inflect the old myth with new value.

I was twenty when I first read "Pomegranate." While I did not understand its impact at the time, I have come to view the poem as a crucial one in my early development as a writer. In direct fashion, it served as a model. A few years after reading "Pomegranate" and influenced as well by Rita Dove's and Eavan Boland's poems responding to the same story, in addition to Lucille Clifton's many poems centered on myth, I wrote my version of the Persephone-Demeter relationship in the poem "Persephone Sets the Record Straight." Fed by my personal history, the persona I created in that poem is indebted to Glück, the aforementioned writers, and the many other women poets who have reckoned with myths and found their own voice in the process.

WRITING PROMPT

Write a poem that adopts the persona of a character from myth. You must use first-person point of view, and you must change the story in considerable fashion (you can change the time period, alter the outcome in some way, present key characters in a revised light, and so on). It might be useful to think of your poem as being "The True Story of X." Through writing the poem, perhaps you will discover the connection between yourself and the character from the myth who gains new life in your rendition.

POMEGRANATE / *Louise Glück*

First he gave me
his heart. It was
red fruit containing
many seeds, the skin
leathery, unlikely.

I preferred
to starve, bearing
out my training.
Then he said Behold
how the world looks, minding
your mother. I
peered under his arm:
What had she done
with color & odor?
Whereupon he said Now *there*
is a woman who loves
with a vengeance, adding
Consider she is in her element:
the trees turning to her, whole
villages going under
although in hell
the bushes are still
burning with pomegranates.
At which
he cut one open & began
to suck. When he looked up at last
it was to say My dear
you are your own
woman, finally, but examine
this grief your mother
parades over our heads
remembering
that she is one to whom
these depths were not offered.[1]

PERSEPHONE SETS THE RECORD STRAIGHT / *Shara McCallum*

You are all the rage these days,
mother. Everywhere I turn, I hear
Demeter in mourning, Demeter
grieving . . . poor Demeter.

Always craving the spotlight,
I know this is what you wanted:
your face on the front page
of all the papers; gossip columns

filled with juicy tidbits
on *what life was like before winter,*
old hags in the grocery store, whispering,
how she's let the flowers go,

while young women hover
in their gardens, fearing their hibiscus
will be next on your hit list.
After all these summers,

you still won't come clean.
Passing me iced tea, instead
you ask, *How's the redecorating?*
Are you expanding

to make room for little ones?
Fanning away flies,
you avoid my eyes, saying,
I've so longed to be a grandma,

you know.
For God's sake, mother,
can't you tell me the truth now it's done?
Just once, tell me

how you put me in that field
knowing he'd come,
that you made snow fall
everywhere to cover your tracks,

that the leaves die still
because you can't punish him
for confirming your suspicions:
not wanting you,

he took me instead.
Of course I ate those seeds.
Who wouldn't exchange
one hell for another?[2]

Notes

1. Louise Glück, *The House on Marshland* (Hopewell, N.J.: Ecco Press, 1975), 28.
2. Shara McCallum, *The Water Between Us* (Pittsburgh: University of Pittsburgh Press, 1999), 52–53.

The Self Made Strange: On Translating Tomasz Różycki's "Iterations"

Mira Rosenthal

My awareness of translation as a vital activity began, as is fitting, when I left the country for the first time to participate in a reforestation project outside of Matagalpa, Nicaragua. I arrived alone at night into Managua, the capital city. Deplaning on the tarmac, I felt like I had landed on a movie set filled with ambient pink light and fake palm trees in rows along the perimeter. There were even extras dressed as guards in khaki who were clutching rifles and pointing the way to the terminal—only, when I asked one of them in English, "Where's baggage claim?," no subtitle automatically appeared in twenty-five characters or less at the bottom of my vision. The guard grinned and chuckled. And suddenly my classroom Spanish was no longer an exercise of filling in the blanks but had become something real and necessary for everything I would do, and this realization scared me. Not only had I been transplanted to a new land and culture, but I had also been dislocated from myself: I could no longer articulate my needs or thoughts or emotions with precision.

Our group of eight college students from the United States traveled to a small mountain town to prepare transplant beds with seedlings. Every day we dug dirt and placed the small trees in rows that looked like neatly written paragraphs, running on and on down the page of land. And at night, we each returned to our separate host families, ostensibly to sow the other kind of seed, that of cultural understanding between individuals. But no matter how earnest I was about learning why the youngest daughter in my host family wasn't attending school, or what exactly had happened to make her right foot lame, or why the mother in the family reused the same coffee grounds—boiled in a tin can and kept by the side of the fire—for an entire week, my Spanish was ultimately inadequate and my gallant attempts at communication inept. Nor could I explain to them how I actually wasn't that tall for an American woman nor that old to be single, or why my twenty-first birthday that they were helping me celebrate was so important, or what had prompted me to come to Nicaragua in the first place. And not being able to be myself, I became even more aware of myself: that I was a woman and single, that I was twenty-one, that I had chosen to come here, self-knowledge like the surprised *oh!* of pain in Elizabeth Bishop's poem about reading the *National Geographic* as a child in the dentist's waiting room.[1] In her companion essay "The Country Mouse," which ends with the same story told in prose, the strange foreign pictures in the magazine prompt "a feeling of absolute and utter desolation" and the realization that "you are *you* and you are going to be *you* forever." Such a thought on the fundamental nature of what it means to be a human being is "like coasting downhill . . . only much worse."[2]

Although it is a cliché to think of translation as defamiliarization and dislocation from the self, I am, however, intrigued by the extension of this idea. As a writer, what draws me to translate is the experience of ultimately being *re*familiarized and *re*located in connection to myself—what Vilashini Cooppan talks about in the context of world literature as coming to know our own selves made strange.[3] When I translate a poem, I step out of my own habits as a writer, my own formulas for lineation, cadence, image, epiphany, and follow another writer's voice and sense of form, a writer who can rescue a poem where I would most likely let it founder. And when I step back into my own poem, I'm never quite the same. This sense of losing oneself also happens with the exercise of copying out longhand the work of a poet writing in one's own language, although the effect is exponentially greater when translating. In struggling to refashion sense-for-sense a poem from another language, nothing is automatic.

Often I have said to myself that a translator is ultimately a very close reader, one who works to become conscious of the nuances in language that are often unconsciously felt and understood. Reading with a translator's mind heightens my relationship to language, both the original and my own, as I cross from one place to another. It heightens my relationship to image, and symbol, and stylistics, and culture, and all the things that embed language with metaphoric significance and make it impossible to simply render a word-for-word equivalence.

When I think about what led me to finally try my hand at translating, I see parallels between my own attraction to being made strange through translation and Robert Hass's formulation of being surprised into self-knowledge through metaphor. I did not set out to become a translator. My speechless month in Nicaragua destroyed any pretense of an innate linguistic ability. But it also instilled a stubborn desire to prove myself wrong, and I ultimately went on to study Hindi and then Polish, possibly more than anything for that feeling of the mind being totally and utterly awake that one gets when learning a new language. And I found that reading as a translator is similar to what Hass calls reading with a "whole mind," which allows the reader "to establish an intimate relationship with himself" as he becomes aware of his own mind's proclivity for metaphoric connection and making sense of the world through relationship. "Metaphor is a participatory act," Hass says, paraphrasing Stephen Dobyns. "It surprises the hearer into self-knowledge. It heightens his relationship to himself."[4] Hass's point is that in metaphor, we have connected two things; but self-knowledge, maybe even pleasure, comes only when we *realize* that we have made that connection.

As soon as I began my translation of Tomasz Różycki's sonnet "Iterations," I realized it posed interesting cultural and linguistic challenges. For example, how could I render the impact of the last line in English? An identity card in the context of Poland's communist past is not the same thing as a passport or driver's license: it is a means for the government to impose authoritarian control, to the extent that being caught without an ID at any time, anywhere, could mean strict punishment and possibly imprisonment. To convey such a political understanding in the brevity of a poem is one of the most difficult tasks a translator can face. Reading with a translator's mind intensifies one's awareness of such gaping cultural differences. It also highlights, for better and for worse, one's own weaknesses. I am a child of counterculture parents who raised me as a Buddhist in California. In translating Polish poetry steeped in the Catholic tradition, I have had to teach myself how to recognize biblical overtones and then find their equivalents in English, which in turn has made me a much better reader of my own English literary tradition as well.

I used to be puzzled when a student would come up to me after class to confess that he didn't "get" poetry, that he wasn't "good at" metaphor. But we use metaphor every day, I would think, in almost everything we say. Take the simple statement "Yesterday I spent time writing." We conceive of time as money without even realizing that we have connected two concepts. But that's precisely the point. In metaphors we use every day—that is, what cognitive linguists have been calling metaphors we live by—the awareness of building conceptual relationships through language largely goes unobserved. Art, on the other hand, calls our attention to relationship building and requires us, as Hass says, to become aware of how we create an understanding of the world. Translation intensifies the discovery and rediscovery of such connections. It insists on the multiple iterations of a word, as in Różycki's poem. It keeps me coming back to literature.

ITERATIONS / *Tomasz Różycki*

In repetition power, in repetition constancy.
Coffee with milk, wine, almonds along with the wine.
A word repeated a hundred times will become a body
in blue sheets, below the mongrel grass.

Food from the Chinese, money from the Jews, the same
pilgrimage a thousand times over the cast-iron Odra—
I go on living and doubting whether the exact same thing
will repeat itself tomorrow outside the black window.

Winter has its own bad habits—snow has buried
the house and all the boy scouts. Just as you taught me,
on my own I keep repeating all the ways love existed.
At that time love was sexier than the Spanish flu,

than this little black-eyebrowed night, than this flagrant
temptress writing down on my ID card her citizenship.[5]

WRITING PROMPT

Strolling across the University of California, Santa Barbara campus one afternoon, poet and professor Kenneth Rexroth saw one of his students lying on the grass. "What are you doing?" he asked. "Oh, I'm reading a book of poetry," the student replied. "How can you be reading poetry?" Rexroth queried. "I don't hear anything." This well-known anecdote about the poet who greatly influenced the Beat generation highlights the fact that there are different kinds of reading. When you read out loud or otherwise alter your automatic understanding of the words on the page, something shifts in awareness, something deepens your sense of the poem and yourself. You go beyond comprehension and begin to embody the words.

Choose a poem in translation that is at least a page in length. Copy out the poem longhand, but ignore the lineation so that the final poem looks like a block of prose on the page. As you go along, pay attention to the significance of certain word choices and note any cultural references that clearly mark the voice as "foreign." Cultural differences may arise at the level of objects, such as the ID card in Różycki's poem. You may also notice differences in terms of tone or even general subject matter that might seem off-limits or inaccessible to a contemporary American poet. Then, putting the original aside and working from your version, copy out the poem longhand again, but this time lineate it based on your own sense of rhythm and form. You may choose to change basic sentence structure or individual word choices, following your own ear, but try to keep the general sense of the original as you understand it. Finally, read both the original and your version out loud. What do the differences tell you about your own tendencies as a writer? How has meaning shifted, even if only slightly, in a way that reveals your interpretation of the subject? Are there similarities that point to the poem's universality? In other words, think about what your version of the poem reveals about you as a writer and what adopting another writer's voice has caused you to do in a new way.

Notes

1. Elizabeth Bishop, *The Complete Poems, 1927–1979* (New York: Farrar, Straus and Giroux, 1983), 160.

2. Elizabeth Bishop, *Collected Prose*, ed. Robert Giroux (New York: Farrar, Straus and Giroux, 1984), 33.

3. Vilashini Cooppan, "World Literature and Global Theory: Comparative Literature for the New Millennium," *symploke* 9, no. 1–2 (2001): 15–43.

4. Robert Hass, *Twentieth Century Pleasures: Prose on Poetry*, 3rd ed. (New York: Ecco Press, 1997), 86.

5. Tomasz Różycki, *The Forgotten Keys*, trans. Mira Rosenthal (Brookline, Mass.: Zephyr Press, 2007), 40.

The Uncanny in the Short Lyric

Deirdre O'Connor

Tomaž Šalamun's poem "To Immerse the Weight" took off the top of my head, as Dickinson would say, when I read it on the Web site *Poetry Daily* last spring. And, in the paradoxical way of poetry, it did so quietly, the way a ghost might take off the top of a head: without fanfare, but with great effect. Here's the poem:

> The hunger of cathedrals, silk, the green silk
> of pastures steps over the threshold. I see smoke,
> a horn, a white mouth. The compactness of the dead
> drinks up the sun, as lapis binds the shadow,
>
> fortified in gold. For an instant in the body
> of others, we lean, we burn in the field.
> Crumbs drink and become bread,
> stigmata find directions. Blackbirds, indifferent,
>
> push aside their prey, for only what is seen
> can be decanted. Where then does hunger come from?
> The frivolity of mountains, laces, fringes?
>
> And their tremendous power to drink up
> the kernel, to turn destiny inside out like a glove
> and play with the fingers, to immerse the weight?[1]

The imaginative force of this poem startles me each time I read it. It illustrates what it means to "think outside the box" of socially constructed reality, which is one way of describing the uncanny. The uncanny, according to Freud, is frightening because, among other things, it evokes an uncertainty in the reader as to whether an object is alive or has come to possess human qualities. Thus, for instance, a doll whose eyes flutter open when one enters a child's room will seem uncanny, as might a moonlit night when the trees seem to have hands, or an experience of profound empathy in which one seems, despite the self's boundaries, to understand the thoughts and feelings of another. Freud says that "the uncanny is that class of the frightening which leads back to what is known of old and long familiar," thus linking the familiar, or that which belongs to the house (*heimlich*), with the unfamiliar or strange (*unheimlich*).[2] Freud relies on examples from German lexicographer Daniel Sanders to illustrate the range of what is *heimlich*:

> This is *heimlich*: "When a man feels in his heart that he is so small and the Lord so great—that is what is truly *heimelig*."

And this:

> "You go to sleep there so soft and warm, so wonderfully *heim'lig*."

On some occasions, however, the distinction between *heimlich* and *unheimlich* feels like the difference between raveling and unraveling: purely semantic, or impossible to determine. Again, Freud quotes Sanders to characterize the interchangeability of the terms:

> "The Zecks [a family name] are all 'heimlich.' . . ." "*Heimlich?* . . . What do you understand by '*heimlich*'?" "Well, . . . they are like a buried spring or a dried-up pond. One cannot walk over it without always having the feeling that water might come up there again." "Oh, we call it '*unheimlich*'; you call it '*Heimlich*.' Well, what makes you think that there is something secret and untrustworthy about this family?"[3]

This shiftiness of names for the uncanny may help distinguish its creepiness from the more routine artistic device of defamiliarization, or *ostranenie*, the artistic practice of "making the familiar strange" in order to more intensively focus the viewer's attention upon it. Defamiliarization can be fun, but there is always something unsettling about the uncanny.

In Šalamun's poem, the uncanny appears subtly but immediately: "the hunger of cathedrals" reveals the cathedral as a creature with an appetite. And pastures, with their "green silk," have agency to step over the threshold and deliver us to a mysterious and fractured image of "smoke, / a horn, a white mouth." I picture an animal's body—a creature of the pasture, maybe a goat or a bull. This animal body is dead, on fire, presumably, and in death the body "drinks up the sun," darkening what also lights it.

In stanza two, the speaker claims that "For an instant in the body / of others, we lean, we burn in the field," here invoking the empathic motion of self into others, who, in this case, burn in the field, resonating with the smoke, horn, and white mouth mentioned a few lines earlier. After this move into the body of others, the poem makes a remarkable turn and claim: "Crumbs drink and become bread, / stigmata find directions. Blackbirds, indifferent, / push aside their prey." Like the hungry cathedral, inanimate objects (crumbs) imbibe, but blackbirds lose their appetites. Things and birds behave in ways they are not supposed to.

The speaker—a disembodied voice, it seems to me—then questions the sensations produced by the poem and its imagery. "Where then does hunger come from? / The frivolity of mountains, laces, fringes?" This questioning of the essence, the core, along with the frivolous edges, remains unanswered by the poem, but both the essence and the edges contain or exude a "tremendous power" to "drink up / the kernel," to render uncanny the familiar and expected, and "immerse the weight" of destiny. The seemingly casual gesture that accomplishes this feat is revealed through simile: "to turn destiny inside out like a glove / and play with the fingers." The simile reminds the reader again of the animal body and its parts, though now the body is clearly human, and the hand's presence is made more startling and strange by having been removed from the glove.

Discussing the architectural uncanny, scholar Anthony Vidler observes that much of the power of the uncanny derives from its ability to "establish" and "destabilize" at once—in a sense, to exhume that which had been buried, an activity that is suggested in the turning inside out of the glove.[4] Perhaps because it ends with the image of the glove and its fingers, "To Immerse the Weight" reminds me of Keats's fragment "This Living Hand." However, unlike Keats's reader, who is confronted with the image of a hand as if it is dead, Šalamun's reader is left picturing the absent hand of destiny. In my mind, this absent presence echoes the way the poem manages both to reify and undermine Christianity. And the poem does so in eerily beautiful language that seems to defy translation, even though it *is* translation.

The strategies of the poem complement and support its uncanny power. It's as if the poem invites us to disturb the expected ground and unbury mystery and, in that act of unburying, to discover that the mystery is greater—and scarier—than what we had anticipated. For me, the uncanny contributes a pleasurable, complicating chill to the lyric poem.

WRITING PROMPT

To experiment with the uncanny in a lyric of your own making, consider the exercise below. I enjoyed tinkering with it myself, and the poem that emerged from it follows the exercise.

First: Read "To Immerse the Weight" often enough that you have memorized it, or almost memorized it. Study it, try to make sense of it, and let yourself be unraveled by it.

Second: Choose an object that appeals to your senses. Šalamun begins with cathedrals; I begin my poem with blankets. Any material object will work, but choose one that strikes your imagination, that might seem ordinary but is not.

Third: Give that object some human feeling that surprises you or creeps you out a bit. "The hunger of cathedrals" led me to the phrase "the longing of heavy blankets."

Fourth: Go wherever this image takes you. Use concrete language. If you get stuck, think about your dream life and try to work it into the poem. Try to keep the poem relatively short, about the size of Christopher Merrill's translation of Šalamun's poem.

Here is the poem I wrote after ruminating on "To Immerse the Weight" in a couple of weeks' spare moments:

WAKE / *Deirdre O'Connor*

The longing of heavy blankets that weigh
upon sleeping bodies, selves removed
to interiors

finite as the hours. I hear the bleat of lambs
being shorn, the squelch and muck of fields,
the hands' grasp of tools.

The distance between blades and flesh:
the imagining mind at rest, eyes rolled back
in sockets, breathing steady except

for occasional gasps of terror, dreams
that dissipate faster than smoke,
never so slowly evaporate

as puddles indelicately stepped in
        or a glass of water left bedside
                in the guest room where no one has

counted sheep in months. The house appears
        to want nothing but to be entered
                and kept, inhabited as by fingers

in a cast-off, reclaimed glove, and the beds inside
        are clean and empty-cool as silence
                where a bloodless battle had been.

Notes

1. Tomaž Šalamun, "To Immerse the Weight," trans. Christopher Merrill, *Poetry Daily*, http://www.poems.com (accessed April 5, 2006).

2. Sigmund Freud, "The Uncanny," in *Writings on Art and Literature*, ed. Werner Hamacher and David E. Wellbery (Stanford: Stanford University Press, 1997), 195.

3. Ibid., 197–98.

4. Anthony Vidler, "The Architecture of the Uncanny: The Unhomely Houses of the Romantic Sublime," *Assemblage*, no. 3 (1987): 12, http://www.jstor.org (accessed August 24, 2007).

TWO

Recording Mortal Sight: The Drama of Prosody

An Interview with Phillis Levin

Phillis Levin: The reason [Anthony Hecht's] "The Transparent Man" seems so appropriate for this anthology is that the process of reading the poem yields profound insights into the creation of voice through prosody, as well as insights into the relation of pattern to meaning. It is one of the best poems for unfolding and illuminating the genius of blank verse, the ways in which one can embody meaning through prosodic variation. The poem contains lines of remarkable textural density and equally stunning moments of textural transparency. I've wanted to write about this poem for a long time, and every time I reread it I learn more about the radiating consequences of seemingly minor variations.

THE TRANSPARENT MAN / *Anthony Hecht*

I'm mighty glad to see you, Mrs. Curtis,
And thank you very kindly for this visit—
Especially now when all the others here
Are having holiday visitors, and I feel
A little conspicuous and in the way.
It's mainly because of Thanksgiving. All these mothers
And wives and husbands gaze at me soulfully
And feel they should break up their box of chocolates
For a donation, or hand me a chunk of fruitcake.
What they don't understand and never guess
Is that it's better for me without a family;
It's a great blessing. Though I mean no harm.
And as for visitors, why, I have you,
All cheerful, brisk and punctual every Sunday,
Like church, even if the aisles smell of phenol.

And you always bring even better gifts than any
On your book-trolley. Though they mean only good,
Families can become a sort of burden.
I've only got my father, and he won't come,
Poor man, because it would be too much for him.
And for me, too, so it's best the way it is.
He knows, you see, that I will predecease him,
Which is hard enough. It would take a callous man
To come and stand around and watch me failing.
(Now don't you fuss; we both know the plain facts.)
But for him it's even harder. He loved my mother.
They say she looked like me; I suppose she may have.
Or rather, as I grew older I came to look
More and more like she must one time have looked,
And so the prospect for my father now
Of losing me is like having to lose her twice.
I know he frets about me. Dr. Frazer
Tells me he phones in every single day,
Hoping that things will take a turn for the better.
But with leukemia things don't improve.
It's like a sort of blizzard in the bloodstream,
A deep, severe, unseasonable winter,
Burying everything. The white blood cells
Multiply crazily and storm around,
Out of control. The chemotherapy
Hasn't helped much, and it makes my hair fall out.
I know I look a sight, but I don't care.
I care about fewer things; I'm more selective.
It's got so I can't even bring myself
To read through any of your books these days.
It's partly weariness, and partly the fact
That I seem not to care much about the endings,
How things work out, or whether they even do.
What I do instead is sit here by this window
And look out at the trees across the way.
You wouldn't think that was much, but let me tell you,
It keeps me quite intent and occupied.

Now all the leaves are down, you can see the spare,
Delicate structures of the sycamores,
The fine articulation of the beeches.
I have sat here for days studying them,
And I have only just begun to see
What it is that they resemble. One by one,
They stand there like magnificent enlargements
Of the vascular system of the human brain.
I see them there like huge discarnate minds,
Lost in their meditative silences.
The trunks, branches and twigs compose the vessels
That feed and nourish vast immortal thoughts.
So I've assigned them names. There, near the path,
Is the great brain of Beethoven, and Kepler
Haunts the wide spaces of that mountain ash.
This view, you see, has become my Hall of Fame.
It came to me one day when I remembered
Mary Beth Finley who used to play with me
When we were girls. One year her parents gave her
A birthday toy called "The Transparent Man."
It was made of plastic, with different colored organs,
And the circulatory system all mapped out
In rivers of red and blue. She'd ask me over
And the two of us would sit and study him
Together, and do a powerful lot of giggling.
I figure he's most likely the only man
Either of us would ever get to know
Intimately, because Mary Beth became
A Sister of Mercy when she was old enough.
She must be thirty-one; she was a year
Older than I, and about four inches taller.
I used to envy both those advantages
Back in those days. Anyway, I was struck
Right from the start by the sea-weed intricacy,
The fine-haired, silken-threaded filiations
That wove, like Belgian lace, throughout the head.
But this last week it seems I have found myself

Looking beyond, or through, individual trees
At the dense, clustered woodland just behind them,
Where those great, nameless crowds patiently stand.
It's become a sort of complex, ultimate puzzle
And keeps me fascinated. My eyes are twenty-twenty,
Or used to be, but of course I can't unravel
The tousled snarl of intersecting limbs,
That mackled, cinder grayness. It's a riddle
Beyond the eye's solution. Impenetrable.
If there is order in all that anarchy
Of granite mezzotint, that wilderness,
It takes a better eye than mine to see it.
It set me on to wondering how to deal
With such a thickness of particulars,
Deal with it faithfully, you understand,
Without blurring the issue. Of course I know
That within a month the sleeving snows will come
With cold, selective emphases, with massings
And arbitrary contrasts, rendering things
Deceptively simple, thickening the twigs
To frosty veins, bestowing epaulets
And decorations on every birch and aspen.
And the eye, self-satisfied, will be misled,
Thinking the puzzle solved, supposing at last
It can look forth and comprehend the world.
That's when you have to really watch yourself.
So I hope that you won't think me plain ungrateful
For not selecting one of your fine books,
And I take it very kindly that you came
And sat here and let me rattle on this way.[1]

Editors: Will you, please, begin by introducing the poem to us?

Phillis Levin: "The Transparent Man" by Anthony Hecht is a poem in blank verse, but it's also a dramatic monologue, a poetic form that is often composed in blank verse. It's a poem in the voice of a young woman, a woman in her early thirties who is lying in a hospital with leukemia. We discover that through what she reveals of herself.

Editors: How would you describe the persona of the poem?

Phillis Levin: Well, the persona unfolds over time, and that's one of the reasons the poem is so compelling. The person speaking is modest; she is self-effacing, so the title, "The Transparent Man," seems to be connected to her, because she sounds transparent. There's a quality of transparency to her speaking; that is, she seems to reveal herself easily. It's not as though she is revealing her emotions, but she doesn't seem to have any guile. She's not witty. Or let's just say that if she's witty, it's more about her condition. She is not at all self-pitying.

We are discovering her through her interaction with Mrs. Curtis, a visitor who brings library books to the different patients. One of the curiosities of the poem is that the speaker, this young woman, is not interested in reading books any more. And I think that is one of the reasons the poem is so interesting: Anthony Hecht, a consummate master of poetry, a great reader, a great aesthete, a great lover of the arts—he knew a lot about music and painting, as well as literature—takes on the persona of a young woman who would rather look out the window at trees than read another book.

Editors: Why do you think blank verse is such an effective means of creating voice and, oddly here, an intimate kind of voice?

Phillis Levin: Again, one of the paradoxes of all art is how, when it's working, you're conscious of the artifice and conscious that it seems natural to be moving within the artifice, giving yourself over to the design. Say if you watch people dancing—you are aware that these are learned moves, patterns that become second nature, and there is the thrill of seeing people perform them. You see the exchange of energy, constant flow and flux, and you know that there is a formula and there is a transcendence of formula simultaneously.

When blank verse works, it's often creating the illusion of the speaking voice, of authentic, vernacular speech. One of the things I've noticed reading this poem is that Hecht interweaves a lot of monosyllabic words with polysyllabic words, and that's one of the ways I think he is able to modulate the voice, creating different textures of transparency and opacity. So both the speaker's humility and her interior complexity are continuously projected through the prosody itself. She'll say things that sound or seem more sophisticated because she's using polysyllabic words. There's actually one line in which she only utters monosyllables: "I know I look a sight, but I don't care." That's completely natural speech, a statement of ten simple words easily forming a pattern of five iambic feet: "I know | I look | a sight, | but I | don't care." Those ten monosyllables occur a few lines after the word "chemotherapy," which is a hard word to utter in a poem. And then there are intricately balanced passages such as this one: "Anyway, I was struck / Right from the start by the sea-weed intricacy, / The fine-haired, silken-threaded filiations / That wove, like Belgian lace, throughout the head."

Weaving is one of the motifs in the poem, one of the overarching metaphors: how, looking through the trees, one sees the way nature weaves and unweaves patterns. So the leaves are full, and she can see the forest, and then she can't see what's there; you get the sense it's a mystery, she can't really see what's there. She's trying to see into and through the landscape. Then she tells us how, as winter comes on, as the leaves fall, things become clearer. But then you see even deeper into the forest, and then you see even more of what you don't see, and then the snows come and they clarify everything, crystallize everything. It's that point near the end of the poem when the speaker actually says, "That's when you have to really watch yourself"—when you think you can see things. I think that's also Hecht's way of saying that, just when we think we see things, just when we think we are in control, we have mastery, that's when we're most likely to fall into a kind of deception, a self-deception or an illusion.

So it's a way, I think, Hecht himself, as an artist, is exploring the limits of sight, the limits of insight and vision—and compassion. Hecht exposes the limits of his art and the limits of artifice, of creating and understanding a character other than himself.

But back to the issue of prosody and blank verse. The whole history of English prosody shows the blank verse line to be the most suitable measure for dramatic speech. It can be heightened heroic speech, but in this case it's really this pretty "plain" person who happens to be lying in bed, dying of leukemia. She sounds "natural," she's an absolutely believable speaker. And that's part of the mystery . . . for she becomes an enchanting, fascinating person that the reader falls in love with, but it's hard to understand why.

Editors: How does the use of blank verse enhance our understanding of the speaker's emotions or emotional stance?

Phillis Levin: Blank verse feels very natural, very flexible, when you work in it and if you read it a lot. But the thing about it is, it's an extremely elastic line. Many of the lines in this poem have feminine endings—that is, they end with an unstressed syllable—and that creates a lilt; you hear that from the very beginning of the poem. The first line ends with the word "Curtis." Then you have "visit." So the first two lines have that softness at the end, which tends to push us onto the next line, eliciting enjambment. The third line is the first one that ends on a full stress, the word "here," and then "feel," and then "way," and then you go "mothers," "soulfully," "chocolates," "fruitcake." Hecht modulates a lot between lines that end with a strong stress and end with a weaker stress; and he plays with where the stress falls at the beginning of the line, sometimes opening with a stressed rather than an unstressed syllable, with a word whose accent falls on the first syllable. Shakespeare does that frequently—so many poets do. It's what makes a line dynamic and unpredictable, in counterpoint to the underlying pattern of regularity. This elasticity is one of the most common qualities of blank verse.

When I say elastic, I mean that you can have five different lines that all scan as iambic pentameter, yet all sound and behave very differently from each other. The question is why. It's the sonic value of the word that contributes to the pace of the line, and the pace of previous lines will affect the rhythmic expression of that word in the line it inhabits. If you have a polysyllabic word (and every polysyllabic word in the English language has one predominant accent, though other syllables in that word may also be more strongly stressed than others), that word will be pronounced more quickly or more slowly, depending not only on the length of vowels and quality of consonants but on the overall environment of the line in which it lives. So if you have

> I'm mighty glad to see you, Mrs. Curtis,
> And thank you very kindly for this visit—
> Especially now when all the others here
> Are having holiday visitors, and I feel
> A little conspicuous and in the way

it just sounds like authentic speech; it sounds idiomatic. You don't say "con-SPIC-u-OUS," you say "conSPICuous." That's part of the dialectic of any prosodic line. The dialectic results from the tension between the abstract pattern of the verse and the idiomatic speech stress pattern. So if you have a word like "conspicuous" that has four syllables, anyone would say the second and the fourth are stressed differently than the first and third. The second and the fourth are stressed more than the first and the third, and yet it's the second that is stressed more than all four. So you have "con-SPIC-u-ous" and you have "con-SPIC-u-OUS," and those two things are happening simultaneously.

The underlying metrical pattern, which is the frame, is an abstraction. Think of Mondrian. As Mondrian develops, his work grows more and more abstract; he formulates a geometry. But if you look at a landscape, or if you look at a painting by Cézanne, you see a landscape, and you see its geometry. You can say here you have this abstraction, which is the blank verse, and then you have the living speech pattern. But the poem slowly unveils a young woman who is dying, who is going to be a skeleton, and underneath it all is the skeleton of the blank verse: you have the abstraction, you have the pattern. Abstraction has a kind of eternity to it, but it's also a kind of death because it's separated from the organic, living, pulsing moment. And you have the pulsing moment in her speech patterns and in the variation, the deviation from the pattern.

Why would you want to write in blank verse, even today? Well, that's because you are able to create these double realities, these polyphonies, where you have deviations from the norm, as is the case in any complex system. You can't have deviation without a norm. The speaker of this poem is a person whose system is breaking down. And the whole poem is called "The Transparent Man." By the middle of the poem, we discover that the transparent man is actually just a toy that this woman's childhood friend received as a birthday present—not a toy to play with, but something to study—a model of the circulatory system. Here's a poem that's trying to look into a person's soul, and inside of the poem we see this girl looking at, looking into, a transparent man. And what does it mean to be transparent, to be seen through, to be seen? The young woman is more and more interested in looking out the window at the trees—and while looking at them, what does she see? She imagines they are the brains of great thinkers. She's projecting her experience of that toy, that anatomical model of the circulatory system, into the forest, and in seeing what she sees, we look inside of her.

It's sort of endless; it's like a fractal of geometry. She has created (Hecht has created) this metaphor: she sees the world through that transparent man, and then she begins to see Beethoven and Kepler, those great thinkers. And then there's also that mystery—what does that mean, to be seeing these great minds? They're not alive; they're in her mind. She's reading them; she's reading the forest.

Editors: How does this poem work like or unlike Browning's dramatic monologues?

Phillis Levin: That's a good question. Well, I think that there's no way to avoid thinking about Browning because he developed the prototypical dramatic monologue as a separate entity that stands on its own, apart from a verse drama. Browning also wrote powerful verse dramas; but his remarkable innovation, the dramatic monologue, must disclose its own context. The difference is, I think, of course, a stylistic difference, but there's a kinship there; that is, the mode is the same. And what Hecht is doing that he learned from Browning is to reveal character through diction and through detail: a character speaks and reveals something about himself or herself that he or she doesn't know he or she is revealing, as in "My Last Duchess," when the duke points out "that's my last duchess painted on the wall." So how are people revealed, how do they reveal themselves? Often through interaction with someone else. Here the young woman is speaking to Mrs. Curtis. It's not a soliloquy. In other words, it's not that this young woman is lying in bed, speaking out loud her final thoughts that we are overhearing. She is speaking to someone else, so we are seeing her in a dramatic exchange. That's what Browning did. What Hecht must have learned from Browning is that you can reveal character this way, that people reveal things about themselves that they don't know they are revealing. There's a lot of pleasure in doing that. It's a challenge.

Editors: Has your opinion of the poem changed over time? Do you discover new things each time you come to it?

Phillis Levin: Yes, actually, yes. I'm amazed at this poem because, more and more, I see it as connected to this issue of surrender and mastery that we confront as artists and in relationship to life. That is, the more we know, the more we don't know, they say. The more we know, we don't know. . . . Humility, I think, is very important, and because of this, I'm especially fascinated by Hecht. Hecht wrote a number of monologues. I think it's not a coincidence that it's much later in his career that he could identify with or at least create a persona of a young woman rather than a man. For example, it's a woman he creates, a woman who is ill and who, according to whatever she says about herself, has never had any sexual experience; the closest she'll ever get to a man is this transparent man, she reveals. Hecht has given voice to someone so other, and he has no animosity toward this female. I think it took him a long time to be able to identify with an ill, young, inexperienced woman who doesn't want to read a book. It's not the likely thing. But I also think he is exploring something troubling, something intriguing; it's not an act of narcissism. And I think it's like Faustus in a way, that Hecht is exploring the limits. But by the end of the poem, I cannot help thinking of Prospero.

There's actually a quotation I found pretty recently that made me rethink everything. It's something that Francis Bacon says: "All depends on keeping the eye steadily fixed on the facts of nature and so receiving their images as they are. For God forbid that we should give out a dream of our own imagination for a pattern of the world."[2] I think all of us would have very mixed feelings about that. What's wrong with giving out a dream of our own imagination for a pattern of the world? But to keep the eye fixed on the facts of nature and receive images as they are, well, we have a lot of skepticism about that; how is that even possible? And yet, that is partly what this poem is trying to do. The girl is trying to be fixed on nature, but she keeps projecting into nature. Hecht keeps trying to focus on her, though. I think he is trying to see what would she really be like—not *me*, but what would *she* really be like. And you know, this whole thing about not being a self-satisfied eye, e-y-e, or I, the end of that,

> If there is order in all that anarchy
> Of granite mezzotint, that wilderness,
> It takes a better eye than mine to see it.
> It set me on to wondering how to deal
> With such a thickness of particulars.

That's one of the most extraordinary phrases, "a thickness of particulars." It's a definition of texture, of the nature of poetry, and of the nature of experience. "Deal with it faithfully, you understand, / Without blurring the issue." That's it, right? How do you not blur the issue, how do you not project? How do you see without projecting? It's almost like wanting to have a scientific vision. It's as if this girl, as she's dying, or this young woman, as she's dying, wants to see things as they are; she wants to lay things bare without illusion. And Hecht is laying her bare. And death will lay her bare.

"Thickness of particulars" also seems to be a description of prosody: he creates a prosody where there are very dense lines musically, semantically, phonetically, syntactically, and then there are lines where everything just becomes clear and transparent again. I think one of the ways Hecht does this is through the counterpointing of polysyllabic and monosyllabic words.

Editors: You already briefly touched on your own work in blank verse. Could you tell us a little bit more about how this poem relates to your own work in blank verse? And also, has your reading of the poem directly influenced your own poetry? Is there a particular poem of yours that you think explores the same kind of strategies?

Phillis Levin: I can't think of any particular poem. I wrote from a very early age; I was very seriously writing by the age of twelve, and my very early work was influenced by hearing a lot of poetry read out loud. And that was largely poetry that was traditional, say Shakespeare, Shelley, Dickinson, but a lot of it wasn't so. For example, I was reading Ferlinghetti and Cummings and Sandburg as well as Dickinson, so I was writing in free verse, in what's now called "open field." I was writing things scattered all over the page between the age of twelve and twenty-one. I was also writing poems in blank verse, and I was writing poems in rhyme and meter. I was experimenting with all of those things from the very beginning. I think that when I returned to working with a line that had meter, what challenged me was the way the structure helped me get out of myself because there's a tension, there's a physicality in prosody. For me, it's more physical when there's discipline in the prosody. I'm solving a problem and it makes me forget myself, and I can surrender to it.

I've always had a very strong interest in philosophy and science, and this poem is also about wanting to see such things. I don't identify usually with people who are ill, and so this girl is very other to me also. But I was fascinated by her imagination, the depth of her imagination, and I was very moved by Hecht's tribute to her, creating someone of such great imagination who is not "special," who would rather look out the window than read. Maybe the relationship to the natural world is so primary for me; that might be one of the reasons the poem touches me. In nature, you always have patterns; you have occurrences of patterns that keep generating themselves and mutating. And so, for me, blank verse is organic. It can keep mutating if you think about it: it is self-generating. There are infinite mutations that are possible within the patterns, and often you have more variety when you have a pattern with deviation than if you have no pattern; that's what I've discovered.

I still write a lot in free verse, but the rigorous underpinning of any metrical structure, I think, creates tensions that allow people to transcend their own limits. Everybody knows this from sports, from dance; for some reason, people don't apply whatever they know about those other things to writing, as much. People think, "Oh, I want to be free." But the thing is, you get on the dance floor, and people usually want to dance with somebody who has some sense of how to move in relation to the rhythm of the music. Spontaneity is not the opposite of that; spontaneity often comes from inhabiting a pattern, a design. There's a degree to which certain things are given in a language. Meaning, if I grew up speaking French, probably the Alexandrine would seem a more natural line to me because, after all, the prosodic strategies and structures evolve from whatever linguistic propensities the language has, and English, because it is so accentual, has all the opportunities for playing with the modulations and sounds.

There are all different kinds of poets, and I think I happen to be very visual and very auditory. For me, these auditory effects, these subtle variations that are possible, give enormous pleasure to me, and I like giving pleasure to the reader. That's why I do it and why I'm drawn to it, but I think there's a degree to which there are certain things that are inexplicable, and one of them is how it is possible to make some things sound so natural. Once you look at it and break it down, at a certain point, the question is: how is it that artifice can seem natural? And yet that is usually how art behaves: when it's working, it just seems like a given, it's like, "Oh, it had to be." "It's like a sort of blizzard in the bloodstream"—that sounds like natural speech, doesn't it? "A deep, severe, unseasonable winter," but that line sounds so different, "Burying everything." Before that there's that flat line, "But with leukemia things don't improve. / It's like a sort of blizzard in the bloodstream." "It's like a sort of blizzard in the bloodstream" has a musicality to it because it's so regular, but the regularity of that and the beauty of that are foregrounded by the line before it, "But with leukemia things don't improve." Inside the poem, he's able to create all of these contrasts. . . .

There's a poem in my very first book, but it's a longer poem, and it's called "The Stairwell." It's actually, I think, the poem that wound up getting me hired at the University of Maryland because it's a poem that Michael Collier had read that he liked a lot, and then he invited me to apply for the job. It's an older poem, but it's a visionary poem about a stairwell and this staircase that I used to imagine was a harp when I was a child. It's in iambic pentameter, and it's a meditative poem, a kind of Wordsworthian poem, I suppose, in terms of how childhood is the source of vision. It's actually very autobiographical; as a child I really did believe that I could fly. Every night I dreamt that I climbed to the top of the stairwell and jumped and that I was floating throughout the house. And I persisted in believing in it because I dreamt it all the time. But I did literally sit at the bottom of the staircase and play with the banister as if it were a harp. So it offers sort of a poetic beginning, this poem. Somehow it has a kinship, probably because there is the constriction in physical space and there's the vastness of imagination in this poem, and I think that probably speaks to this girl who's even more constricted; she's in a hospital bed, but she's looking out and her imagination has endless freedom. "The Stairwell" is a kind of emancipation poem, as well as an *ars poetica*: it's about the discovery of the boundlessness of one's imagination, and so maybe in some way it's very appropriate.

Oh, there was one very personal thing I didn't say . . . you asked me why this poem means so much to me. Last summer, my aunt had heart surgery. She is a very vital, lively person. She's doing very well now. Jack, my now fiancé, is a cardiac anesthesiologist, and he took the case (and when he agreed to take the case, he must have had a much better sense of what he was getting into than I did, that the experience would be charged with emotion), working with a top heart surgeon. I was seeing step by step the kinds of things involved, just what a patient has to go through. I was a witness to the conversation Jack had with my aunt the night before the operation, his interview with her as the patient. I listened to him speaking with my aunt; I could hear and see the exchange of words and gestures that led her to trust her life in someone else's hands. And after the operation was over, I visited her every day and saw the humiliation and all of that—how vulnerable people are. Watching Jack in his daily interactions with my aunt, from the day before the operation to the period of critical care and then recovery, made me understand "The Transparent Man" in a whole new way. He happens to be someone of great humility. A lot of people in medicine are egocentric; he happens to have a lot of humility. And watching him day to day dealing with managing moment to moment somebody's life and realizing it took enormous detachment and control, somehow it became an analogy for what happens in art. There's an enormous amount of healing, and then you have to have all this other control. . . . It just hit me that, especially in medicine, very high-level medicine, you are dealing with unbelievable sophistication, and yet there is a degree beyond which you have no control: you don't know what is going to happen. You have all of the equipment, you have the great minds, etc., and something can go wrong that you can't explain. I was in the hospital every single day watching this, and I was watching him. And I was watching how he interacted with her, the respect he had for her as a person. It's very hard for me to articulate, but it really affected me because it made me understand that human touch that's needed no matter how much control you have. And I somehow felt that the poem, for Hecht, was a very mature moment for him because it was this exploration of a non-heroic subject, of a subject who wouldn't be remembered, who was ordinary, and showing something absolutely extraordinary in that person. Somehow the experience of this life and death thing, it has to do with technique and pathos. You act as if you don't have any feeling. These doctors, they just—they have so much feeling when you talk to them, but they can't show it.

You have to have enormous detachment in order to function, and maybe that's what it is; maybe that's what I'm attracted to as an artist and why I loved the sciences always. There's a part of me that loves dealing with a problem, solving a problem in language. And that's so different from the realm of feeling. You know how it is: when you work on a poem, it can be about the greatest heartbreak, and there you are wondering where the line break should be. And you're like, "Wait a minute." It's not just a distraction; there's a pleasure in the heightened relationship to the craft, and at the same time there's all this feeling and you're juggling all these things simultaneously. So I guess somehow I've just been spared that. I've had very little experience in life with illness or with people being ill. It was the first time I had spent a lot of time in the hospital. So probably it did bring back the poem because "The Transparent Man" is set in a hospital ward, and its speaker is someone who can't really do much more than look out the window.

> What I do instead is sit here by this window
> And look out at the trees across the way.
> You wouldn't think that was much, but let me tell you,
> It keeps me quite intent and occupied.

I love that, "It keeps me quite intent and occupied." And then she goes further, "Now all the leaves are down, you can see the spare, / Delicate structures of the sycamores, / The fine articulation of the beeches." That's an incredible articulation, articulating the nature of blank verse, "The fine ar-ti-cu-la-tion-of-the-beech-es,"—you don't say it that way, you say, "The fine articulation of the beeches," but it's this absolutely mellifluous line articulating the nature of blank verse—you hear the beauty of it, it just sings . . .

Hecht has created somebody who has such a vivid imagination; we get lost in her imagination. We become part of her imaginative projection. He's created a world in a world in a world. Now what that has to do with blank verse, it doesn't go without saying. It doesn't have to be in blank verse. But I think the weaving of the spell has to do with the relationships between regularity of pattern, which is calming, which is soothing, which is enchanting, which creates a lull, you just sort of relax, you trust him, you're with him. And after all, this is somebody who is breathing. To be alive means you have regular repetitive rhythms continuing. And yet what it means to be alive isn't just inhale, exhale; it's what we're doing while we're doing that. It's as if the prosody itself is the metaphor, is the frame for the baseline of living.

WRITING PROMPTS

One idea is to read different lines of blank verse out loud and see how differently they behave, and try to figure out why. Why does one line of blank verse sound so different from another? What is that? A lot of it has to do with syntax, as with every other metrical line. Also, what's happening is that it affects the way you handle syntax because, in a metrical line, the line ends where the meter runs out; maybe there's one less or one more syllable. You actually are enhancing your enjambments, but the enjambments feel more natural than they would in free verse because in free verse you are making a decision every time you break a line, whereas in a metrical verse, the line has to break. So there's the feeling of inevitability. The paradox is that you can have a more dramatic enjambment that seems more natural.

Also, to play with the values of words, that's a lot of fun. For example, try to write a blank verse line with as few words as possible, and then try to write one with as many words as possible. So with ten monosyllables you could have a blank verse line, but it's possible, as well, to compose a blank verse line with only two words. And then you can see what happens when you say it out loud, and then you can talk about relative speed. Speed is so important in a poem. And you control speed through the modulation of the length of words. If you have a series of lines with predominantly short words, and then you introduce a line with longer words, you're going to pronounce that line the same way. If you have five lines in a row that seem to take the same amount of time, you'll tend to give the sixth line the same amount of time. So, if it's a line with fewer words, suddenly you'll be pronouncing that line more slowly. Do you see what I'm saying? With blank verse, another fun thing is once you have the pattern, the environment of blank verse, then you can see the effect of introducing a longer or shorter line into that environment; for example, a shorter metrical line, a very short line, just one or two stresses, and then you see, oh, you've come up short, and there's a sort of thrill or shock there.

"The Transparent Man" is also so compelling because Hecht deploys a very broad range of diction. That would be an interesting prompt: write a poem in which you can have a technical term like "chemotherapy," and then you can have a phrase like "Belgian lace." Part of the reason the poem is so rich is that it includes all of these different realities: Kepler and Beethoven, a toy, the word "plastic" is in here. Even the syntax—the word "impenetrable" is a single word sentence. You know, "And the eye, self-satisfied, will be misled"—to me that's the key to the poem. "And the eye, self-satisfied, will be misled, / Thinking the puzzle solved, supposing at last / It can look forth and comprehend the world." This is really a poem in which Hecht is saying we really can never comprehend the world. That's pretty amazing. It's a vision. And though this poem bears no real resemblance to "The Hill," an earlier visionary poem of Hecht's, both of those poems are visions that occur in unassuming, bland, uninspiring places. That would be maybe another sort of prompt, emphasizing something separate from the prosodic element, for instance a poem in which you develop a way of seeing that then could be applied to something else, say as an analogue. It's also a dramatic monologue, so it's a poem showing the opportunities possible to explore in a mode.

Another prompt could be to write a poem in which you imagine yourself as someone you could never imagine being. Also, I think it's very important that poems be heard aloud. I think it is really interesting to take someone like Frost or somebody like Elizabeth Bishop or a lot of different poets who have written in blank verse and to look at the way their blank verse sounds, and you look at Stevens and you ask, What is the value of these sounds? What makes one line sound slow and one sound fast? Because once you have the constant of a pattern, you can see the difference. That's one reason I think the poem is very suited for teaching, because it's long enough, it develops a vision, it has many layers of language and imagination, and you can compare all these different kinds of lines and say, "Oh, this line is so different from that line."

One of the things I've found useful with teaching on any level—people get so confused about stress and accent and all of that—is just to ask people to write their names down and look at their names and ask them how they pronounce them. Everybody knows that if somebody mispronounces his or her name, it often has to do with putting too much weight or stress on the wrong stress, accenting the wrong syllable. You may not respond or even recognize the name as your own when you hear it pronounced; if it doesn't sound like you, then it isn't you. Your fundamental sense of identity is connected with where that syllable is weighted. And in a word like "Elizabeth," the second syllable is stressed, but it's "Eliza-beth." If it were in an iambic pentameter line, you would go "Eliza-beth," right? And "-beth" would also get a stress, too, though somewhat less so. We know that the second of these four syllables is the strongest, and so just by looking at a name, one discovers the music of the name—how it is made up of four syllables, one of which is more strongly accented than the others, and yet how two of the four are more weighted than the other two. If one experiments with pronouncing names aloud, the power of accent and stress pattern comes to the foreground. We learn what we take for granted about how integral those accents are to identity. Everyone knows this, but most people don't think about it, aren't conscious of it, until someone mispronounces their name.

THE STAIRWELL / *Phillis Levin*

The deepening glissando of steps
Where the banister spokes became a harp
On which my untuned song was played,
At night became the shrine of my unfolding,
A meeting place for dreams on the sublime.
In the dark, I rose from my bed
And moved across the threshold of my door
Into the hall, where the stairwell
Shone in the glow of the night-light.

At the top of the staircase I posed
Like a diver, held my breath and jumped
The full flight, hitting the landing,
Then gliding and floating through the house,
Lifted by the flare and fission
Of a thousand thoughts.
The stairwell
Was my night garden, where I returned,
By day, to bask in the light
And shadow of the spokes, considering
Generations of cloud shapes
Recurring like rhythms I strummed on the harp
While I sat at the bottom of the stairs,
Chin on the railing's lustrous wood,
Fingers flying swiftly on resistant strings,
Making music hollow as an echo.
There I plucked the fruits of isolation
And reason, for there logic took its turns,
A philosophy was born, and the disobedience
To a life which seemed the pale shadow
Of my dreams.
But the world that moves
All worlds imagined was shifting and teeming
Outside, where a tall pine grew,
Knocking against the second-story window
By the time I was ten. By then
I was done with hunting for treasure
In dirt and dead needles under that tree
And instead, in the heat of summer,
Descended to the basement, where thick-bodied
Books with thin, fine pages cooled
The spaces between my fingers; and upstairs,
In autumn and winter and spring, reading
In the parlor by the light of the bronze
Torch lamp, alone in the embrace
Of grandfather's armchair, I'd turn
To face its old, broad back—tracing,

In the network of cracked leather,
A faded map whose veins
Led through wavering tributaries
To countries and cities
Where I was explorer and ruler, unaware
That my world was unpeopled
And bare.
So children are brought
From the womb into various lights
And darks, barely distinguishing
The forms and terms of their imprisonment,
But imagining, wherever there is a space
Resembling the mind (or a simple thing
Well-wrought), a new world—that does not
Breed and bury what should be cleared
And uncovered. For the way of growth
Is wound in a spring
Of information and viscera
Invisibly weaving patterns
The loving and watchful beholder
Divines. Looking into the mirror,
The child sees the beautiful petal
Of its face, reaches with the hands,
And begins to search the planet
For something that will match
This consciousness: first in the mirror,
Then in the window, the winding walkway,
The opus of light and air.
So to live
In a world shutting out
The danger at every turn of being
Alive is to rent a room doomed
To destruction by collapse or explosion.
The mind finds the analogue
For implosion in itself, for expansion
In itself; and soon the imagination
Sketches and fills in

A design that seems the blueprint
Of a memory—and thus, unwittingly,
Engineers the ruin of the prison
Before it has even been named.
The roof creaks open and folds back
Like an antique book, leaving the house
Utterly exposed to earth and sky.
Now the skull must cover
What the brain recovers, the heart
Regulate the rhythm of its rage
Inside its scaffolding of labor and desire—
Less a function of traffic and dread,
More the correlative of body and head.
Root systems: cosmology of coils and knots
That, in time, unravel and untwine,
Raying upward, where stars tangle
In the moonlit twigs, limbs bow
Under changing leaves, death visits
And departs, sunlight always casting shadows
In the mind's corridors, its beckoning
Branches and abysmal mines.
The self unwinds
To let the world be wound in all its ways;
The body reclaims the valley of the soul,
And from its rich well of darkness
Seeks the blue uncharted regions of day.[3]

Notes

The editors conducted this interview on October 2, 2007.

1. Anthony Hecht, *The Transparent Man* (New York: Knopf-Random House, 1990), 69–72.

2. Francis Bacon, "The Great Insaturation," in *Collected Works*, ed. James Spedding (London: Routledge, 1996), 32.

3. Phillis Levin, *Temples and Fields: Poems* (Athens: University of Georgia Press, 1988), 43–46.

The Physics of Persona Poems

A. Van Jordan

When we talk about the short story, we think of a moment in a character's life that defines who this person is. In the persona poem, we have a similar artistic problem: we need to locate that person's voice, but, more important, we need to locate where that voice is at this time in his or her life. The question I often ask of the persona is, why are we hearing this story *now?* That is to say, I want to know what the defining moment in the poem is that will reveal character. And if character *is* revealed, I want to know something as simple as *What am I supposed to learn from this? What's at stake here?* These are valuable questions to ask of any poem, really, but I think the necessity is more pronounced when we talk about the persona. Indeed, the persona will surely fall short without attending to these questions.

I like poems that take emotional risks. My first drafts often have emotion in the foreground of the poem; 90 percent of my revision process consists of pushing the emotions into the background. The emotional revelation of the first draft cannot be captured in subsequent drafts. After the first draft, the revision process becomes more intellectual than emotional. The persona poem calls for emotional resonance almost as a tenet of its tradition. I became particularly attracted to the persona poem because I found I just didn't have the chops for it early on, so I started writing a lot of bad, sentimental personas and reading poets who had mastered this poem: Rita Dove, W. H. Auden, Robert Hayden, Ai, Patricia Smith, Norman Dubie, Chaucer, and others.

In the process of the workshop, I find that many poets steer clear of sentimentality, often at the expense of emotion. As a result, I started asking poets in workshops to point out an emotional risk they were taking in the poem, to locate where the poem risked being sentimental. I started this because I was tired of reading so many sterile, emotionless poems in workshops and even literary journals. Some poets admitted that they didn't "go there" because it was too close to family, it was too soon after a relationship, or they were afraid to reveal male vulnerability, and so on.

The emotion in a poem is intimately connected to the tone of the poem. Tone not only holds emotion but also *conveys* emotion. And if we can say that tone conveys emotion, then there are ways in which the tone also conveys the character or persona. Going back to "memorable characters" in poetry, it's often the tone of the persona that we remember: the enigmatic tone and truncated syntax of the alien in Hayden's "American Journal"; the minstrelsy of Henry/Mr. Bones in John Berryman's *Dream Songs*; the humor of the Wife of Bath.

In fiction and drama, characters are developed through their actions. Speech, appearance, and even thoughts contribute to the development of character, but character is ultimately created through seeing characters in motion. In fact, these personas often *do* take action in the poem and, through an equation of action and tone, create character.

But when we speak of the persona poem, "action" should be bracketed in quotes. There are moments in which the action is more in line with what Isaac Newton referred to as potential energy. Potential energy exists whenever an object that has mass holds a position within a force field. That is, it exists whenever an object has the potential to attempt to resist gravity. His equation was potential energy = mass × gravity × height above the earth's surface. Thus, the legend of the low hanging apple (mass) falling (gravitational acceleration) from a tree's limb (height above the earth's surface).

In a persona poem, the thoughts, history, motivations, and situation of a persona can all be potential energy. The persona, through any one of these elements, can be motivated to take action.

Newton called action "kinetic energy." Kinetic energy takes the equation for potential energy and factors in the *velocity* of the apple falling from the tree. So, one would ask how much potential energy is in a rubber band stretched to capacity. Answer: Possibly enough to shoot it across a classroom. How much kinetic energy is that? Answer: Enough to send it across the classroom at 10 miles per hour. Or, if you think of a golf ball approaching you at 5 miles per hour, you can probably catch it. But if that same golf ball is traveling at 150 miles per hour, you'd better duck.

It's easy to think in terms of action in poems; we simply follow the verbs. In the moments of potential energy, the speaker usually speaks in past tense (recalling history) or in the subjunctive (expressing a wish or possibility).

It's when the speaker moves to the present tense or the affirmative that we see the shift in action, which often coincides with a shift in tone. More simply put, we take action once we make our minds up to do so.

My concern here, though, is what is the potential energy that leads to the action in the poem? And, more to the point, what motivates this persona? Are there tonal cues that we can hone in on that work associatively with action in the poem?

I've identified five categories of the persona, five routes leading to the persona that call for us to stay true to the emotion in the poem. These are just a few possibilities for the persona; they're conduits for the emotion they can carry and the tone that will bring them to life:

1. Voices we don't know but characters with which we're familiar. We don't have a preconceived idea of the voice of this persona: the voice of Leadbelly's guitar in Tyehimba Jess's book *leadbelly*, the voice of a house one grew up in, the voice of the unknown soldier, and the like.
2. Voices we know publicly but not intimately: the voice of Patricia Smith's poem "Skinhead," the voice of Mr. Rogers, or the voice of Superman.
3. Voices we know intimately *and* publicly from their own confessions: the voice of Anne Frank, the voice of Frederick Douglass.
4. Voices we know in a vacuum but not in challenging situations. This is simply the fish-out-of-water persona, such as the voice of an alien on earth in Robert Hayden's "American Journal."
5. Voices we know but not in the context of counterpoint characterization: Berryman's *Dream Songs*; Mr. Rogers sitting at Andy Warhol's table at Studio 54.

I've been asked to explain my approach to one of my own persona poems, so I'll attempt to do so from my latest book, *Quantum Lyrics*.

THE FLASH REVERSES TIME

DC Comics, November 1990, #44
"Never Look Back, Flash,
Your Life Might be Gaining on You"

When I'm running across the city
on the crowded streets

to home, when, in a blur,
the grass turns brown
beneath my feet, the asphalt
steams under every step
and the maple leaves sway
on the branches in my wake,
and the people look,
look in that bewildered way,
in my direction, I imagine
walking slowly into my past
among them at a pace
at which we can look one another in the eye
and begin to make changes in the future
from our memories of the past—
the bottom of a bottomless well,
you may think, but why not dream a little:
our past doesn't contradict our future;
they're swatches of the same fabric
stretching across our minds,
one image sewn into another,
like the relationship between a foot and a boot,
covariant in space and time—
one moves along with the other,
like an actor in a shadow play—
like a streak of scarlet light
across the skyline of your city
sweeping the debris, which is simply confetti,
candy wrappers, a can of soda,
all the experience of a day discarded
and now picked up
even down to the youthful screams of play
that put smiles on the faces of the adults
who hear remnants of their own voices
through a doorway leading back
to a sunrise they faintly remember.[1]

The tone of this poem is controlled by the point of entry: When. The adverb opens with the question of what time and at what point action takes place. Strangely enough, the persona doesn't take direct action until he begins to "imagine," employing the present tense verb:

> I imagine
> walking slowly into my past
> among them at a pace
> at which we can look one another in the eye
> and begin to make changes in the future

The adverb "when" allows for the *potential* to take *action*; the sentence is then stretched like a rubber band through dependent clauses until we get to "I imagine." The tone and pace of the poem is set, and we get a sense of the voice of this speaker.

The Flash is a persona that most comic book readers know, but we may not know The Flash's most intimate feelings, and, most important, we don't know his vulnerabilities aside from his battles with his villains. In this way, the poem may serve in two categories: voices we know publicly but not intimately and voices we know in a vacuum but not in challenging situations. I'll deal with the latter first, because I think this category calls for justification. That The Flash, a DC Comics superhero, is a formidable character with the superpower to travel at the speed of light and to cross time barriers is no breaking news. With the responsibility of being a hero, we are seldom privy to his insurmountable desires, the desires that have nothing to do with nabbing a villain. His desire to stand still with someone, to have a level of intimacy that calls for a slow hand, is something we have not witnessed. To talk about his speed is cliché; we know this already. So my curiosity with this figure, the artistic problem of capturing the voice of this persona, falls under the category of authenticity. How do I reveal something about this icon that hasn't been revealed but that's believable? The one tool at my disposal as an artist is emotional experience. That level of experiential knowledge is universal, so I'm trying to approximate the emotion of a man who wants to go back in time to make changes, to do things differently. I chose a one-sentence, strophic structure to convey the intensity and the fluidity of his struggle through time and space. Everything else is an observation of a life in the span of a day:

> sweeping the debris, which is simply confetti,
> candy wrappers, a can of soda,
> all the experience of a day discarded

and now picked up
even down to the youthful screams of play
that put smiles on the faces of the adults
who hear remnants of their own voices

The voice of this persona is a public figure, of sorts, but we don't know him intimately. When we think of The Flash, we see him with a streak of red in his wake, arms pumping, knees pointing, and his feet in a blur: this man is not easy to pin down. So another artistic problem arises singular to this figure: how do we get him to stand still, so to speak? I decided the voice needed a sense of reverie, reflection, and contemplation. So, my attempt was to slow him down long enough to hear his thoughts and concerns and, ultimately, regrets.

Let's look at one more example from a poet who is masterful in this tradition. When asked about the enterprise of writing in the voice of others, Rita Dove—in an interview from the *Swansea Review*—had this to say: "I do find relationships to be kaleidoscopic and infinitely changing; no relationship is ever clear or safe, no matter how intrinsically wonderful it is and all that."[2] In "The House Slave," Dove delves into that "kaleidoscopic and infinitely changing" relationship of slave plantation owner and slave:

The first horn lifts its arm over the dew-lit grass
and in the slave quarters there is a rustling—
children are bundled into aprons, cornbread

and water gourds grabbed, a salt pork breakfast taken.
I watch them driven into the vague before-dawn
while their mistress sleeps like an ivory toothpick

and Massa dreams of asses, rum and slave-funk.
I cannot fall asleep again. At the second horn,
the whip curls across the backs of the laggards—

sometimes my sister's voice, unmistaken, among them.
"Oh! pray," she cries. "Oh! pray!" Those days
I lie on my cot, shivering in the early heat,

and as the fields unfold to whiteness,
and they spill like bees among the fat flowers,
I weep. It is not yet daylight.[3]

The tension of daybreak opens the poem, on the verge of possibilities and limitations. The point of view in the first stanza offers a more comfortable perspective; we're seduced into thinking this is a narrative in third person, with the distance of third person, but by the second line of stanza two, we realize that the narrator is more reliable and more intimate: this is the first-person narration of a slave beginning his day. "The House Slave" offers an example of voices we know publicly but not intimately and voices we know publicly and intimately from their confessions. That is, we know that there are African American slaves in America's history, but we may not know their voices, their everydayness, intimately, unless we've spent time with the singular voice of the slave narrative, unless we read their intimate confessions. Here, Dove makes an amalgam of the two genres: poetry *as* slave narrative. This is not *Incidents in the Life of a Slave Girl,* or the narrative of Henry Bibb or Frederick Douglass, but we know other slaves had their narratives to tell, so we buy it.

The potential energy is infused in the temporal/spatial orientation of the poem—its setting. We realize that we're in a slave's quarters at the start of a day. The potential for kinetic energy is certainly high here, but we assume that the action of the poem will take place once the slaves are out of the quarters and in the fields.

Dove moves us to this place with the sounding of "the second horn" when "the whip curls across the backs of the laggards." This comes after we know that "mistress sleeps" and "Massa dreams," but our speaker "cannot fall asleep again." The dichotomy of the mistress and master sleeping and the slave who cannot sleep provides not only a tension but also a transition into the action of the day via the awake dreaming—or nightmares, more appropriately—of the slave narrator.

The possibility of what the speaker's sister will face in this day as she cries, "Oh! pray," provides enough tonal desperation to get a sense of what's at stake: the everyday routine and the danger of the unexpected. And once this work is done, we're brought back to the moment at hand: "It is not yet daylight." We have a marriage of narrative and the lyric. We get a sense of the speaker's "story" and also of the voice and circularity of his experience.

There's the need to get the story out, but there's also the music rumbling beneath the terror. The tone is of a speaker in tune with his vulnerability—"Those days / I lie on my cot, shivering in the early heat"—and there's the music beneath this "as the fields unfold to whiteness, / and they spill like bees among the fat flowers," and the evidence of emotion in "I weep." The narrative offers vulnerability and good reason for caution, but the lyric of the poem offers the hope to survive. The narrative and the lyric are contrapuntal in this persona, as the *strength* to face the day is contrapuntal with the *fear* of facing the day.

WRITING PROMPT

The power of the persona comes from speakers who have something to lose, speakers who contemplate their actions or are forced into their actions, and speakers we already know placed in extraordinary situations. The persona should challenge poets to say what they never thought to say in their own voices and, as with all poems, it should challenge us to say what has not been heard before.

Notes

1. A. Van Jordan, *Quantum Lyrics: Poems* (New York: W. W. Norton, 2007), 13–14.

2. Rita Dove, "Rita Dove Talks to M. Wynn Thomas," *Swansea Review* 19 (1995): 158–63, also found as "An Interview with Rita Dove by M. Wynn Thomas," *Modern American Poetry*, 1995, http://www.english.illinois.edu/MAPS/poets/a_f/dove/mwthomas.htm (accessed March 11, 2010).

3. Rita Dove, *The Yellow House on the Corner: Poems*, 2nd ed. (Pittsburgh: Carnegie Mellon University Press, 1989), 33.

"For he can creep": Christopher Smart and Anaphora

Joelle Biele

I have always loved Christopher Smart's poem "My Cat Jeoffry" from *Jubilate Agno*. It grabbed my attention when I discovered it as an undergraduate, and it has held my attention ever since. Written during Smart's 1756–63 confinement at St. Luke's Hospital, the poem uses anaphora to build to a quiet resolution. Considering that Smart was institutionalized for a religious mania that found him in a state of almost constant prayer, his use of a poetic form that can be found in religious texts from around the world makes complete sense. That the poem is about his cat is something I find deeply appealing.

The word "anaphora" comes from ancient Greek and means "a carrying up or back." As a rhetorical device, anaphora makes its first appearance in the first century B.C., in the *Rhetorica ad Herennium* and in Cicero's *de Inventione*, where it is defined as the same word or phrase starting each line. In Greek, anaphora is related to the word for "offering" in the sense of sacrifice. This connection between the use of repetition and religious rites suggests anaphora's oral roots. You find anaphora used throughout the Bible, particularly in the Old Testament. Take Ecclesiastes, chapter 3—"To every thing there is a season, and a time to every purpose under the heaven: A time to be born, and a time to die; a time to plant, and a time to pluck up that which is planted"—or Psalm 23: "The Lord is my shepherd; I shall not want. He maketh me to lie down in green pastures: he leadeth me beside the still waters."[1] It is found in Celtic chants, Navajo prayers, and Malaysian spells, in Roman Catholic and Eastern Orthodox liturgies, African American sermons, and Baptist hymns, in Hebrew response poetry and Yoruba and Zulu praise poems. The Aztecs used it, and so did the ancient Egyptians, along with Chaucer, Rabelais, and Shakespeare, to varying degrees. After Whitman, there is, of course, Allen Ginsberg followed by contemporary poets like Joy Harjo and Gerald Stern.

What draws me into the poem is the sheer delight Smart takes in describing his feline companion. He begins, "For I will consider my Cat Jeoffry," and continues by using "For" to start the next seventy-three lines. The way Smart structures the poem is to make a statement or series of statements about the cat's devotion to God, which he then follows with an example or series of examples that elaborate his original claim. This pattern emerges in the third line with the assertion: "For at the first glance of the glory of God in the East he worships in his way." Next comes the clarification: "For is this done by wreathing his body seven times round with elegant quickness." Employing the religious and persuasive uses of "for," the speaker calls to mind both a priest leading a congregation in prayer and a lawyer presenting a reasoned case. Smart then brings in an image by using the metaphorical "wreathing" instead of "circling," shifts his diction to the conversational "seven times round," and succinctly qualifies his description with "elegant quickness."

What keeps me in the poem is Smart's humor. Utterly serious about what he is saying, Smart shades each line with a gentle grandeur and a playful irony. His joy is abundant as he pairs the philosophical with the quotidian and glides between the devotional and the everyday.

> For the Lord commanded Moses concerning the cats at the
>   departure of the Children of Israel from Egypt.
> For every family had one cat at least in the bag.
> For the English Cats are the best in Europe.
>
> . . . .
>
> For he is tenacious of his point.
> For he is a mixture of gravity and waggery.
> For he knows that God is his Saviour.

Smart's juxtapositions work so well because of the repeating "for"; anaphora is the thread that holds the beads of the poem together. Occasionally, he expands on the original "for" by adding a few words that will also repeat. You find it in lines nine to eighteen, where he whimsically outlines his cat's day, beginning each line with "For first," "for secondly," "for thirdly," "for sixthly," "for eighthly," winding up the series with "For tenthly he goes in quest of food."

Quickly and quietly, the poem comes to a near-ecstatic close. By repeatedly jumping off "for," packing in as much information as he can about his cat and his relation to God, Smart embellishes his descriptions like a musician working through a theme. He even touches on one of the major scientific discoveries of his day, electricity. Smart ends by listing the cat's movements: "For God has blessed him in the variety of his movements. / For, though he cannot fly, he is an excellent clamberer." These lines, for me, call up the Beatitudes: "Blessed are the poor in spirit: for theirs is the kingdom of heaven. Blessed are they that mourn: for they shall be comforted."[2] The last three lines have six stressed syllables, followed by three, then two:

> For he can tread to all the measures upon the music.
> For he can swim for life.
> For he can creep.
>
> (63–65)

Rhetorically speaking, this ending is tight, but metrically it is still a little open. Lines 64 and 65 almost combine to balance out 63 with five instead of six stressed syllables, but since the lines are missing the final syllable, the ending does not quite close, leaving the reader to dwell upon the image of the cat getting ready to spring or disappear around the corner. It's up to the reader to experience the close. Ending with the cat's actions suggests a belief in the material world, a belief that God can be found not just in St. Paul's Cathedral but also in Smart's home. The cat never becomes a symbol or metaphor for the believer; he is first and last a cat. Written entirely in the present tense, the poem, through anaphora, continually reaffirms the value and passing of the individual moment.

One of the reasons that Smart landed in the madhouse was his habit of stopping his fellow Londoners in Hyde Park and demanding that they join him in prayer. Smart felt that God's presence was continually around him, and he was unabashed in declaring his devotion. The story goes that at St. Luke's Hospital, in an environment that must have been extremely difficult to bear, Smart used a key to etch his poems into the walls and that he shaded his words with charcoal so he could read them. True or not, the story and Smart's poetry suggest that words have the power to transmit the presence of the divine.

For me, anaphora has been useful in bringing together disparate images and stories that come from a central theme. I have used it to try to convey the feeling I had a good part of the time I spent traveling in Europe and to link together passages from Gerard Manley Hopkins's notebooks. Anaphora was also a tool that helped me shape material I found difficult to address in a direct, narrative way, such as in my poem "Family Stories." This poem is made from my mother's experiences and those I recall from my childhood. I had tried to write individual poems about some of the incidents in the poem but was never satisfied with the results. Once I decided to try bringing the stories together, the material became much easier to work with. Anaphora seemed to reflect the way the stories rattled around in my brain. It is a form I am always drawn to, and whenever I hear it in a poem, on the radio, or in a prayer, I simply love the way it sounds.

WRITING PROMPT

Using Smart as a model, write a sixty-line poem that begins with "For" that considers as many attributes of a concrete object. Try to avoid abstract nouns like "love" or "happiness." Use metaphor, simile, comparisons, actions, folklore, history, and etymology to get to sixty lines. Don't worry about the order or making logical sense. Read what you've got and come up with twenty more. Perhaps a kind of sense will start to emerge based on sound or image.

FROM *JUBILATE AGNO* / *Christopher Smart*

For I will consider my Cat Jeoffry.
For he is the servant of the Living God, duly and daily serving him.
For at the first glance of the glory of God in the East he worships in
  his way.
For is this done by wreathing his body seven times round with
  elegant quickness.
For then he leaps up to catch the musk, which is the blessing of
  God upon his prayer.
For he rolls upon prank to work it in.
For having done duty and received blessing he begins to consider
  himself.
For this he performs in ten degrees.

For first he looks upon his forepaws to see if they are clean.
For secondly he kicks up behind to clear away there.
For thirdly he works it upon stretch with the forepaws extended.
For fourthly he sharpens his paws by wood.
For fifthly he washes himself.
For sixthly he rolls upon wash.
For seventhly he fleas himself, that he may not be interrupted upon
  the beat.
For eighthly he rubs himself against a post.
For ninthly he looks up for his instructions.
For tenthly he goes in quest of food.
For having considered God and himself he will consider his neighbor.
For if he meets another cat he will kiss her in kindness.
For when he takes his prey he plays with it to give it a chance.
For one mouse in seven escapes by his dallying.
For when his day's work is done his business more properly begins.
For he keeps the Lord's watch in the night against the adversary.
For he counteracts the powers of darkness by his electrical skin and
  glaring eyes.
For he counteracts the Devil, who is death, by brisking about the life.
For in his morning orisons he loves the sun and the sun loves him.
For he is of the tribe of Tiger.
For the Cherub Cat is a term of the Angel Tiger.
For he has the subtlety and hissing of a serpent, which in goodness
  he suppresses.
For he will not do destruction if he is well-fed, neither will he spit
  without provocation.
For he purrs in thankfulness when God tells him he's a good Cat.
For he is an instrument for the children to learn benevolence upon.
For every house is incomplete without him, and a blessing is lacking
  in the spirit.
For the Lord commanded Moses concerning the cats at the depar-
  ture of the Children of Israel from Egypt.
For every family had one cat at least in the bag.
For the English Cats are the best in Europe.
For he is the cleanest in the use of his forepaws of any quadruped.

For the dexterity of his defense is an instance of the love of God to
 him exceedingly.
For he is the quickest to his mark of any creature.
For he is tenacious of his point.
For he is a mixture of gravity and waggery.
For he knows that God is his Saviour.
For there is nothing sweeter than his peace when at rest.
For there is nothing brisker than his life when in motion.
For he is of the Lord's poor, and so indeed is he called by benevo-
 lence perpetually—Poor Jeoffry! poor Jeoffry! the rat has bit thy
 throat.
For I bless the name of the Lord Jesus that Jeoffry is better.
For the divine spirit comes about his body to sustain it in complete
 cat.
For his tongue is exceeding pure so that it has in purity what it
 wants in music.
For he is docile and can learn certain things.
For he can sit up with gravity, which is patience upon approbation.
For he can fetch and carry, which is patience in employment.
For he can jump over a stick, which is patience upon proof
 positive.
For he can spraggle upon waggle at the word of command.
For he can jump from an eminence into his master's bosom.
For he can catch the cork and toss it again.
For he is hated by the hypocrite and miser.
For the former is afraid of detection.
For the latter refuses the charge.
For he camels his back to bear the first notion of business.
For he is good to think on, if a man would express himself neatly.
For he made a great figure in Egypt for his signal services.
For he killed the Ichneumon rat very pernicious by land.
For his ears are so acute that they sting again.
For from this proceeds the passing quickness of his attention.
For by stroking of him I have found out electricity.
For I perceived God's light about him both wax and fire.
For the electrical fire is the spiritual substance which God sends
 from heaven to sustain the bodies both of man and beast.

For God has blessed him in the variety of his movements.
For, though he cannot fly, he is an excellent clamberer.
For his motions upon the face of the earth are more than any other
  quadruped.
For he can tread to all the measures upon the music.
For he can swim for life.
For he can creep.[3]

FAMILY STORIES / *Joelle Biele*

Some stories will never leave you alone.
They work their way into the blood, the brain,
they flash in corners of your dreams
with laundry drying in the halls,
lemon oil rubbed into wood, bristles and soap
working their way under your nails until it's your arm
in the winter Hudson, the eel in your hand,
and you stand on the bridge with your aunt
about to jump. She's your breath
blowing over uncles who didn't exist,
the baby born on the living room floor,
women rushing with water and sheets.
They are in your skin with the boy
practicing bugle, warm bread in the mouth
and salt on the tongue. They are in your laugh.
They sit in your rooms, declare they're in love,
and it's your ear pressed to the door,
the money-lender on the other side, the daughter
locked in the closet, brooms, coats, and stacked cans,
the daughter who was not born. They flush
the skin, live behind the eyes, sink in the throat
with the other loves, the other children,
the wind off the ship, the bark of dogs.
They speak in the ache in the shoulder,
with the fear that lurks in the mute, the son
hanging from the shower rod, the man,
the doves, on the roof, the daughter tripping
on the beach, her children playing in the sand.

They are in your voice with the knives,
the cattle in the street, the race out of town.
It's your gun to the boy's head telling him
to choose, and you're calling out the window,
stopping for dandelions on the side of the road,
bitter leaves and pale roots, and you're
the mandolin shaped like a pear, mother-of-pearl,
swinging away from the world, a woman's hips
stepping in song, pulsed in blood, your beating heart.[4]

Notes

1. Scriptures are from the King James Version.

2. Matthew 5:3–4.

3. Christopher Smart. "For I will consider My Cat Jeoffry," in *The Norton Anthology of Poetry*, 3rd ed., ed. Alexander Allison et al. (New York: W. W. Norton, 1983), 470–71 (lines 697–780 from *Jubilate Agno*).

4. Joelle Biele, *White Summer* (Carbondale: Southern Illinois University Press, 2002), 20–21.

The Burden of Seed, the Seed of Burden: "Repetitional Schemas" & Pace in Terrance Hayes's "Sonnet"

Metta Sáma

Recently, on two electronic mailing lists, "performing poetry" was a popular topic. Not performance poetry, but performing (one's) poetry. Members on both lists lauded Auden, Yeats, Eliot, and Dylan Thomas & (genially) harpooned slam poets. I take it that the great difference between "performance" and "performing" has a lot to do with the poem itself, as well as the poet herself. A performance poem (aka slam or Spoken Word) is often defined as a cutout pattern—think McCall's: the pattern is factory-approved, designed by someone with supple fingers and a general sense of shape but who remains faceless; she gives you wiggle room by suggesting fabric (rayon and polyester-cotton blends are highly recommended; use silk and linen at your own risk) and leaving color choice to you. The so-called standard slam poem has been called formulaic: political or social situation as topic; assonance, consonance, and internal rhyme to provide a stage; a few quiet pauses to show gentle compassion; and a steady rise and fall of pitch to keep the body & the audience rocking.

By contrast, then (since we are in the dichotomous realm of assumption), what is a (regular? normal? traditional? conventional? non-slam?) poem? If a slam poem is said to rely on sound elements, what does the () poem rely on, if any elements at all? Let's allow me to suggest that a () poem uses the tools of poetry-making to create an image (a poem on the page is, in fact, a visual image) that can be lifted from the page, entered into the body, and (silently) uttered. No, that can't be right. Perhaps a () poem is one in which, as Wordsworth intimated in "From Preface to Lyrical Ballads," the everyday is made extraordinary by "tranquil recollection," "spontaneous overflow of emotions," & "language of the every man."[1] Is the () poem designed to sit idly, dead, on the page? Is it designed to be "yowled"? Are some () poems written for the page, while some are written for the stage? Can we (do we dare?) hold () poems up to the same standards as we hold the slam poem? In other words, if the slam poem fails because it doesn't "hold up on the page," does the () poem fail if it doesn't "hold up on the stage"?

It's with these (engaging, frustrating, adventurous) conversations that I enter. If a performance poem is one that is constructed merely for vocal, onstage theatrics, what is a () poem? In what tradition does it rest, particularly if a () poem is, say, experimental, quiet, & provocative?

Did you, by any chance, read the *New York Times* article about chamber music looking for a new direction, taking the chamber from the music? Literally. Playing this music in bars and clubs and hotel lobbies. Changing the name to "ensemble music." Changing the venue to better articulate the heart of the music. Take the chamber from the musicians & what do you get? Take the poem from the page & how many ways can you, then, see/hear/experience "moon"?

With all the discussions around me about performance in poetry, I've found myself living inside of one poem that has never quite evicted itself from my mind. More than the images (watermelons, seeds, slices), the potential of the vocal performance has wrapped around me; think: strangler tree; think: that lover whose legs always found a home around your waist. How (& has he?) does Terrance Hayes vocally perform "Sonnet"? I've had the luck of seeing Terrance Hayes be poet Terrance Hayes. I've not had the luck of hearing Terrance Hayes read this poem. Has he ever read this poem to an audience large?

Hayes's "Sonnet" consists of fourteen lines. Ten syllables per line. Iambic, really. It's a sonnet. Its fourteen lines (seven burdens, in a way) all say the same thing: "We sliced the watermelon into smiles." Why am I so eager to hear Hayes read this poem? Because the poem is fourteen lines that say the same thing. How does one read fourteen lines that say the same thing, in order to make the same thing not the same thing but some thing entirely different fourteen times? Where are the inflections, the intonations, the pauses, the pitches? Where oh where is the sound barrier? Is there a sound barrier? (Have you, dearest reader, by now thrown aside this essay and put pen to paper and written Hayes's fourteen lines so you yourself can perform it? I did, and it's worth the ink. Do it. Now.)

Okay, so now that you see the [noun] and [noun] and [noun] of these seven burdens, tell me where you dropped the voice, where you raised the pitch, where you peeked under the letter, where you polished the vocal chords to tune the next word. How many times did you read this poem all the way through, and in how many variations? Imagine: "We sliced the watermelon into smiles" said the exact same way fourteen times. Are you *mad*? Are you *machine*? Is it *even* possible? I don't know, but I tell you, "Sonnet" has me using italics for emphasis (& check this, pacing). Hayes achieved emphasis and pacing in "Sonnet" with ten syllables. Used over and over (+ twelve times) again.

I want to slow down.

A woman told a little story. Someone read E. E. Cummings's "Buffalo Bill" for thirty minutes, repeatedly. Of course, she said, he had to alter the way he read the poem: speeding up, beginning in one emotion, raising the pitch to anger, and ending somewhere in despair. I recalled Thomas Sayers Ellis, who'd recently read to an audience "more eccentrically" than he had previously.[2] The poems coming from his voice box felt unfamiliar to me. Were these the poems engraved on the page I thought I knew intimately? Had Ellis, in his "eccentric" vocal performance, created a new poem? A new line? Pacing beware: we're talking page versus stage. Ellis read all of his poems with the same breath, the same stops and starts, the same fissures, the same, if I may, hurricanes. I went home & Googled Ellis, found his other readings of these same poems. He varied the pacings, varied the sound waves, & sometimes carried the poems, gingerly, from the page to his voice. Tori Amos–fashion: each performance was fresh & gave the "dead word" (to use Ellis) an opportunity to be resurrected.

Since poems can be lifted from the page & vocally performed to fit whatever mood and space a poet enters, what happens to pace for the reader? Pacing on the page is what? If we, as alive writers, If we, as alive writers who read our poems out loud, If we, as alive writers who read our poems out loud for an audience of more than a few, If we, as alive writers who read our poems out loud for an audience of more than a few, have the (precious) right to alter the feel of a poem, despite what it looks like on the page, If we exercise that vocal performance right, what do we hope to achieve on that page? (This anaphoric strategy I borrow from Juliana Spahr's *This Connection of Everyone with Lungs*.)

One can only imagine that one wants to achieve *something* at a precise moment and that once that moment has passed, it's gone. To paraphrase Ellis:

"Why don't nobody write a stutter, hunh? You meet somebody who stutters, & they write perfect sentences. You meet somebody who trips when they walk, they write perfect sentences. *Why **is** that?*" Stephen Dobyns, in *Best Words, Best Order,* says pacing can be defined thusly: "controlled variations in the forward momentum of the poem. . . . [P]acing is controlled by tension, and tension is energy."[3] Tension is also "desire + danger."[4] In Hayes's "Sonnet," the poem is left-justified; all the lines are end-stopped. The tension, then, can be seen in the tightness of the box, the almost claustrophobic feel of the tight little box. The rhythm doesn't change, or the sounds; the metric is just as solidly stubborn as the punctuation. The extended burden also drives this poem forward. This is not a skipped record; Hayes is a sophisticated stylist, capable of stuttering and record-skipping. No, this is a deliberate utterance, a hand that forces and pushes and antagonizes and jokes. (Yes, I said jokes. I find this poem funny in its audacity, its whimsical ease.)

There is nothing threatening about the words in the sentence. There is everything threatening in this form. (Tension is "desire + danger.") This is a non-movable object, suffocating, and yet the poem moves from page top to page bottom, from left to right. There are several reasons to continue to read through this poem, although we can be almost certain nothing will change in the presentation of the poem.

For my eye and quiet ear (the non-read-out-loud ear), the poem must shift somewhere. This is my imposition on the poem. I want something to change. I want to see flow of thought, emotion, spirit, and intellect. & I've trained myself to believe that thought cannot shift in seven burdens. In fact, what can shift and what does shift is the way I read & the way I perceive. "We sliced the watermelon into smiles" is, for me, a wonderful example of poetic pacing. I can pause whenever I want, if I want, how I want, but the poem on the page has established its parameters: iambic pentameter, fourteen lines, end-stopped, start to finish, same sounds, rhythms, and (possibly) moods. I can also see the (witting? unwitting?) brilliance of slicing the pentameter by slicing the fruit. The extended burden performs as a series of movements: the breath as movement, the spirit as movement, the thought as movement, the emotion as movement, & more subtly, the reader's demands as movement. & if I think of movement as a kind of pace, then in "Sonnet," pacing, as vocal speed, can be slow (look at those mirrored long "i"s in "sliced" and "smiles"; the laze of the sibilants; the soft "we," "the," "wa-," "-ter"), and pacing, as vocal speed, can be sped up; turn that dial from 33 1/3 to 45, I hear a (dare I say it) song.

WRITING PROMPT

Hayes has written a rather fresh, politically charged, nondidactic poem primarily because he created a form to articulate a social problem, which frees him up to state a problem & question that problem without making demands about how we, the readers, should respond to the problem. Does the extended burden give him the playing space to write provocatively, boldly, unapologetically? I'd say yes, certainly. I'd also say the extended burden could work for many kinds of "genre" poetry: love poems, for example; erotic poems; childhood poems; and so on.

My charge to you: create a form that makes use of repetition in order to find a new way to talk about old topics. You can take a look through Lewis Turco's *The New Book of Forms* to learn the different types of repetition, but here are a few to get you started: anaphora, ploce, anadiplosis, symploce, repeton, epizeuxis, refrain, & the list is long. The twist: take the form to its limit, & then push some more. Create your own repetitive strategy, or as Turco calls it, schema, that best articulates and creates the mood & tensions you want to achieve. Keep your ear and eye alert to pace and how "repetitional schemas" create pace. Pay attention to line, sentence, placement of words on a page, language, diction, and sound. Pay attention to what earns you your repetitional schema.

SONNET / *Terrance Hayes*

We sliced the watermelon into smiles.
We sliced the watermelon into smiles.
We sliced the watermelon into smiles.
We sliced the watermelon into smiles.
We sliced the watermelon into smiles.
We sliced the watermelon into smiles.
We sliced the watermelon into smiles.
We sliced the watermelon into smiles.
We sliced the watermelon into smiles.
We sliced the watermelon into smiles.
We sliced the watermelon into smiles.
We sliced the watermelon into smiles.

We sliced the watermelon into smiles.
We sliced the watermelon into smiles.[5]

THE UNIVERSE IS MOVING AWAY FROM US / *Metta Sáma*

Yes. The moon metaphors you. A pulse of
Yes. The moon metamorphoses you. A push of
Yes. The moon metathesizes you. A pucker of
Yes. The moon meteorites you. A puddle of
Yes. The moon. Metonym. You. Pukka.
You. A punch. A meta-. A muse. The yes.
You. A metallic puff. The powdered mood. Yes[6]

Notes

1. William Wordsworth, "From Preface to Lyrical Ballads," in *The Norton Anthology of English Literature,* 7th ed., vol. 2, ed. M. H. Abrams (New York: W. W. Norton, 1999), 242.

2. Thomas Sayers Ellis, lecture (Juniper Summer Writing Institute, Amherst, Mass., June 27, 2007).

3. Stephen Dobyns, *Best Words, Best Order: Essays on Poetry,* 2nd ed. (New York: Palgrave Macmillan, 2003), 322.

4. Heather Sellers, *The Practice of Creative Writing* (New York: Bedford/St. Martin's, 2008), 141.

5. Terrance Hayes, "Sonnet," *Hip Logic* (New York: Penguin Books, 2002), 13.

6. Metta Sáma. "The universe is moving away from us," in *Letters to the World: Poems from the Wom-Po Listserv,* ed. Moira Richards, Rosemary Starace, and Lesley Wheeler (Los Angeles: Red Hen Press, 2008), 328.

"Slapped:with;liGhtninG": Poetry and Punctuation

Susanna Rich

> Punctuation gives us the human voice, and all the meanings that lie between the words.
>
> —Pico Iyer

When language was chiseled into stone slabs in ancient Greece, the writers had to save space, so they left none between words. Words ran together and became confused. So the first punctuation element was a dot suspended between words to separate them. Later, space itself was used to separate—to punctuate—words. White space includes word spacing; paragraph, stanza, section, and chapter breaks; and book covers. Capitalization—a word derived from the Latin *caput*—was originally used to indicate either a new head(ing) or the name of a head of household. So white space and capitalization are punctuation, as well.

Let's remember that poetry has changed from the predominantly oral and physical art of the itinerant bard to an increasingly visual medium on the page. The voice inflections of the live poet have to be recorded on the page, like sound on a musical score, to indicate pacing, meaning, and emotional nuance. But we must also reconstruct the physical gestures of the poet. W. B. Yeats tells us that art comes from the "fountain jetting from the entire hopes, memories, and sensations of the body."[1] Through punctuation, we can record and re-embody the gestures of a bard.

Considering that in terms of punctuation, most poetry falls somewhere between the pyrotechnics of E. E. Cummings and the spareness of W. S. Merwin, who punctuates only with white space, capitalization, and traditional apostrophes, we can better appreciate the synaptic and expressive power of punctuation. Here is an eleven-line excerpt from section XXXVIII of Cummings's *W [ViVa]*, which includes the title of this essay:

n(o)w
the
how
dis(appeared cleverly)world
iS Slapped:with;liGhtninG
!
at
which(shal)lpounceupcrackw(ill)jumps
of
THuNdeRB
loSSo!M iN[2]

Cummings renews our sense of the uses of punctuation by playing meaningful counterpoint with the norms. For example, in the first line he parenthesizes the "o" in "now," creating a tension between the words that that suggests: "now," "no," "o," "ow," and even "nw." How appropriate a response to a lightning storm, which forces a sense of urgency and nowness on us, and the ambivalent reactions of "no," "o," and the wincing "ow." With the "o" dropped out, "nw" feels clipped, as if by a sudden stroke. Visually, the parentheses create a whirlwind around the eye-of-the-storm "o."

In line 5, Cummings capitalizes the second instead of the customary first letter of "iS," thus aligning and amplifying the sound "S" with the capital "S" in "Slapped," the following word. The sound effect sizzles, as lightning does. Had Cummings not capitalized the "S" in "iS," the "is" would have had merely a "z" sound. Also, he would have lost the surprise effect of "S," which mimics the surprise of lightning. Instead of white spaces to separate the three linked words in line 5, Cummings uses a colon and semicolon, punctuations traditionally used to separate much larger units of language. The colon functions like two pointing index fingers: LOOK AT THIS. "Slapped," like lightning, is sudden and clipped, especially with the colon following it. The word "with" is slapped—struck—between the muscular punctuation marks of the colon and the semicolon (half comma and half period), as lightning is surrounded by the expansive dark before and dark after it. Because we have become accustomed to white spacing between words in the five centuries since Gutenberg, there is tremendous tension between our expectations and the surprise of this line. Even more unexpected is the word "liGhtninG," whose capital "G"s flash and flash into our eyes, as lightning would. Cummings's choice of capitalizing the "G"s is especially meaningful, since the letter is often an initial morpheme in words related to visual experience, as in "glow," "glimmer, "glance," "goggles," and "gaze."

In contrast to Cummings's punctuational exuberance, Merwin has an ascetic aesthetic. Consider the last three lines from his poem "Just This," in which Merwin also works with lightning:

> how did this haste begin this little time
> at any time this reading by lightning
> scarcely a word this nothing this heaven[3]

By not punctuating the first line of this excerpt, Merwin encourages us, as readers, to enact the haste about which he writes. We can read "begin" as a transitive verb with "this little time" as its object, so that haste literally "begins" time. This is quite true: to be in haste is to be pressed for time and so very aware of it and its passing. We lose our sense of time when we are absorbed and leisurely. So time does begin when we are in haste. "Begin" can also function as an intransitive verb, with "this haste" and "this little time" parts of a series of subjects. In either case, the rushing through to figure out the syntactical relationships in the line (which the lack of punctuation creates) is like a rush of lightning. That we may be confused on first reading reflects the usual consequences of haste. If Merwin had punctuated these lines according to the second, intransitive reading of the verb, it might have yielded the following possible translation:

> How did this haste begin, this little time
> (at any time), this reading by lightning
> (scarcely a word), this nothing, this heaven?

So marked, the poetry changes significantly. The commas cut in, cut off, and weigh down. We are certainly more sure of how to interpret this version of the lines and less, therefore, in the more hesitant experience of "reading by lightning." The parentheses show the paralleling of the "this ____" constructions but minimize the import of the phrases they peripheralized. The final question mark is a strong end punctuation. Although a question, it nonetheless creates a finality that the unpunctuated words do not imply. On some readings, the lines become a rhetorical question, which actually is an assertion inviting no further response. In Merwin's version, "nothing" and "heaven" are followed by a drop off into white space—a far more provocative experience for the poem. By providing only white space in these lines, we are left to our own interpretive devices. And that, after all, is the truth of reading poetry, of reading by lightning—that there is no final meaning.

In my own poetry, one of my favorite punctuation breakthroughs was in a work originally titled "F.Y.I.: An Interoffice Memo." In this poem, a young woman addresses an office colleague who both attracts and repels her by his sexual overtures. In the early drafts of the poem, I used traditional punctuation, clearly marking off phrases and sentences and lines. I soon realized, however, that these clear demarcations contradicted the psychological blurring and testing of boundaries between the two characters. Here are the first two of fifteen stanzas:

F.Y.I.: AN INTEROFFICE MEMO

Behind the sweating cinderblock wall between them,
he sucks Merit butts and True Blue.
Smoke smolders around his doorjamb.

She emerges from her side to ask him not to.
He responds, Open your window, and belches
the belch of someone who always can.

The title is too sure of its boundaries, the periods after the abbreviated words "For Your Information" too defining. The colon functions like two pointing fingers that know what they are indicating. Period/end of sentence: there is nothing smoky and wavering about "Smoke smolders around the door."

The current first-person version is as spare of punctuation as Merwin's poetry is. Here are the title and first two of thirteen stanzas:

F Y I NEED TO TALK

Between us the cinderblock wall
Its sweat grit and empty cores
You puff True Blues and Now

To smoke a frame around your door
Where I wait to ask you
Again to open your window

The first highly punctuated title was rhythmically and thematically inappropriate. Pulling out the punctuation, I realized that what followed the colon was dull and too self-explanatory. "FYI" is only used as a memo heading for "For Your Information," so why define it as such? When I tried "FYI," I saw a further opportunity for ambiguity. "FY" can be an acronym for "F____ You," and the "I" can either be the first-person pronoun of the sentence "I Need to Talk" or short for some slur, such as "Idiot." But there were not enough cues in "FYI" to invite alternate interpretations. I brought my puzzlement to my senior writing seminar as a punctuation challenge, and my student Abigail Avis cleverly suggested the title I finally kept. "F Y I Need to Talk" allows for several groupings/interpretations by a reader, including, but not limited to, what would be suggested by the following punctuations: (1) a traditional office memo—"F.Y.I.: Need To Talk"; (2) a curse and request—"F.Y.: I Need to Talk"; (3) a curse and slur of the other—"F.Y., I(diot): Need to Talk"; (4) a curse of other and self (although it should be "me")—"F.Y. (&) I: Need to Talk."

Syntactically, the poem shifts and reshifts as the woman experiences her ambivalence—her connection to and separation from her colleague. The white spaces mimic the undefined spaces between them. The unmarked enjambments rush us toward the next lines, much as the woman approaching the man, and the man approaching the woman. As readers, we may be tempted to read in the missing punctuation, thus inviting us into a voyeuristic relationship with the characters. Honoring Merwin's punctuation aesthetic enriched the poem and made it more dynamic.

WRITING PROMPTS

1. Revise a poem of your choice with four different kinds of punctuation strategies: (1) an alternate traditional; (2) a Cummings; (3) a Merwin; (4) your own experimental.

2. Write a poem with standard punctuation. Create three other versions with a range of punctuation strategies: (1) a Cummings; (2) a Merwin; (3) your own. Remember that white space is a punctuation and that the line endings are followed by white space. What do you learn about punctuation from this process? What insights and breakthroughs emerge about your poem and about the uses of punctuation?

JUST THIS / *W. S. Merwin*

When I think of the patience I have had
back in the dark before I remember

or knew it was night until the light came
all at once at the speed it was born to
with all the time in the world to fly through
not concerned about ever arriving
and then the gathering of the first stars
unhurried in their flowering spaces
and far into the story the planets
cooling slowly and the ages of rain
then the seas starting to bear memory
the gaze of the first cell at its waking
how did this haste begin this little time
at any time this reading by lightning
scarcely a word this nothing this heaven

F Y I NEED TO TALK / *Susanna Rich*

Between us the cinderblock wall
Its sweat grit and empty cores
You puff True Blues and Now

To smoke a frame around your door
Where I wait to ask you
Again to open your window

You will belch the belch of one
Who has no need to state
My office my lungs my gut

Words to stun
My eyes will tug at your eyes
Don't gaze down the length of my hair

To my left breast
My hand a cameo at my throat
My elbow a shield

I'll say something about breathing
Tantric yoga you'll say
Best kind of breath   I won't

Understand   You'll say
All those naked yoga positions
I'll tell you love

Is a poem   You'll say
Emily Dickinson was an S&M
Lesbian black leather and studs

Under white piqué   I'll say
Love is an art
You'll say Sex is a ribbed Trojan

My ears like vacuums will draw
Forth your words to hang
Like swollen tongues from your lips

Your sentences will build around you
Like the cathedral of excrement
One tropical caterpillar

Sculpts around itself to say
To birds You don't want me Please
Don't eat me I lift now my fist

Miss Liberty
Rock of desire chisel of
Despair strike the match

Notes

1. W. B. Yeats, "The Thinking of the Body," in *The Collected Works of W. B. Yeats*, vol. 4, ed. Richard J. Finneran and George Bornstein (New York: Scribner, 2007), 212.
2. E. E. Cummings, *Poems 1923–1954* (New York: Harcourt, 1954), 250.
3. W. S. Merwin, "Just This," *New Yorker*, June 6, 2005, 98.

The Active Blank: The White Space Speaks

Elline Lipkin

As poets, we depend on words to do our work. What happens, however, when words alone aren't enough? We labor over their precise arrangement in order to convey the most minute of nuances, to have words serve as the best vehicle for our conceptions. Spelling, grammar, and punctuation, as well as form within a poem, are all meant to serve the poet's meaning, and their regularization is intended to draw attention from the "madeness" of words (of course, essentially visual symbols themselves) so that intention, whether connotative or denotative, can shine.

In the past few years, however, I have found myself more and more drawn to poems that break with this expectation and to those that use unexpected means to convey what can't be conventionally expressed. Sometimes, this seems a choice because the poet can't find the words to define a subject or wants the deliberate unfixedness that not using words strikingly allows. Sometimes, the decision means a turn toward the visual: by veering from conventional word placement on the page, a new layer of emotion or meaning builds the reader's understandings. Not quite concrete poetry, poems that incorporate visual elements often potently layer meaning in correlation with their subjects.

When I first spotted Alice Fulton's poem "==" in *Sensual Math*, her fourth collection, I was momentarily stunned. What was this mathematical symbol doing in a poem? How should I read what she calls "the double-equal sign" or "the bride sign"? I've never heard Fulton read the work, but I understand that she simply pauses when she comes to the sign in order to create a moment of silence in the air, setting a space for what cannot be said:

> It might mean immersion, that sign
>   I've used as title, the sign I call a bride
> after the recessive threads in lace ==

the stitches forming deferential
space around the firm design.
It's the unconsidered

What does it mean for a poet to come to a place where words don't suffice? Is it a failure, I wonder, on the part of language to provide enough meaning for the writer, or is it a failure of the poet to come to the end of his or her use for words and to turn to the visual instead?

Throughout *Sensual Math,* and especially within this poem, Fulton reveals an attraction to places of instability, both literal and metaphorical. Her poems often hover in their un-fixedness, momentarily alighting on an image before layering what's found with another pattern or discourse. The poem continues:

mortar between the silo's bricks == never admired
when we admire
the holdfast of the tiles (their copper of a robin's
breast abstracted into flat).

It's a seam made to show,
the deckle edge == constructivist touch.
The double equal that's nowhere to be found
in math. The dash
to the second power == dash to the max.

Suggestions of betweenness abound, as in her mention of the "unconsidered / mortar between the silo's bricks," "a seam made to show, / the deckle edge," "the acoustic signals / of things about to flame," or

wheels on snow

that leave a wake == that tread in white
without dilapidating
mystery == hinging

In perhaps a reference to Dickinson, she writes that it is the "dash / to the second power" and a "dash to the max." The poem's final phrase, left unpunctuated, and ending image, "the white between the ink," seem particularly powerful to me—as if the white space surrounding the black print of words is not an empty void but rather an open field, equally filled but traditionally unseen.

I believe Fulton's incorporation of the sign also serves as her own form of punctuation to stress an imposed pause for what goes unsaid but needs to be there. After introducing the symbol in the poem "==," she goes on to use it throughout the rest of the book and then in her next, *Felt,* as its resonances shift and demonstrate correlations between subjects that she doesn't want to pin down in exact words.

Fulton's "==" symbol represents the tension of wanting something symbolized that cannot, in fact, be represented. In a 1995 interview with critic Alec Marsh, Fulton comments, "I think of the double equal as a metaphorical sign and a feminist sign, imbued with the qualities of the background, of negative space, of reticence. Yet, it's also very visible." She correlates this to what she labels "the way that women have been in the background historically."[1] The sign itself does this, she argues, since it is a mark no one has ever seen within a poem.

There aren't always the words to say what we want to say, but still we want to chart the fissures, missing links, and attempts. The sinuous lineation Fulton employs, with unevenly spaced lines that add visual rhythm to the page, also seem another way in which she paces the absences present in her work. I love the idea of marking a place for what cannot yet (or perhaps ever) be expressed and conveying meaning (literal and figurative) through other senses.

Another favorite poet of mine, May Swenson, is also concerned with this challenge. Her book *Iconographs* reveals her own variation on shape or concrete poetry. Swenson activates the white space around the printed words as she breaks with the expectation (perhaps the tyranny?) of the left-hand margin. Swenson, too, was concerned with expressing what was deemed unacceptable, and many of her subjects, particularly her highly coded lesbian love poems, cleverly and craftily address her covert, sometimes overt, sometimes dancing-on-the-line concerns.

In a note, she comments on her visual intentions in *Iconographs,* saying that she wanted "to have material and mold evolve together and become a symbiotic whole. To cause an instant object-to-eye encounter with each poem even before it is read word after word." Swenson wants there to be a sensuality and physicality with her words that parallel the intense sensuality often found in her metaphors and images: "With the physical senses we meet the world and each other—a world of objects, human and otherwise, where words on a page are objects, too. The first instrument to make contact . . . the quickest to report it, is the eye."[2]

Swenson insists on a physicality with her poems that is unusual; not unlike Fulton, who arrests the reader's eye with the introduction of a new sign, Swenson's use of space on the page gives pause as the reader must sometimes figure out how to read differently and map new correspondences between the words presented, both through their physical placement and content. One of Swenson's most famous iconographs is the poem "Bleeding," in which an internal caesura opens up down the poem's center like a jagged wound:

> Why must you   bleed in the first place said the knife.
> For the same   reason maybe that you must do what you
> must do said   the cut.
> I can't stand   bleeding said the knife and sank in farther.
> I hate it too said   the cut I know it isn't you it's
> me you're lucky to be   a knife you ought to be glad about that.

The dialogue within the poem, between a knife and a cut, is gendered as male and female and is painful to read. The knife taunts the cut, and the cut sounds like a subservient housewife sacrificing itself and apologizing to its abuser in what almost seems a parody of gender politics.

Is Swenson offering social commentary? It's hard to tell, but she suggests other nuances: the phallic symbolism of the knife and cut interacting, the association of blood with women and menstruation, a sense of shame and willfulness. The reader encounters a ragged gap stopping the words as she shows (rather than tells of) the hesitations between the objects personified as speakers and, at moments, emblemizes their closeness and, at moments, their distance. As one's eye follows the path created between the words, there is a visceral frisson created when one sees the cut tear between the words, as the reader witnesses, as well as comprehends, the embodiment of this battle.

Some of her other poems visually exemplify their subjects, such as "The Lightning" with its diagonal bolt of blank space slicing the side of the poem (as if just struck) and the gaping awe the speaker feels has also forced the letters' sudden separation. One of her most wry poems, "Women," imitates, through the text's placement on the page, a sway of shifting shapes that reflects the various roles women inhabit throughout their lives. The words stack in precariously mounting rows, each edged a bit farther out and interrupted by an unpunctuated phrase driving across the base of each column. It's hard to know the direction in which to read, and Swenson's visual disorientation lends multiple meanings to her words. She asks in the poem if women should be like

> sweet
> oldfashioned
> painted
> rocking
> horses

later adding,

> joyfully
> ridden
> rockingly
> ridden

It's a sexual metaphor that is mimicked through the motion of the words themselves. Again, Swenson is deft in suggesting compliance, defiance, and difficulty in ascertaining various meanings by keeping the reader just as off-kilter as the text. She explores different roles women can inhabit, including

> Immobile
> sweetlipped
> sturdy
> and smiling

while also saying they should be

> moving
> pedestals
> moving
> to the
> motions
> of men[3]

In one interview, Swenson claims that she began to be a "feminist at age three-and-a-half." Her questioning of gender hierarchy and expectation is done subtly, and insistently, as she shows (given the time period in which she published) subterfuge, especially through this dislocating use of the visual. This device is her strongest strategy in saying what she otherwise seems to feel could not be said outright.[4]

I've always been a poet who works loosely with a variety of formal techniques, trying to create a prosody that organizes itself around a poem's inherent logic. As I sought a form for a poem whose subject I wanted to leave deliberately unclear, it occurred to me to borrow the whiteness of the page, to highlight what is not there, as Fulton and Swenson both do within their work. By activating the blankness that surrounds the text, the words' visual separation would reverberate along with the poem's intent. While I don't turn to the invention of a new symbol like Fulton does, I feel satisfied that I've let out an idea, at a comfortably coded level, whose pressure had long built. Just as Swenson's words blow across the page in her poem "Untitled," airing out her images and causing their own associations, so I wanted the space between words to evoke a visual mood, a nuance of distance, that could be both initially seen and then, after reading, also felt.

EPITHALAMION MANQUÉ

Rose, Pearl

June me quick,
a brown-edged bloom.

Rice me right,
luck this gaped womb.

Gold, Kiss

Sieve my glove,
palm years' lined loom.

Ring one left,
my Manx-tailed groom.

White, Wind

Veil this day,
scar-scarved, hope-sewn.

Nimbus nipped,
again, alone.[5]

I had long thought of writing a very wry poem that revealed its subject through subterfuge, a dancing around the edges of its main theme. Although an epithalamion is always a poem written for the occasion of a wedding, I wanted to allude specifically to what wasn't there, to what hadn't taken place. I put "manqué" into the title but didn't want to give any more location than that. Alongside eschewing traditional grammar and syntax, I decided to let the paired words, unbothered by traditional lineation, stand together to see what shape they could sculpt and to let the angles of the poem, especially the white space let in around the tight lines, display a solitariness, a loneliness, that would visually connote a mood and emote a feeling of abandonment, as the words group in rigid lines, a half pace away from the mentioned governing symbols of a wedding day, floating above them.

Saying what we want to say in a poem is a fraught concept, an endless conundrum, where meaning meets form and the work of expression is complexly wrought. When I began to study poets who added a visual layer within their poems, I saw a way to create a space for other things to be expressed, a place to mark nuances literally and figuratively, to invite words both written and unwritten into the poem.

WRITING PROMPT

Write a poem that incorporates a visual element. Either invent or reinscribe a symbol for use within the poem or work with the white space of the page in a meaningful way. How can you layer the poem's meaning through incorporation of the visual? Does this allow you to express something that you feel can't otherwise be said? Finally, consider making one theme of the poem the act of writing about something you can't or feel you shouldn't write about.

== / *Alice Fulton*

It might mean immersion, that sign
        I've used as title, the sign I call a bride
after the recessive threads in lace ==
the stitches forming deferential
                space around the firm design.
                    It's the unconsidered

mortar between the silo's bricks == never admired
                    when we admire
the holdfast of the tiles (their copper of a robin's
      breast abstracted into flat).

      It's a seam made to show,
the deckle edge == constructivist touch.
      The double equal that's nowhere to be found
                    in math. The dash
      to the second power == dash to the max.

It might make visible the acoustic signals
of things about to flame. It might

      let thermal expansion be syntactical. Let it
add stretch

                    while staying reticent, unspoken
as a comma. Don't get angry == protest == but a

comma seems so natural, you don't see it
when you read: it's gone to pure
transparency. Yes but.
                        The natural is what

poetry contests. Why else the line == why stanza == why
       meter and the rest. Like wheels on snow

                that leave a wake == that tread in white
                    without dilapidating
                    mystery == hinging
                one phrase to the next == the brides.

Thus wed == the sentence cannot tell
whether it will end or melt or give

                way to the fabulous == the snow that is
the mortar between winter's bricks == the wick that is

                  the white between the ink[6]

BLEEDING / *May Swenson*

Stop bleeding   said the knife
I would if I   could said the cut.
Stop bleeding   you make me messy with this blood.
I'm sorry   said the cut.
Stop or   I will sink in farther said the knife.
Don't   said the cut.
The   knife did not say it couldn't help it but
it   sank in farther.
If   only you didn't bleed said the knife I wouldn't
have   to do this.
I know   said the cut I bleed too easily I hate
that I   can't help it I wish I were a knife like
you and   didn't have to bleed.
Well   meanwhile stop bleeding will you said the knife.
Yes you   are a mess and sinking in deeper said the cut I
will have   to stop.
Have you   stopped by now said the knife.
I've almost   stopped I think.
Why must you   bleed in the first place said the knife.
For the same   reason maybe that you must do what you
must do said   the cut.
I can't stand   bleeding said the knife and sank in farther.
I hate it too said   the cut I know it isn't you it's
me you're lucky to be   a knife you ought to be glad about that.
Too many cuts around   said the knife they're
messy I don't know how   they stand themselves.
They don't said the cut.
You're bleeding again.
No I've stopped said the cut   see you are coming out now the
blood is drying it will rub   off you'll be shiny again and clean.
If only cuts wouldn't bleed   so much said the knife coming
out a little.
But then knives might become   dull said the cut.
Aren't you still bleeding a   little said the knife.
I hope not said the cut.
I feel you are just a little.

Maybe just a little but I can   stop now.
I feel a little wetness still   said the knife sinking in a
little but then coming out a   little.
Just a little maybe just enough   said the cut.
That's enough now stop now do   you   feel better now said the knife.
I feel I have to bleed to   feel I   think said the cut.
I don't I don't have to   feel said   the knife drying now
becoming shiny.[7]

Notes

1. Alec Marsh, "A Conversation with Alice Fulton," *Alice Fulton Website*, 1997, http://alicefulton.com/interviews/tq.html (accessed March 8, 2010), originally appearing in *TriQuarterly Review 98* 98 (Winter 1996–97): 22–39.

2. May Swenson, *Iconographs* (New York: Scribner, 1970), 87.

3. May Swenson, *New & Selected Things Taking Place* (Boston: Little, Brown, 1978), 105.

4. Karla Hammond, "An Interview with May Swenson: July 14, 1978," *Parnassus: Poetry-in-Review* 7.1 (1978): 62.

5. Elline Lipkin, *The Errant Thread* (Tucson, Ariz.: Kore Press, 2006), 61.

6. Alice Fulton, *Sensual Math: Poems* (New York: W. W. Norton, 1995), 56–57.

7. Swenson, *Iconographs*, 13.

Back to Back: An Epistolary Essay on Collaboration

Alice George and Cecilia Pinto

MONDAY

Alice and I are writers. Sometimes we write to each other. We write for each other. This is an interesting process that involves spontaneity and serendipity. Put another way, Alice is like lightning. I am like mud. We are essential. We are unknown to each other. We are making this up.

Alice and I are friends. We have had many meals together, and her lovely blue eyes keep me honest. I am writing this and will send it to her. She will do the same. Although I don't know what she's writing until I read it. We'll exchange work for a few days, reacting to and stealing from each other and braiding (that's Alice's word) until we have something that holds together and is both strong and pretty. Eventually, we'll sit side by side and create a final version.

The braiding is fun. Sometimes I throw something in just to see if Alice picks it up, like *anodyne*, which is a word I just learned this morning and the title of a poem by Yusef Komunyakaa whose meaning I don't understand. And because I work in mud, meaning slowly, and not always with much glee, it's nice to steal some fantastic idea from Alice and run with it, or at least lift myself a little closer to her crackling sky.

Having written in this way for a while, there are some things I can now predict. Alice is better with the rules, and she's faster. I never know what she'll send me, even when we've discussed a project in advance. This can be exciting and a little troubling. Sometimes what she does causes me to want to be like her, sometimes the opposite. I've written my part; now I'll hunker here in the muck and the reeds and wait to see what happens next.

—Cecilia

*

C. beat me this morning, writing her first bit toward this essay, so her words go first. Banter abides between us, tonic and sister-like. Her e-mail subject line: *Beat ya.*

One metaphor that comes to mind when thinking about our process is parenting—and how collaborative work feels like raising a child with two parents—while most of our solitary work is unitary, mythic. Athena springing from Zeus's forehead. Ferns asexually emitting spores. But, when we make something together, C. and I, we can err and exceed, posit untenable ideas, speak in extreme or odd terms. Leave our sentences unfinished. Because we'll be countered, doubled, added to and subtracted from. Someone has our back. Someone will stop us from threatening to ground our teenagers until they start smiling.

That sounds too comfortable, though, because sometimes what happens to my original words is scary. She sees something I didn't see. Which is what readers do. But then she responds to what she sees in a way that makes me see it strange. Often that strangeness is amplified by our way of writing blind, writing back to back, each e-mailing the other, not knowing what the other has just written. The process can feel transgressive, because when you're used to making something alone, making something with someone else feels uneasy. Lopsided yet complete. Askew.

—Alice

(P.S. I've set my iTunes to party shuffle while I write this, mixing my daughter's music with mine. Another kind of influence. Not knowing what comes next.)

TUESDAY

Reading what Alice wrote on Monday, I'm struck by the friction between our lines. I know what Alice wants. She knows what I want. We can appease, we can tease.

Usually, Alice is the grown-up. She organizes, keeps us on track, prods me to write. And occasionally, she reminds me of what's true: her eyes are green, she says. (I'm pretty sure they're not.) However, I've taken responsibility here for being the one who explains things, so she can waft and be ethereal, write unfinished sentences, posit, shuffle, be lopsided.

Alice said that writing with someone else causes unease. I guess, since she continues with me, that she likes that uneasy shifting, someone getting in and out of her boat. That's me, my muddy feet scraping against her hull.

Alice is lightning. Alice is a boat.

—Cecilia

*

O mud woman o. Things like adobe and cattails arise from the mud, whereas I'm good for scaring dogs and starting fires. So be it. We shall egg each other on, upping the ante.

I feel our collaborations have given us license to lie and tell the truth, and sometimes to fill in the blanks of each other's stories. Perhaps the scariest version of our collaborative experiments (at least for me) was when we wrote between the lines, creating twenty-line poems out of ten-line beginnings. Both of us took the risk of trying some narrative. How the hell can we tell each other's stories when we don't share each other's memories? We can't. We did. And sometimes it felt just wrong (I remember C. saying "my sister wouldn't say that"), but, without sounding too postmodern, it was great having my story welcome another story, without a wound. Somehow an anodyne, a way to say "pshaw" to the singular self!

—Alice

WEDNESDAY

No longer giddy and exhilarated, all this has made me suddenly sad and lonely. It feels pointless. I don't even know what color Alice's eyes are, for God's sake. What kind of a friend am I? There is nothing to be gained by this writing to each other. It cures nothing. It is no anodyne; it doesn't mitigate pain. This writing only illustrates distance and makes those crossroad moments more poignant, more desperate.

I am not explaining anything, just complaining. And I know, because I know Alice, that what I've just said, about the futility of this, will irritate her. Alice isn't really a boat.

Clearly, I'm done being the grown-up. I'm not writing.

Sorry, Alice. You can laugh at me. Then, please fold the paper over and write me back.

—Cecilia

*

Bossiness is important here, in this essay, because collaboration is about friendly power, index fingers shaking commands like a patch of black-eyed Susans in the cold wind that's just sprung up. Here in Illinois, in September.

So. I want everyone to do it, all writers, to find mud-fragrant writers and then to figure out some ground rules, some ideas of how to mix two voices. It's political (honoring the other) and liberating and wonderfully intimate. It will make you a better writer. I'm beginning to learn from C. to use fewer words and tell awkward truths.

I want C. right now to know that even if she's not writing me back, she is still the great blue heron that's oddly stalking this house I'm living in. She is noble and stern. And intent on catching fish. Bird muse.

And finding a muse that's a friend is something. That's something.

—Alice

THURSDAY IS A BLANK.

FRIDAY

So when we sat together earlier this morning we were a temporary spell. Our brunette heads a bit powerful. Against the sadness that C. had so articulated. When we sat together, C. said she thought we were writing about atheism and our different take on the voids. And then I said I'd realized we were talking about loneliness.

We sat there, lightning and heron, though also all bristling with the practical facts of ourselves like weird jobs and short money. And she said that was part of it, of our process, resisting influence, resisting orders, while still working together.

And I said I was a little nervous, because our essay was so personal. And she said that was part of it. (We sounded a bit like Frog and Toad but in a feminist kind of way.)

intimacy + resistance = collaboration?

C. said once our whole essay should be like a bouquet of flowers. And I am still waiting to hear how she intends to pull that one off.

—Alice

MONDAY

Alice and I met on Friday to review what we'd written individually and to determine how to mesh the two pieces. We read our work aloud, enjoying some intersections. We quibbled over some differences.

We agreed to write a little further after discerning some threads to possibly bind or braid. We agreed on loneliness. I think we agreed to disagree, or at least to think that our disagreements were interesting. She allows me my petulance.

We enjoyed a good lunch of salami, goat cheese, hard bread. There were two apples that neither of us ate. Alice showed me her eyes.

She has turned me into a bird, as though she had the power. I told her I could make this piece disintegrate like a bouquet of flowers, the petals browning and falling, the water dank and fetid. I could do it really easily; it wouldn't take but a few words to wreck everything.

If this was just a piece of writing, ending with a threat might be satisfying. But I can't in good conscience because Alice is my friend and because it seems worth noting that what's at stake here is the fragility of any friendship and the power of language to bind and braid. We are in this together.

Three years ago, when Alice and I wrote our first piece together, the stakes were different. We—well, I was interested in entertaining, and we didn't know then that our words together would mean something to anyone. We didn't know they'd mean something to us. Sitting at Alice's picnic table the first time we edited our work together, there were moments of creative magic and connection that I have not experienced outside of myself. Who is this person, I wondered, looking into her green eyes? Who am I?

With Alice and me, it's not us against the world but something riskier, I think. We square off, back to back. Looking away from each other, we walk twenty paces, turn, and run until we collide. There are bound to be accidents, but there are other possibilities, and what we've written here is one of them.

—Cecilia

WRITING PROMPT

Find another writer whose work interests you. It may be helpful if their style or content is quite different from yours. Each partner writes a ten-line poem, leaving space in between each line. Then each partner hands the poem to the other and proceeds to write in between the lines, resulting in two twenty-line poems. Then switch the papers one more time, allowing the original writer to title the poem and perhaps give it a final edit. Note that both of our poems reprinted here use some version of this method; however, "Your Five + My Four = Nine" was written "blind"; that is, we merged our lines without seeing the other's work, relying completely upon serendipity.

THIRST / *Alice George and Cecilia Pinto*

I could tell you of my daughter's backseat lamentations,
how strange each day has its particular grief

as we leave our Maine vacation, her weeping for water,
a dry throat, a longing for the left behind, the lost.

Or my painting of my father-in-law's temporary gravestone,
how strange the way even loss lacks permanence,

the way his widow leaned over the work, politely nervous,
following the rituals of mourning, counting on the solace of duty

until I found the right botanical image: a willow.
There are other trees, lean out any window, find them and the
fluttering birds.

Or the way each morning my hands can count,
number them, name them, remember

the new dead in the Middle East. But my tongue—
Robin, Blue Jay, Raven, Crow—

could turn black and nothing would change
names carved in stone. How strange that a name in stone is enough

except some settling in me, and perhaps in you.
I could tell you of tears wept under a willow, roots that go into
the ground.

Instead, let's make new things to mourn, let's forget, let's eat.
Our names will remain for strangers to consider, our thirst,
however, will end.[1]

YOUR FIVE + MY FOUR = NINE / *Alice George and Cecilia Pinto*

I keep forgetting
I have it
people fear people
broken washing machines
every little day
I wish that

x-rays showed my
house was clean
dark coat draping.
*

Are you feeling
the unsettled feeling
sexy I am
beneath my skin
so angry today
makes everything taste
wish I was
different this morning
smack someone's ass.
*

I always sit
stealing the stars
in an office
I'm doing that
or the woods
I've got them
trying to find
in my hat
the right words.
*

If the pheasant
spring rain falling
why not me
the heavenly lilacs
all seeking water
make me remember
flash of fire
my grandmother's passing
scouring the bones.
*

Everything is flying
parchment and canvas
wind, rain, ideas

blue and white
choppy and blue
yellow bird billow
but no wings
sleep well tonight
sing out tomorrow
*
Black pickup truck
in the middle
on the road
late last night
R.I.P. Tina
my son descended
in the night
on the window
and ate fruit.
*
Red round there
working this hard
and yellow too
feel stony yet
hands in hair
glorious and steaming
lips on face
snapping yet sleek
name this place.
*
Yesterday you told
anoint these eyes
me to forget
for everything's seen
the past but
lids are swollen
if I do
irises gasp open
I won't remember
what you said.

*

The story goes
there are numbers
everything will rinse
that I can't
and fall away
understand a magic
if the storm
that floats above
really knows me.

Note

1. Alice George and Cecilia Pinto, "Thirst," in *Saints of Hysteria: A Half-Century of Collaborative American Poetry*, ed. Denise Duhamel, Maureen Seaton, and David Trinidad (Brooklyn: Soft Skull Press, 2007), 279.

The Quarrelsome Poem

Michael Theune

We make out of the quarrel with others, rhetoric, but of the quarrel with ourselves, poetry.[1] While William Butler Yeats's famous formulation is gorgeously and almost convincingly mellifluous, as is the case with so many declarations about poetry in general, it is simply not true: many poems are arguments composed specifically to quarrel with others.

Poems in fact argue in a host of ways, employing all the argumentative and rhetorical maneuvers and strategies employed in both everyday life and scholarly discourse—too many ways to enumerate, let alone treat in any detail here. However, if critic and theorist Gerald Graff is correct when he states that a "summary-and-response pattern represents the deep structure of most written argument," then it might be best to examine one very specific manifestation of this pattern in order to show clearly both the existence of quarrel in poetry and how an openness to such quarrelling can be used to create new poems.[2]

Graff's notion of argument-as-summary-and-response is as uncomplicated as it sounds: an argument consists of first recounting and then replying to an opponent's views. In the clear poetic manifestation of this pattern, the simple, two-part structure first reveals a problematic, clichéd representation and then turns to provide an alternative to that troublesome, overused language.

This cliché-and-critique structure, as it will be referred to here, has long been and remains a vital pattern for making poems. Unsurprisingly, as the act of turning suggests, an early instance of the cliché-and-critique structure can be found in the midst of the Renaissance sonnet tradition, a formal tradition that also requires a *volta*, or a turn, a major shift in the rhetorical progress of the poem:

> Some blaze the precious beauties of their loves
> By precious stones, and other some by flowers,

Some by the planets and celestial powers,
Or by what else their fancy best approves;
Yet I by none of these will blazon mine,
But only say her self herself is like,
For those similitudes I much mislike
That are much used, though they be divine.
In saying she is like herself, I say
She hath no like, for she is past compare.
Then who aright commends this creature rare
Must say, "She is"; and there of force must stay,
  Because by words she cannot be expressed;
  So say, "She is," and wond'ring owe the rest.[3]

In the opening quatrain of this sonnet, poet John Davies of Hereford notes how others use the standard methods of the blazon tradition (a tradition in which a poet employs flowery, rich, celestial imagery and metaphors to enumerate the beautiful features of the beloved) to praise, or "blaze," a beloved. However, as signaled by the opening "Yet" of the fifth line (the most significant *volta* in this sonnet), Davies believes such conventional descriptive methods are inadequate to express the virtually impossible beauty of his own beloved, and so he employs a new poetic approach to do justice to his singular, wondrous love. Davies responds to the blazon tradition by noting that its weakness is that it thinks it can actually approximate the beloved's value, but he trumps this strategy by suggesting that his own beloved is simply beyond compare, that her glorious beauty is unutterable, leaving whoever sees her speechless.

Though initially it might look very different from Davies's Renaissance-era sonnet, Staceyann Chin's twentieth-century "I Don't Want to Slam" also follows the same cliché-and-critique pattern:

I've decided
I don't want to be
a poet who just writes
for the slam anymore

I want to stop writing
poor excuses for poems
that do nothing but

stroke my ego and fool
the crowd into thinking
my bucking and screaming
was actually their orgasm

I don't want to be a poet
writing to slam anymore

I don't want
to join the staged revolution

don't want to be a part of just
some spotlight-slamming solutions
don't want to go to Austin or Chicago
simply because I think I have
the rapidly moving metaphors
smashing off the Nuyorican walls
or similes like a silver bullet
bee-lining for the finals on a balloon
full of nothing but hot air
making the room smell like a fart
from a bad poem that somebody
should have said excuse me for

I don't want to just slam anymore

I don't want to sit
in smoke-filled rooms
listening to women who rhyme
creating lyrics that rock
making sure they fit within
the confines of some judge's ticking clock
smiling with people I've only seen
on the corner of an old SlamNation flyer
trying to get them to tell me
how to record that first CD
how to really work a crowd
how to fuck those hard to please judges
so I can give birth to a bastard TEN

I'm tired of igniting blazes on the mike
pimping poems about my lover's private life
sipping iced tea over superlatives
eating spring rolls over hyperboles
juxtapositioning myself in vegetarian cafes
between guys with funny sounding names
like Guy and Procope and Dot
hoping some of what makes them real poets
will rub off on a pretender like me

I want to be like them
when I finally grow up
because I've watched them
rewrite stolen histories
in breathtaking three minute pieces
doing only honest performances
so that every time they go on
they kick a poem with heart
fighting the fanfare of this
slamming pseudo-revolution
changing the world
one poem at a time

Now that I've actually been a poet
been romantic and been poor
I don't want to be a slam poet anymore

Today I want to write
from a place where I change lives
and change people and places
cross over boundaries
of sexes and cultures and races
paint the skies deep red
instead of boring blue
write the true history of me and you
crawl deep inside the lines
of every poem I write
I want to speak about the stars
as if I had become the night

Tonight I want to be
intimate with my muse
Hell—I want to bed the woman
I want to have her so close
she gets up inside me
so when I am asleep
she can rouse me
No!
I want her to arouse me
have her way with me
have her play with me
so that when I wake up
I will be inspired
to write honest poems
poems about grandmothers
and babies and truth
poems that don't care
about the meter or the rhyme
poems that really couldn't give
a flying fuck about the time
poems that will not sit
within the squares of any chart
poems that are written in blood
flowing straight from the heart

I want to write
I left my lover and
now I want her back poems
I miss Jamaica
but I'm never going back poems
I know it's not a ten
but it sends shivers down MY back poems
poems that talk about life
and love and laughter
poems that reveal the flaws
that make strikingly real people
real poems
poems that are so honest
they slam[4]

Although she eventually concedes that there are some slam poets doing interesting and valid work, for virtually the first half of this poem, Chin critiques slam poetry by enumerating what she perceives to be its numerous problems: too often it is ego-driven (slam poets are portrayed as striving more for publicity than for true expression), inauthentic (slam's passions and desires are largely "staged," "hot air" intended to "fool" the audience), and surprisingly confining (slam poems can be no longer than three minutes) and goal-oriented (some slam poets aim at getting a "ten," the highest possible score). Instead of this, Chin wants something that is more powerful because it is more personal; she wants poems that break the rules, and perhaps even fail, in pursuit of the personal in order to be more "honest" and "intimate."

The cliché-and-critique structure used in both Davies's and Chin's poems has two essential features. The first, and most obvious, is the necessary turn from an initial revelation of a clichéd representation to a critique, which often involves trying to surpass that problematic representation. The second, perhaps less obvious, feature is the strategic use of contrast. Generally, the two parts of a cliché-and-critique poem are very different from each other. After stuffing his sonnet's initial quatrain with the material from the blazon tradition, Davies's critique section is noticeably abstract and thus clearly differentiated from the tradition from which it wants to distance itself. Davies presents the blazon tradition as being a bit gaudy; in contrast, Davies's own approach, like his own beloved, is statelier. Chin's slam poem opens with the noise of slam, both referring to it by using slam lingo and recreating it with frenetic stanzas packed with slam "superlatives" and "hyperboles." In the poem's critique portion, the poem gets quieter, softer; it refers to "grandmothers / and babies and truth"; its orgasm isn't loud and fake, it's intimate and deep.

By sharing the same cliché-and-critique structure, both Davies's and Chin's poems also share that structure's many benefits. If, as with so many poems, one often can read a poem and wonder what it is doing, what its import is, this does not happen with the cliché-and-critique poem, which clearly presents its own context. Additionally, because the cliché-and-critique strategy requires a clarifying contrast, a reader can understand and perhaps even feel much more distinctly the author's viewpoint after first having examined another view. This is especially helpful when assuming stances like Davies's and Chin's, which want to ratchet down the noise of poetry. A whole poem about quietness might sound very loud (or at least it would seem obviously paradoxical: such wordiness to try to convey such quiet!), but when that quietness is represented over and against a contrasting noise, that quietness stands a better chance of seeming actually quiet.

The clear contrast of the cliché-and-critique structure also provides a poem with the drama of contention, or at least the semblance of such contention, and this adds a clear element of suspense to the poem, giving the poem's reader/audience something to anticipate. When a sonneteer writes "Some blaze," immediately one is on the lookout to see how this particular sonneteer will blaze, what this particular sonnet will do differently. When a slam poet slams "I don't want to slam" and complains about slam *while slamming*, one wants to see how this slam poet will get out of this dilemma. Of course, a big part of watching such a drama is the thrill of witnessing a poem establish a challenge for itself. Beyond just offering explicit indications of a poem's import, the cliché-and-critique pattern establishes a marker by which a poem's success or failure can be judged: does the poem accomplish the critique it attempts?

The writer of a cliché-and-critique poem, however, is assisted in overcoming the challenges inherent in this structure by the facts that, first, the poet gets to control the representation of that to which the poet is responding and, second, this structure helps the poet to clearly establish ethos. Do all blazons work the way Davies says? Are slam poets really so concerned with the ten to the extent that Chin suggests? Perhaps or perhaps not, but at least for the space of the poem, the cliché-and-critique poem's pronouncements hold sway. Perhaps paradoxically, what might be seen as this structure's cunning is reinforced by the fact that this structure creates ethos for the speaker of each poem. The speaker in a cliché-and-critique poem comes across as smart and self-aware; the speakers in both Davies's and Chin's poems prove that they have intimate knowledge of the traditions to which their poems respond. (And one imagines Chin getting the additional bonus of being able to perform a send-up of the versions of slam she critiques.) And the effect of accumulated ethos spreads: because the speaker in a cliché-and-critique poem clearly knows so much about one thing, the reader/audience might more likely believe that the speaker knows something about other matters and, thus, whatever claims are made in the critique portion of the poem are more likely to be accepted.

While it is tempting to say that in a cliché-and-critique poem one should carefully and honestly represent the opposition, the only criteria needed to guide a poet in this endeavor are the poet's own conscience, the poet's sense of the knowledge and integrity of the poem's speaker, and a sense of what an audience will believe or let the poet get away with. Of course, poets should remember that if one advances a view too easily critiqued, one's own poem could become the subject for another poet's cliché-and-critique poem.

And one should beware: poets *are* apt use the cliché-and-critique structure. While Davies's sonnet and Chin's slam poem show very clearly the cliché-and-critique pattern, its rhetorical structure is used in a variety of ways by a number of poets. Framed by a walk with friends, the meditation at the heart of Samuel Taylor Coleridge's "The Nightingale" largely follows the cliché-and-critique pattern, arguing against what Coleridge claims is the merely poetic notion of the melancholic nightingale and replacing it with a true representation of the nightingale as joyous. In "Death's Valley," a poem written in response to a painting by George Inness, Walt Whitman composes a poem that critiques Inness's dark and gloomy portrayal of death, replacing this picture with one in which death is "[s]weet, peaceful, [and] welcome."[5] Wilfred Owen's "Dulce et Decorum Est" very strategically inverts the cliché-and-critique structure so that his response to his opposition occurs at the beginning and lasts for the majority of the poem. In this way, by the time the poem is done showing the horrors of war, the notion that it is, as Horace says, "[s]weet and noble . . . to die for one's country" has been shown to be completely untrue, an outmoded cliché.[6] In Zbigniew Herbert's "I Would Like to Describe," a poem in which the speaker tries to describe various feelings but can come up with only clichés such as "shafts of rain or sun" for "joy or sadness," this structure interestingly fails—Herbert's poem ends up incapable of finding the new language it so wants; however, the failure of this effort, dramatized at the end of the poem, is so beautifully and convincingly portrayed that the effort to try to dream up new language comes to seem authentic and valuable in itself.[7] John Ashbery's "And *Ut Pictura Poesis* Is Her Name" is a playful version of the cliché-and-critique poem, opening with the broad, general proclamation that "[y]ou can't say it that way any more" and so establishing an initial ground from which he can do—and does!—whatever he wants, making poetry new in his own way.[8]

Used by so many poets, past and present, the cliché-and-critique structure clearly has been a generative tool for poem-making. And it will continue to be, as long as the world keeps offering up its versions of what is to be valued (versions of love, beauty, sexiness, paradise, good poetry) and in what ways and to what extent these values should be esteemed, and as long as thinking and feeling individuals make the effort to react and respond by recognizing what the world is offering up and by providing other options. Indeed, if anything, in a world that grows more and more homogeneous, it virtually is a duty of art to demarcate alternatives. The cliché-and-critique structure encourages and helps poets to see the arguments the world makes, to take a stand, and so to enter the fray.

WRITING PROMPT

"Time heals all wounds." "Look before you leap." We are surrounded by such adages, such commonplaces. Sensitive to the language around them, poets often find such coinages invitations for their own (often critical) response. Edna St. Vincent Millay writes a sonnet that begins, "Time does not bring relief; you all have lied / Who told me time would ease me of my pain!"[9] W. H. Auden writes the poem "Leap before You Look." In order to participate in this vital poetic tradition, take up a contemporary popular saying—perhaps a proverb, perhaps a slogan—consider its appeal, but then launch your own critique of the saying and the actions or the worldview that it endorses.

THE VALUE OF MAN / *Michael Theune*

In a museum in London there is an exhibit called
"The Value of Man": a long coffinlike box with lots of
compartments where they've put starch—phosphorus—
flour—bottles of water and alcohol—and big pieces of
gelatin. I am a man like that.
—Stéphane Mallarmé, letter dated May 17, 1867

One man feels lifted up.
Another, drained.

One man is frightened:
Our emptiness is so *real.*
One man takes comfort:
So our emptiness is *real.*

One man marvels.
Another can't stand that
Our vision rises up just
To give us . . . *this*—

Indignant, one man
Thinks this is in bad faith.
Indignant, another
Thinks this is in bad taste.

One man does the math,
Works it out: about
Three pounds and change.
One man wants to know
What is the value of woman?
Is it the same?

One man decides to marry.
Another, to leave his wife.

One man feels angelic.
One man thinks he'll run amok.
One man wants to know exactly
What phosphorus and gelatin are.

One man decides Christ
Was lucky to have been
Butchered—at least that way
He felt right up to the end
That he had a soul.

Looking at his reflection
In the case's glass, one man
Sucks in his cheeks a bit.
Another brushes his hair.

Aghast, one man thinks it is too ugly.
Another wonders if it's too aesthetic,
If the neatly arranged boxes
And the crystal decanters might
Give someone the wrong idea.

One man thinks, *Just as I thought.*

One man thinks science instills
An appreciation of design.
Another thinks, *Evolution.*
Another, *The Fall—*

One man thinks of a grocer's shelf.
Another of a cold crucible
To purify the mind.

One man thinks it is too antiseptic.
Another wants to know, *What's that smell?*

One man thinks, *I could do this.*
Another wants to purchase one of his own.

One man begins to imagine equality,
A Brotherhood of Man.
Another thinks, *Mixed right, this*
Material could make a bomb.

One man looks up quizzically at another man.
One man thinks, *I am a man like that.*

One man finds the experience educational.
Another feels quite simply he has paid
Too much for his admission.

Notes

1. William Butler Yeats, "Anima Hominis," in *The Collected Works of W. B. Yeats: Volume V, Later Essays*, ed. William H. O'Donnell (New York: Scribner, 1994), 8.

2. Gerald Graff, *Clueless in Academe: How Schooling Obscures the Life of the Mind* (New Haven, Conn.: Yale University Press, 2004), 156.

3. John Davies, "Some blaze the precious beauties of their loves," in *The Penguin Book of the Sonnet: 500 Years of a Classic Tradition in English*, ed. Phillis Levin (New York: Penguin Books, 2001), 35.

4. Staceyann Chin, "I Don't Want to Slam," in *Poetry Slam: The Competitive Art of Performance Poetry*, ed. Gary Mex Glazner (San Francisco: Manic D Press, 2000), 206–9.

5. Walt Whitman, "Death's Valley," in *Complete Poetry and Selected Prose*, ed. James E. Miller Jr. (Boston: Houghton Mifflin, 1959), 389.

6. Horace, Book III, Ode 2, in *The Complete Odes and Satires of Horace*, trans. Sidney Alexander (Princeton: Princeton University Press, 1999), 96.

7. Zbigniew Herbert, "I Would Like to Describe," in *The Collected Poems: 1956–98*, ed. and trans. Alissa Valles (New York: Ecco Press, 2007), 65.

8. John Ashbery, "And *Ut Pictura Poesis* Is Her Name," in *Houseboat Days* (New York: Viking Press, 1977), 45.

9. Edna St. Vincent Millay, "Time does not bring relief; you all have lied . . . ," in *Collected Poems*, ed. Norma Millay (New York: Harper and Row, 1956), 562.

"Memento Mori" and Terza Rima: A Revision Narrative

Diane Thiel

For years, I had the idea to write about a memory of an odd middle-school project I did on Dante's *Inferno*. The narrative itself existed (in my mind and memory), but the piece hadn't yet found its form. Would it be cast as an essay, a story, a poem? Choosing poetry to tell the story of first encountering Dante's epic seemed most appropriate, but the choice of terza rima for the poem occurred later in the process. Terza rima ("triple rhyme") is a verse form invented by Dante, with a rhyme scheme *aba, bcb, cdc,* and so on. The middle rhyme of each tercet becomes the first and third rhyme of the following stanza. The interlocking rhyme scheme gives the form a natural forward-moving momentum that is often well-suited to a narrative poem.

Reproduced here is an early draft of "Memento Mori in Middle School." It is not the first draft (I write everything initially by hand) but the first typed draft. In the early stages of writing a poem, I often find myself putting "Notes for a Poem" at the top of the page because I hardly think of the draft as a poem but more as a free-write. As I looked through the twenty-some drafts of this poem, I chose this one to illustrate the revision process because it is the point at which a crucial realization about the form of the poem took place. What could I do with this story? How should I render it? And then it came to me—terza rima—of course! The form Dante invented for *The Divine Comedy* suddenly seemed the only choice.

In the first typed lines of this draft, as well as in my handwritten reworking in the lower right hand corner, you can see the new incarnation of the poem beginning to take shape. The first lines are rewritten with a tentative terza rima, testing out the new idea. Subsequent drafts show my changes of various parts of the poem to arrive, finally, at a version of terza

The Divine Comedy

When I was twelve, I chose the Inferno
for a project - an oral presentation
with visual aids. My brother ~~was a better~~ artist.
He offered to draw the tortures.
It took ten posterboards. We were always over-achievers.

That Monday I arrived with my nine circles,
and spread them out around the class.
The students were impressed.
The teacher seemed amused,
most clearly by the tiny tortures drawn
into the rings. By reputation, she was cruel.

The students, nearly always bored,
were awakened by the tortures,
perhaps as we all had been conditioned.
They requested permission to round the room
with me as I presented, to see each circle up close.
We passed the first one, full of poets and philosophers
their imagined likenesses cut out from an article
in a Scientific American. The class thought
they were a boring lot. They probably deserved their fates.

For the second, I had drawn the wind
as best I could, with tiny figures blown about.
I pointed out Paolo and Francesca.
We had a boy named Paolo in our class,
and people laughed.

Everyone liked the gluttons and fistfulls of slime
and the river Styx - a popular band at the time.
And the city of Dis would easily become
the city of dis and dat for weeks to come.
For the three furies, shrieking and tearing
their breasts with their nails, and for the harpies,
I had cut out certain teachers faces
from the school paper, but then thought better of it.
and left their cut out heads at home lying on the table.

Everyone quieted a little at the monstrous trees,
the wood of suicides.
I think everyone thought of Fred,

Memento Mori

though no one said a word.

People moved on quickly to Geryon
and rode the flying monster down.
The wicked counselors we knew by name.
They occupied the office right below us.
But again, I had resisted pasting in their faces.
A last minute decision. Their little cut-out heads
remained on the table at home.

always wanted to know
"what ~~about~~ happened to those sweet
poems I used to write.

For the ice in the last circle, where my brother
had expertly drawn the traitors with unfeeling hearts,
my mother had insisted I take with me
a freezer full of popsicles — to end on a lighter note,
she said. After all, it is a comedy isn't it?
Always a bit disturbed by my projects, she hadn't seen
the end result. But she thought, by the end,
everyone would need it.

I wanted to be liked.

Encouraged by the treat, the class moved quickly
to the last circle, and chose their colors.
The teacher, mildly confused, but knowing
they would melt, reluctantly allowed them.
And when the bell announced the change of class,
we left her room with red and purple mouths.

became kids
again.

nearly forgotten

the concerns
amidst the
nearly forgotten by everyon
I carried the posters back
home.

we all had secrets by then.

Bird
Imagery
(Penne:
wings).
Francesca

Present some philosophy —

A + E - fortunate fall

We understood descent.

and still have
them
somewhere in the house
that.

rima. You can see, even in this early reworking of the opening lines, that I chose to soften the rhymes into *chimes*, perhaps, by using assonance and off-rhyme. Examples of these chimes are "Inferno" and "fabbro" in lines one and three of the poem and "presentation" and "ten" in lines two and four. The exact rhymes then attain a more emphatic quality.

Most of the narrative details are already present in this early draft: the speaker's choice to do an oral presentation on Dante's *Inferno* at the age of twelve; specifics of the way each circle of Hell was depicted by this twelve-year-old presenter; the speaker's mother insisting that the child take a "freezer full of popsicles" to reflect the ice in the last circle of Hell; and the children leaving school with popsicle-stained "red and purple" tongues. Creating the poem had to do, mostly, with finding the right lyrical path. The heightening and clarification of certain details, however, became an important aspect of revision. In the second line of the poem, for instance, adding the small detail about the "gifted class" gives the narrative more credibility. An average class of twelve-year-olds would not be reading the *Inferno*. The detail also begins establishing the tongue-in-cheek tone. How odd those gifted class projects (and students) were. The union of the *Inferno* with that trial-filled middle-school age became a reflection of threshold crossings that burn themselves into our memories.

One important point that had to be expanded in later drafts was the introduction of Fred, who the children thought of "at the monstrous trees." In the early draft, the narrative moves quickly past what may have happened to him, with merely a hint of Fred's story during Dante's wood of suicides. In reality, this detail becomes the dark heart, the memento mori (recognition of our mortality), perhaps even the motivation for "Memento Mori in Middle School." The mention of Fred needed a longer moment to reverberate. The early version states:

> Everyone quieted a little at the monstrous trees
> The wood of suicides
> I think everyone thought of Fred,
> Though no one said a word.
> People moved on quickly to Geryon. . . .

In the final version of the poem, this brief moment is expanded upon, with additional details such as "His name was in the news" and "he might have just been playing with the gun." This important moment in the poem becomes significantly more intense and simultaneously more lyrical with the use of more exactly rhymed terza rima:

> At the wood of suicides, we quieted.
> Though no one in the room would say a word,
> I know we couldn't help but think of Fred.
>
> His name was in the news, though we had heard
> he might have just been playing with the gun.
> We moved on quickly by that huge, dark bird
>
> and rode the flying monster, Geryon. . . .

The change in title, from "Presenting *The Divine Comedy*" to "Memento Mori in Middle School," reflects the importance of this point in the narrative and sets up both the dark and the light in the poem. You can see the new title making its first appearance at the top of the second page of the draft, close to the point where Fred is introduced. The lighter aspects of the poem, with all the details about a child's interpretation of Dante's poem, might make a reader laugh aloud, but the suggestion of Fred's likely suicide gives the poem important contrasting darker shades.

WRITING PROMPTS

1. Write a poem responding to a famous work of poetry, using the form of the chosen poem.

2. Take a poem you are working on and try recasting it. Does the form you have chosen thus far serve the poem thematically? Are there any repetitions of themes, lines, or words that might suggest using a form of repetition, such as a villanelle or sestina? If it is a narrative, you might want to consider terza rima, the ballad, or blank verse. Look closely at any rhythm or rhyme scheme that may be trying to emerge in your draft.

3. Write your own revision narrative. An important aspect of revision involves knowing when to stop, an issue that often troubles both beginning and established writers. Save drafts of each essay and number them. You may find yourself returning to earlier drafts, or at least sections of earlier drafts. It is useful to put your writing aside for a while before revising. Take a particular poem that has several drafts and write a short piece of prose

describing what your revision process has been with the piece. You might begin to notice your own patterns of revision.

MEMENTO MORI IN MIDDLE SCHOOL / *Diane Thiel*

When I was twelve, I chose Dante's *Inferno*
in gifted class—an oral presentation
with visual aids. My brother, *il miglior fabbro,*

said he would draw the tortures. We used ten
red posterboards. That day, for school, I dressed
in pilgrim black, left earlier to hang them

around the class. The students were impressed.
The teacher, too. She acted quite amused
and peered too long at all the punishments.

We knew by reputation she was cruel.
The class could see a hint of twisted forms
and asked to be allowed to round the room

as I went through my final presentation.
We passed the first one, full of poets cut
out of a special issue of *Horizon.*

The class thought these were such a boring set,
they probably deserved their tedious fates.
They liked the next, though—bodies blown about,

the lovers kept outside the tinfoil gates.
We had a new boy in our class named Paolo
and when I noted Paolo's wind-blown state

and pointed out Francesca, people howled.
I knew that more than one of us not-so-
covertly liked him. It seemed like hours

before we moved on to the gluttons, though,
where they could hold the cool fistfuls of slime
I brought from home. An extra touch. It sold

in canisters at toy stores at the time.
The students recognized the River Styx,
the logo of a favorite band of mine.

We moved downriver to the town of Dis,
which someone loudly re-named Dis and Dat.
And for the looming harpies and the furies,

who shrieked and tore things up, I had clipped out
the shrillest, most deserving teacher's heads
from our school paper, then thought better of it.

At the wood of suicides, we quieted.
Though no one in the room would say a word,
I know we couldn't help but think of Fred.

His name was in the news, though we had heard
he might have just been playing with the gun.
We moved on quickly by that huge, dark bird

and rode the flying monster, Geryon,
to reach the counselors, each wicked face,
again, I had resisted pasting in.

To represent the ice in that last place,
where Satan chewed the traitors' frozen heads,
my mother had insisted that I take

an ice-chest full of popsicles—to end
my gruesome project on a lighter note.
"It *is* a comedy, isn't it," she said.

She hadn't read the poem, or seen our art,
but asked me what had happened to the sweet,
angelic poems I once read and wrote.

The class, though, was delighted by the treat,
and at the last round, they all pushed to choose
their colors quickly, so they wouldn't melt.

The bell rang. Everyone ran out of school,
as always, yelling at the top of their lungs,
the *Inferno* fast forgotten, but their howls

showed off their darkened red and purple tongues.[1]

Note

1. Diane Thiel, *Echolocations* (Ashland, Ore.: Story Line Press, 2000), 29–31.

The Eccentric Discipline

Michael Waters

During the past decade or so, I've been writing, often but not always, sometimes without intention, syllabic verse. I don't count syllables as I draft a poem, but have found that certain cadences, those of decasyllabic lines or their variation—alternating lines of thirteen and seven syllables, for example—insist themselves as the poem takes shape. "There are those who say that you cannot hear syllabics," Eric Pankey has stated, "that as a form it is only an obstacle for the writer. But I believe that we can train our ears to listen for the most subtle patterns in the language, syllabics being only one such pattern."[1] For a long time I have written by ear, allowing the sounds of words to suggest other words as the poem progresses, trusting "the sound of sense," as Robert Frost called it.[2] Such chiming effects help to keep the entire poem in the foreground, each word snug in its line, each equally important. "A poem is not a poem," John Logan insisted, "unless it has an essential surface to it which is musical in character."[3] Rhyming all along the lines while the lines themselves remain taut yet shapely creates a tension that may suit the emotional content of my work. The fluidity of the diction ripples across linear paths like water winding through a creek bed. Each line surprises, hurtling forward or slowing to gather more force or shifting direction, yet seems the inevitable result of all preceding lines. "As systems go, syllabic verse has little to recommend it," writes Brad Leithauser, "except for one puzzling thing: It works. With some frequency, the eccentric discipline it imposes seems to push everyday utterance into memorability."[4]

"Beloved" was written in the fall of 2005 on the island of Malta, where I was enjoying a five-week residency fellowship at the St. James Cavalier Centre for Creativity. I wrote each day, starting in early morning, then strolled the waterfront promenade for several hours in late afternoon, a walk that became part of the process of revision. I carried the poem with me and stopped often to add a line, or delete several, or strike one word and substitute another, then stopped again to replace the stricken word.

I had made several decisions, all arbitrary, regarding my writing before arriving on Malta: I would work every day, almost all day; I would move forward every other day with a new poem rather than keep deepening into one poem, as was my habit (otherwise I might work on only one poem the entire residency); I would keep the poems short; and I would avoid syllabic scaffolding. I came home with fourteen new poems, all short, all but two strictly decasyllabic. Go figure.

My wife, Mihaela, accompanied me to Malta. She had grown up in Romania, not leaving until 1996, when she was twenty-four, seven years after the violent revolution that ended with the execution by improvised firing squad of dictator Nicolae Ceauşescu and his wife, Elena, on Christmas Day 1989. Her stories of life under communism were fascinating and horrifying, and I felt strongly that they should remain hers, to be told in her own poems, in her own style. Yet in writing this love poem, I filched, with permission, one detail from that life: she had to bring her own lightbulb to the library in order to read there. All other details in the poem are imagined, except for the reference to the death of Ceauşescu and the fact that Mihaela and I would have dinner with Toni Morrison in 2001. The title is borrowed, of course, from the novel of the same name by Morrison but might be mistaken for a sticky bit of romantic drivel until that association is revealed near the poem's close, muting the sentimental gesture. The decasyllabic lines mean to urge the poem forward, both vertically and horizontally, their cadences inexorable, while the threat of imminent violence is mitigated by the leap from Romania to New England, that brief opening of landscape and promise that becomes, with the book's absence, suddenly and cruelly impossible, until the evocative prose of another novel braces the girl.

I revised this poem during the act of composition rather than taking it through one complete draft, then another, then another . . . Revision often reveals how craft and luck seduce each other. "I have never started a poem yet whose end I knew," Robert Frost stated in an interview, and Theodore Roethke expressed the same inchoate method in iambic pentameter, his own ten syllables advising what perhaps remains the best approach to writing a poem: "I learn by going where I have to go."[5]

WRITING PROMPT

If, as Joseph Conrad stated, "a work of art should carry its justification in every line," it might follow that a line of poetry should carry its justification in every syllable.[6] While the idea may be attractive, the practice may be forbidding. The cadences should flow, not stumble forward as the poet counts each syllable finger by finger. The lines must break naturally, not be chopped off when the determined number of syllables is reached. You might start with an eight-syllable line. British poet Roy Fuller noted that the difference between an octosyllabic line and a decasyllabic line is like the difference between going for a swim in a pond and swimming across the ocean. Eventually you can lengthen the lines and vary them, alternating, for example, lines of thirteen syllables with lines of eight syllables.

Such lines lend themselves more readily to narrative and discursive modes than to the lyric. Often the traditional elements of fiction—character, setting, plot—suit poems as well. You might rewrite and update a biblical story, deepen into the particulars of a legend (the baker proclaimed Pope Fabian in 236 when a dove alighted on his head), or select a brief, evocative item from the newspaper, such as this one from an account of the Madrid train bombings: "'On many bodies, we could hear the person's mobile phones ringing as we carted them away.'"[7] All of the elements are in place and need only, as Coleridge insisted, "the best words in the best order."[8]

BELOVED / *Michael Waters*

Romania
1989

She cradles the rag-swathed, 40-watt bulb
Like a hand-painted egg in woolen gloves
With holes scissored at forefinger and thumb
For turning pages in the icy nook.
The library looms beyond gritty drifts,
Past blood-soaked slats and the empty, grease-glossed
Hooks beckoning from butcher shop windows.
Last week she began reading *Ethan Frome,*
A donated copy—some Fulbright prof's—
And felt that New England snowscape her own,
But the volume's vanished between visits.
She hopes Ethan chose love over duty.
Still, she can't bring herself to steal a book;
Ceauşescu won't be shot until Christmas.
She scours shelves for American novels—

Overhead bulbs fizzled out years ago—
Then finds the harrowing tale of a slave
That makes her bulb seem to surge with power
Hour after hour in the cold cubicle.
(A decade later she'll meet the author.)
Sixteen now, she can't anticipate much,
Except to be loved as she loves these books.

for Mihaela[9]

Notes

This essay originally appeared in *Making Poems: Forty Poems with Commentary by the Poets*, ed. Erin Murphy and Todd Davis (Albany: State University of New York Press, 2010).

1. Lee Newton, "Interview with Eric Pankey," *Pleiades* 20.1 (2000): 104–16.

2. Qtd. in Harvey Breit, "In and Out of Books," *New York Times*, October 16, 1955, BR8.

3. John Logan, "A Conversation with Anthony Piccione and A. Poulin, Jr.," ed. S. Tobie Hewitt, in *A Ballet for the Ear: Interviews, Essays, and Reviews*, ed. A. Poulin Jr. (Ann Arbor: University of Michigan Press, 1983), 29.

4. Brad Leithauser, review of *Inner Voices*, by Richard Howard, *New York Times Book Review*, November 21, 2004, C18.

5. Theodore Roethke, *The Collected Poems of Theodore Roethke* (Garden City, N.Y.: Anchor Press, 1975), 49; Frost qtd. in Breit, "In and Out of Books."

6. Joseph Conrad, preface to *The Nigger of the Narcissus*, by Joseph Conrad (Garden City, N.Y.: Doubleday and Company, 1914), 11.

7. Keith B. Richburg, "Madrid Train Blasts Kill at Least 190; 10 Bombs Detonate Almost at Once; Nearly 1,500 Hurt," *Washington Post*, March 12, 2004, A01.

8. *The Collected Works of Samuel Taylor Coleridge, Volume VI: Table Talk*, ed. Kathleen Coburn and B. Winer (Princeton: Princeton University Press, 1990), 293.

9. Michael Waters, "Beloved," *Poetry International* 13 (2009): 77.

THREE

"Winter Gulls": Toward Authenticity

Nancy Eimers

At first I narrow my eyes
because I think that maybe the gulls want more from me
than simply my observation of them. . . .

I first read that passage—the opening to Marcia Southwick's "Winter Gulls"—as a graduate student getting my MFA.[1] If I could have borrowed forward in time from a poem I hadn't read yet, I think I would have thought of Muriel Rukeyser's lines "I want to speak in my voice! / I want to speak in my real voice!," exclamation points and all.[2] What Southwick's poem enacted for me was a quality I didn't then know to call authenticity. What W. H. Auden said "ought to be a writer's chief preoccupation." Sadly, it seems old-fashioned to be using such a word now—authenticity—but it still rings true for me. Auden: the writer "can always know, not immediately perhaps, but certainly in a short while, whether something he has written is authentic—in his handwriting—or a forgery."[3] Michael Ryan: "As for authenticity, we are dying for it amidst all the fakery and fragmentation."[4]

I seemed to recognize the handwriting in Southwick's poem as something like what mine could try to be.

Southwick's poem begins unabashedly with a direct articulation of thought, what for lack of a better word I'll call a statement, not an image—OK, "I narrow my eyes" calls up an image, a facial gesture, but it's an image that acts as a threshold crossing to a thought:

but then I realize I'm mistaken,
it's just that they are usually thought of as beautiful,
while to me they look like scraps of dirty cloth. . . .

a thought that makes possible this passage on distance and loneliness later in the poem:

And I think of myself as elsewhere,
how around me there are always other people
and to them I am always *there* but never *here*,
and it seems to me that this is a terrible tragedy
like losing a best friend,
though everyone keeps talking nevertheless
or calling to each other over what they think
is the not too serious distance between them.

At that point in my writing, I hadn't realized one could write not about things but about thoughts. I hadn't read "Tintern Abbey"—

While with an eye made quiet by the power
Of harmony, and the deep power of joy,
We see into the life of things. . . .[5]

—or "Frost at Midnight"—

Therefore all seasons shall be sweet to thee. . . .[6]

—or Rukeyser—

Whoever despises the clitoris despises the penis
Whoever despises the penis despises the cunt
Whoever despises the cunt despises the life of the child[7]

—or William Carlos Williams's "Asphodel"—

It is difficult
to get the news from poems
yet men die miserably every day
for lack
of what is found there[8]

—or Rukeyser, again—

Who will speak these days,
if not I,
if not you?[9]

—or the poems of Jon Anderson, my then teacher—I was just beginning to read them—which soon would teach me much about statement and authenticity:

Give me a little time—
Eternity—
& I will mend.[10]

I didn't yet know any of the things that statements could do. Stumbling on Southwick, I began to understand what the poems of Wordsworth, Coleridge, Williams, Rukeyser, and Anderson would further unfold.

The statements in Southwick's poem—moments of someone's trying to talk about things she was thinking—had the authenticity of handwriting, or of someone on the other end of the phone. Is "statement" right, though? It was an utterance so conversational in Southwick's poem, thought that mimicked casual talk, that allowed for the wobbliness of the present, in which thought and feeling are not formed but forming, still unsure, precarious.

But sometimes, like now,
I can feel that distance becoming acute. . . .

I remember a moment in *The Catcher in the Rye* when Holden Caulfield compares writers one would and writers one would not want to call up on the phone after reading his or her work. For me, the Southwick who had written that poem would have been in the dearer first group. In the end, she opts in "Winter Gulls" for a simile, as if there were no getting closer to knowing one's distance from everything:

It's as if I were asleep
and trying to open my mouth.

I was awed by the implied disorientation, the admitted ineffectuality of thought.

For the next few month's, when I felt my own poem's handwriting veering toward forgery, I would reread "Winter Gulls" and feel like myself again, restored to my own uncertainty and the ongoing mystery of feeling and thought.

WRITING PROMPT

My suggested exercise for any young writer is to find a poem that functions as a kind of Geiger counter for authenticity and keep it handy, reading it when you feel yourself faking it, emotionally, intellectually, stylistically. That model needn't be the poem you want to write—just one that reminds you why you want to write.

Here's the second part of the exercise: don't refer to a listener, but imagine you are speaking to someone in the poem. This isn't original advice. When you write a poem, speak as if to an intimate, someone you know well enough that you can speak to him casually in your most intelligent voice, said Jon Anderson in a long-gone conference I am sure he wouldn't have remembered, though I never forgot. To this I'd add, speak from a particular place. From a room or outside an abbey or in a cottage of sleepers or on a beach in winter. It seems like a way to cross the distance Southwick is spooked by at the end of her poem. Or maybe it is simply a way of speaking from somewhere to distance itself.

BOOK OF INVISIBLE THINGS / *Nancy Eimers*

And all our gestures go no further than our bodies
And we can reach only as far as our arms go . . .
—Fernando Pessoa

Somewhere trees are vanishing beautifully in a fog. Not on this street. Trees go on with a silence so deep it is going to be chainsawed limb by limb so it disappears from the earth. They're on a hit-list early this morning, wind in their leaves like pages turning in the book of invisible things. If I could reach far enough outside my body I could find out where the beginning begins and why at the toes and fingertips there are so many capillaries bearing so much blood. As for skin, does the soul come out safely on the other side? In a movie rerun I just saw, an extraterrestrial revives a dead deer strapped to the hood of a hunter's car. In the movies a spiritual act takes place from the outside in, unless the actor is a method actor. This one moves haltingly for his character's body is borrowed; as he looks on the deer, he wears a holy strain on the musculature of his face. First its front legs, then its head wakes up. Limb by limb it struggles back into itself. And it vanishes, simply by running across the highway into the woods. The extraterrestrial turns to his human companion and says, *You must be a very primitive species.* A woman's voice on the radio has gone crackly with the distance from Pakistan to an early morning in Kalamazoo. She was raped by decree of a village tribunal she was at the hands not at the mercy of. She was not, she was *not* to disappear from her body yet. Having spoken out, she is under house arrest. She is asked by the interviewer, is she safe and well, is her family supportive, when will she be given her passport back? Her answers travel out of the mouth of her translator in an English that is simple and undramatic. Yes. Yes. Soon. But there is the problem of her real voice coming out of her real mouth. Voices come to us out of our radios in the early morning as static. Which is what she is. Which is why her body is not going anywhere. Wind through leaves sounds like pages turning; leaves are not voices and do not need throats. Below and above there are small and large thunders—somebody rolling a garbage can to the curb, a storm on its way inland from the lake. *If we could hear light, it would sound like the pitter-patter of individual raindrops falling on a tin roof* said a scientist on TV last night. Did she want at first to crawl out of her body? Is it going to rain? Will rain bring the lake down into the trees? If everyday speech were visible, it might be rain. If silence were, it might be trees. If only you could look down from the treetops you would see no houses, no cars in their driveways, no people. Hard shine of leaves in place of each. Nowhere on earth does anything actually *vanish*, there are lovely synonyms, such as: ash, or shrug.

—NPR Interview with Mukhtar Mai, June 2005

Notes

1. Marcia Southwick, *The Night Won't Save Anyone* (Athens: University of Georgia Press, 1980), 42.

2. *A Muriel Rukeyser Reader*, ed. Jan Heller Levi (New York: W. W. Norton, 1995), 107.

3. W. H. Auden, *The Dyer's Hand and Other Essays* (New York: Vintage Books, 1989), 18.

4. Michael Ryan, *A Difficult Grace: On Poets, Poetry, and Writing* (Athens: University of Georgia Press, 2000), 153.

5. William Wordsworth, *Selected Poetry*, ed. Mark Van Doren (New York: Modern Library, 1950), 105.

6. *The Selected Poetry of Coleridge*, ed. Harold Bloom (New York: New American Library, 1972), 82.

7. *Muriel Rukeyser Reader*, 228.

8. *The Collected Poems of William Carlos Williams,* ed. Christopher MacGowan (New York: New Directions, 1991), 2:318.

9. *Muriel Rukeyser Reader,* 232.

10. Jon Anderson, *The Milky Way: Poems 1967–1982* (New York: Ecco Press, 1983), 13.

Longfellow's Ghost: Writing "Popular" Poetry

Angela Sorby

Nineteenth-century poets—Lydia Sigourney, Alfred Lord Tennyson, Henry Wadsworth Longfellow, and others—had something precious that we latter-day poets have lost. They had readers. They had *thousands* of readers. Ordinary people not only read poems such as "The Charge of the Light Brigade" but read them aloud and committed them to memory. By pointing this out, I do not mean to express nostalgia for the days of drugless dental work, bad roads, and compulsory schoolroom recitation. But I do wish to suggest that we can profit (though not monetarily—that's hopeless) by thinking more carefully about questions of audience. My poem "Asphalt" was written for my grandfather's funeral, but I want to consider it not as an elegy but as a *social act*, a poem aimed at a community of readers (or in this case, auditors) who are themselves neither poets nor aspiring poets. This is not a matter of moving from, say, the college poetry workshop to the slam bar; it's rather about moving into realms (imaginatively, and sometimes literally) where people do not expect good, original, contemporary poetry at all. At best, picturing poems as social acts can help poets to understand their poems not just as forms of self-expression but as other-directed events that connect audiences to themselves and to one another.

Literary theories of reception often emphasize the "dialogical" nature of meaning; that is, meaning is an unstable phenomenon produced by the author and (re-)produced by the reader. In other words, writers begin texts and readers finish them—and in finishing them, revise the meanings of texts to match their readerly expectations and wishes. But the reader is never simply an abstract ideal; reading always takes place in a specific setting that reflects specific cultural values. Poets and poetry readers are, on the one hand, happily diverse in terms of race, gender, and sexual orientation, but "we" have this in common: most of us are aligned with and/

or dependent upon educational institutions. We often delude ourselves that these institutions are not really relevant to our work as poets, hence the "great divide," most recently bemoaned by Marjorie Perloff, between literary critics and practicing poets in English departments.[1] But the fact remains that most poetry reading these days takes place in colleges and universities, and this means that readers are likely to have some of the following traits: (1) they are reading the poem on the page rather than just hearing it; (2) they are willing to work to decode fairly obscure metaphors and allusions; (3) they want to "succeed" as students or teachers; and (4) they have internalized (at least for school purposes) a "high cultural," as opposed to a "popular cultural," aesthetic, valuing innovation over repetition, difficulty over accessibility, and ritualized dissent over consensus. I hasten to insist that none of these traits are "bad," since, as an English professor, my own reading habits reflect them. But it's worth pointing out, with a little help from our nineteenth-century counterparts, that there are other ways to write and read poetry.

Longfellow's poems, for example, were typically read aloud rather than silently. As a writer, he did not ask his readers to decode challenging metaphors; instead, in a poem like "The Village Blacksmith," he constructs the metaphor of "the forge" and then carefully explicates its meaning for his readers:

> Thanks, thanks to thee, my worthy friend,
> For the lesson thou hast taught!
> Thus at the flaming forge of life
> Our fortunes must be wrought;
> Thus on its sounding anvil shaped
> Each burning deed and thought.[2]

Moreover, Longfellow did not shy away from clichés. His ideal readers were not working (as students or teachers) and didn't necessarily want to work hard at poetry; they appreciated familiar tropes over unexpected images and ideas. And precisely because Longfellow and his ilk were so widely popular and visible, this type of rhyming, predictable verse is still what springs to mind when many people (outside of colleges and universities) think of "poetry."

In beginning undergraduate poetry workshops, there are often a few "naive" poets who write from within a nineteenth-century popular aesthetic. A typical poem by such a poet might begin:

On the steady road of life,
We are walking, full of strife,
Hardships soon will come our way,
Night falls on the sunlit day.

Such student poets are slowly acculturated into a more sophisticated understanding of how poetry works. They learn to ditch the rhyming dictionary, to banish clichés, and (if I may quote one cliché we have yet to banish) to "show, don't tell." But as these students become more sophisticated academic poets, they also drop the assumptions that informed much nineteenth-century verse and that made poetry a popular art. Clichés, after all, are common cultural codes that bind people together in a shared understanding of their world. And many, if not most, people like to hear rhyming, resonant, reassuring poetry.

As I contemplated the likely audience at my grandfather's funeral, I had to rethink my own assumptions about the function and reception of poetry. I had to balance two value systems: the "academic" and the "popular." I was writing for a "popular" nonacademic audience, rather than simply for the purposes of self-expression or aesthetic pleasure, and I did not want to write a poem that emphasized my own quirks and intellectual preoccupations. The originality that is so prized in academic settings would seem incongruously self-aggrandizing during a funeral, which is, after all, a ritual of collective mourning. At the same time, I did not want to write doggerel; I wanted to honor my grandfather's particularity, not his generic qualities—and to do him honor, I needed to draw on, while simultaneously revising, my own understanding of what makes a "good" poem.

"Asphalt," then, is the result of a balancing act, and it remains one of the few poems I have written for a specific community of people. Its opening line recalls an old chestnut of nineteenth-century recitation culture (though one actually written in the 1790s), "John Anderson, My Jo," by Robert Burns:

John Anderson, my jo, John,
  When we were first acquent;
Your locks were like the raven,
  Your bonie brow was brent;
But now your brow is beld, John,
  Your locks are like the snow;

But blessings on your frosty pow,
  John Anderson, my jo.[3]

Burns's poem is charmingly archaic and reads well aloud. One way to write accessible poetry is to engage with the popular tradition that "John Anderson, My Jo" represents. In "Asphalt," I begin with a nod to Burns, addressing my grandfather directly. An early version of the poem actually retained the phrase "my jo," but I ultimately dropped it because Scottish dialect seemed out of place in a poem about a Swede. I did maintain, however, what Annie Finch has called "the ghost of meter" even as I moved away from Burns's archaic elements:[4]

Harold "Andy" Anderson, grand
dad, you were a crack shot, touch jerky,
and so tan that all winter it seemed
you were just back from a dream
vacation. Why, if the midnight sun
burns twenty-four hours in Sweden,
are Andersons so white?

My poem retains the idiosyncratic details that I value as a contemporary poet, but its internal rhymes, straightforward images, and celebratory tone (stressing consensus rather than dissent) implicitly address an audience that wants to be comforted, not challenged. And like Longfellow, I end with a fairly explicit announcement of the poem's theme: "My roads run / Out of yours, Harold Anderson." Thus, while the poem has an aesthetic dimension, it was also able to serve a pragmatic social function when I read it at my grandfather's funeral.

WRITING PROMPT

Nineteenth-century people used poems as social texts, not just at funerals but also at political gatherings, banquets, holiday celebrations, and in many other places. Inspired by this tradition and by my own experience with "Asphalt," I offer the following writing prompt in closing: Write a poem for a group of people who are not poets, a poem to be read to a gathering of children, at a family holiday celebration, at a political meeting, at a wedding or a funeral, or in some other social context. Use language and images that this particular group will appreciate, even as you retain your own sense of what makes a "good" poem.

ASPHALT / *Angela Sorby*

Harold "Andy" Anderson, grand
dad, you were a crack shot, tough jerky,
and so tan that all winter it seemed
you were just back from a dream
vacation. Why, if the midnight sun
burns twenty-four hours in Sweden,
are Andersons so white? You alone
browned, as you worked pouring asphalt
downtown, then steamed yourself red
at night in the full body steamer
with only your head sticking out,
like John the Baptist's, on a platter.
When I come home to Washington
in summer I drive over blacktop
that glitters darkly in the industrial
district around the Port of Seattle.
You are not there, among the warehouses
full of office supplies, but if you were alive
you'd steal me a box of pencils.
No CEO, not you, but you poured
terra so *firma* that my roads run
out of yours, Harold Anderson.[5]

Notes

1. Marjorie Perloff, "President's Column: Teaching in the Wired Classroom," *MLA Newsletter*, Winter 2006, 3–5.

2. Henry Wadsworth Longfellow, *Selected Poems* (New York: Gramercy, 1992), 20.

3. *Robert Burns: Selected Poems* (New York: Penguin Books, 1993), 157.

4. Annie Finch, *The Ghost of Meter: Culture and Prosody in American Free Verse* (Ann Arbor: University of Michigan Press, 2000), 82.

5. Angela Sorby, *Distance Learning* (Kalamazoo, Mich.: New Issues Press, 1998), 37.

Pimpin' Out

Maria Melendez

The first poem I ever published in a nationally recognized literary journal was called "For a Teenaged Chicana in Phoenix." In the years since its publication, I've learned to become ashamed of it. I wrote it as an undergrad and was trying, as I wrote, to synthesize hope and distill meaning from work I'd done leading groups of "underprivileged" Denver preteens on excursions to Colorado parks and natural areas. During one of our trips, I'd overheard two twelve-year-old Mexican American girls talking about a friend who had been shot; other program counselors told me about another girl in our group who sometimes got "slapped around" by her dad. Even though we hiked together, did "team-building exercises" together, and argued together in the vans over radio stations, to me, these girls' most outstanding feature was what they didn't have: safety at home or school, parents with the time or money to take them on leisure outings. All the brilliance of what they did have—lively minds, loyalty to their friends, humor and healthy skepticism about authority—reached me dimly through the heavy layer of lack I'd mentally thrown over the batch of them. Because of this, I was, subconsciously or not, casting around the entire summer for talismanic images, "signs of hope."

My original draft narrated a Saturday morning with the girls that stood out in my mind as emblematic: we began the day early, eight o'clock, the Denver mist just beginning to think about moving over to make room for the day. On a green hill in the city park where we met to load up, a white man played a bagpipe solo, notes curling through the mist, the spruce trees, and our little group gathering on the grass. When we went inside the natatorium to use the bathrooms before heading out on our day's adventure, I saw teenaged Chicanas swimming laps, hanging around together on benches beside the pool. One young woman curled up at the edge of the water and hugged her legs to keep from shivering. In a park I knew to be associated with gangs and drugs at night, I took these daytime images to heart as "good signs": a man on a hill making spontaneous music, a brown woman preserving her body heat. This early draft had its share of flaws—was, in fact, truly a piece of prose chopped into lines—and I knew it needed stylistic improvement. But I also knew that the images of the bagpipe player and the swimmer had real resonance for me and that this was something I wanted to be able to transmit through the poem.

My Introduction to Poetry Writing professor told me, during a manuscript conference in her office, that this poem would be a lot stronger if the images showed a greater sense of "cultural relevance." When I asked her what she meant, she circled the two images I'd felt held the most metaphoric promise, those of the swimmer and the bagpipe player. I don't remember what she said, but the clear implication was that the bagpipe as an object and swimming as an action just weren't "relevant" in a Chicana poem.

Aside from a few pot-smoking months in ninth grade, I'd never been one to tell off teachers, or even, at that point, to question the wisdom of their own perspectives and judgments. I see this unquestioning acceptance of authority in creative writing students today as they wring their hands or twist their hair and ask each other "What does she WANT?" when they're given critical feedback by myself or my colleagues. It's natural. Much of the time, writing is guesswork for all us, and especially so for beginning writers. In my case, I knew this professor to have published a couple of well-regarded books of her own poetry, and I especially admired her internationally known work as a translator and anthologist of Latin American women's poetry. That she was a white reader calling for an essentialized version of "culture" in my work would not occur to me until years later.

Following our conference, I set to revising the poem to be more cohesively "Chicana," in the readily identifiable sense of the word. The closer the poem moved toward what my professor had looked for as Chicana authenticity, the further it moved from my sense of the authenticity of my lived experience. I intuited the standard ingredients expected of me to add "salsa" to my literature, the "ethnic" fragments I should piece together for this so-called cultural relevance. (Relevant to what, I now ask? Some nostalgic notion of Chicanismo as static and utterly sealed off from interface with "other" cultures?)

The setting, Denver, became Phoenix—in the ro-sham-bo of prepackaged Chicano identity, the Southwest beats the Rockies any day. I threw in a serape, God help me, rain-soaked and clinging to shoulders, to stand for despair. I cut the swimmers altogether, supposing women's sports might not be heavily featured in Aztec myth. The white musician became brown, and the bagpipe became not just a guitar but a "guitarra." Oh yes, the poem hung together well—hung together like a plastic *chile ristra* sold as decoration to enhance "southwestern" decor. And it appeared, a year later, in all its fundamental irrelevance, in a well-regarded literary magazine. And what had the experience taught me? When it came to gaining recognition from some white poets and editors, I could sometimes win by cheating, by fitting the mess and miracle of life in a mixed-race body into some easily identifiable, categorizable, safety-deposit box of stock images. This "winning by cheating," a poetic means of playing to societal expectations around so-called identity politics, is a risk inherent to all poets who either self-define, or are defined by others, as operating outside the norm, be that in economic class, physical ability, sexuality, religion, or any other category on which contemporary definitions of "normal" might have a stranglehold.

One of my Raza poet peers, Paul Martínez Pompa, would call what I did "pimpin' out," a phrase that here means the ratcheting up of multi-culti elements in a piece of art to make it more appealing to some readers as authentically "other," or outside the dominant norm. Fair enough. Such a gesture could be seen as analogous to the black minstrel artists of the early twentieth century who performed, in blackface, as exaggerated caricatures and were materially rewarded by white audiences for doing so. They made a living, some might say, being stereotyped versions of themselves. Others might argue that they were folk artists in their own right. Such men made a career in the arts in a way that activated their societal positionality, making this positionality work for them as one among many available tools, indeed the most viable (read "readily rewarded") tool in certain settings.

The dismissal of these caricatured performances (on stage, in the visual arts, in writing) is a slippery slope. Who will arbitrate, for example, when "culturally relevant" elements are deployed in a spirit of sincerity and when they are simply an example of "playing the race card"? To whom should such judgmental authority be given? Do white writers face such scrutiny when they deploy pop culture elements in their work? Yet I do feel, in judging my own poem, embarrassed by the fact that I supplanted my own sense of poetic value with a prepackaged view of what Chicana poetry should be in order to make the piece more "interesting" and "cohesive."

As a young writer trying to revise this poem following its critique by my professor, the only feeling of unease about the process that I could have articulated would've been the old "but that's how it really happened" objection, an inkling I'd been taught, through workshops, to ignore. Conventional workshop wisdom holds that the artistic success of a piece is the literary writer's highest goal, with accurate expressiveness being what personal diaries are for. In reflecting on my own situation, I see that teasing out the nuances of my regret at losing "how it really happened" would have been one way I could've come to a fuller understanding of why and how cultural *complexity* was key to my initial conception of the poem. I might have been able to articulate that I liked the swimmer precisely because she *wasn't* wearing a *china poblana* and dancing the *cucaracha*—because she could have been me, or the girls I was with. If my professor had asked me, "Why is having a bagpipe player important to you in this narrative?," I might've been able to clarify that I wanted the concept of interracial harmony, vitally and personally important to me as a mixed-race writer, to factor into this poem somehow.

Literary power structures—meaning teachers, editors, writing peers, publishers, readers—can and will exert conflicting influences on emerging writers. The process of negotiating which influences to embrace and which to reject can be painful and confusing, particularly for those writers who choose to identify with, or who find themselves co-opted into, various literary camps/categories. From the comfortable distance of a few years out, reevaluate the standards and biases of your early mentors. Position yourself in relation to them in a way that makes you feel powerful and inspired. The "that's how it really happened" objection, raised in opposition to revision suggestions, might not always need to be summarily dismissed. Latent in that expression could be the fuse at the core of a young writer's inspiration for beginning a poem in the first place. Gentle inquiries of yourself or your peers, when you hear this objection surface, might yield important illumination for both poet and reader. In the end, the poem does need more sense of form and style than a news report or a diary entry, but there may be original elements of the first draft that, transformed with a good eye and ear, can help make the final poem unique and powerful.

WRITING PROMPT

Write a poem in which the speaker of the poem takes on caricatured qualities of your own, or another, identity. Then write a reflective poem or journal entry on the process and aftermath of writing the first piece. Was the process liberating in some ways, restrictive in others, infuriating, comical, empowering, embarrassing? Find a metaphor for what the process felt like and try to identify, from as many angles as possible, the outside forces that might be influencing your response to this process. Last, write a poem drawing on the entire arc of this process that illustrates the difficulties, tensions, and potentials inherent therein. Begin this last poem, if you like, with the words "I can say ____, but I can't say ____."

[UNTITLED] / *Maria Melendez*

Everywhere, I am talked to by silence.
Who do you think you're kidding?—it says.
And—Chrissakes, give me break.
Apparently, silence has no problem swearing.

Meanwhile, uncurling leaves burble
like springs, or grate and squeal
as metal train wheels;
the sun alone hears leaf-birth

the way bees can see u.v.,
the way snakes sense dimensions of heat.
What sensory spectrum is our specialty?
The ear's guess-work, the heart's deep fabrications—[1]

Note

1. Maria Melendez, *Flexible Bones: Poems* (Tucson: University of Arizona Press, 2010), 43.

Breaking with Strategy

William Olsen

When workshops incline toward questions of form and audience, they tend to talk in terms of strategy. That word has both a military and a competitive ring to it. Whom or what do we imagine we are fighting against?

As poetry is about the business of attaining to an active peace, perhaps strategy is a condition a poem ought to break with altogether, insofar as this is possible.

It first occurred to me that a poem could do this after I memorized James Wright's "Speak." It is a poem the generous sanity of which I'd missed my first few times around Wright's work. It was not flashy enough, there was no mining of the unconscious for deep imagery, and it was done up too formally to interest the innocent sensibility I mistook to be a sophisticated one. I can't say any understanding of this poem came in a Pauline flash of light. It was a slow, partial awakening without premeditation. Memorization is a matter of taking a poem into one's brain, blood, guts, and nervous system. On some level you have to "get" the poem to memorize it, but memory itself is no guarantee of comprehension.

Something about the music of "Speak" and the simultaneous flattening of that music, or, as Frost says, "a tune that's different from the tune of music," must have drawn me to it.[1] It has too fully rendered a sense of the human voice to be set to music. It has a good deal of Yeats to it, but it refuses, or attempts to refuse, Yeats's euphoric syntax. It is a series of stratagems meant to protect the self from coming upon the soul in its hiding place. These stratagems break down. It couldn't be more inconsistent in tone, and yet it turns back again and again from hysteria:

SPEAK

To speak in a flat voice
Is all that I can do.

I have gone every place
Asking for you.
Wondering where to turn
And how the search would end
And the last streetlight spin
Above me blind.

Then I returned rebuffed
And saw under the sun
The race not to the swift
Nor the battle won.
Liston dives in the tank,
Lord, in Lewiston, Maine,
And Ernie Doty's drunk
In hell again.

And Jenny, oh my Jenny
Whom I love, rhyme be damned,
Has broken her spare beauty
In a whorehouse old.
She left her new baby
In a bus-station can,
And sprightly danced away
Through Jacksontown.

Which is a place I know,
One where I got picked up
A few shrunk years ago
By a good cop.
Believe it, Lord, or not.
Don't ask me who he was.
I speak of flat defeat
In a flat voice.

I have gone forward with
Some, a few lonely some.
They have fallen to death.
I die with them.
Lord, I have loved Thy cursed,

The beauty of Thy house:
Come down. Come down. Why dost
Thou hide thy face?[2]

Seldom in poetry does an awareness of separation happen with such a roughed-up grace. This poem's ingenious use of something resembling the ballad form, only foreshortened—a three-beat–two-beat variation instead of the ballad's four-beat–three-beat variation and the balladic *abab* rhyme scheme concealed in an eight-line stanza—ensures that its music works on us subliminally. In other words, the poem keeps escaping its own desire to be appealing. I think of another bit from Frost: "There is such a thing as sincerity. It is hard to define but it is probably nothing but your highest liveliness escaping from a succession of dead selves."[3] This poem expends the notion of sincerity to embrace irony, self-deception, rage, hurt—all the petty feelings, even the lies that make us recognizable to one another. And it dramatizes its self-deception by concealing from us and from itself its passions for as long as it can. Which isn't very long. For really, the flat voice the poem ascribes to itself—emphasized by the leaden spondee of the phrase "flat voice"—lasts exactly two lines. These two lines propose that the poem is over, defeated, the instant it has begun. In fact, the voice is so neutral in these lines that so far, for all we know, we could be in one of James Wright's free verse poems. But any emotional stoicism breaks down, at least temporarily. The next two lines introduce a rhyme scheme and the balladic prosody, but that strategy breaks down as well with the two-beat fourth line—again in the interest of flatness—dropping a foot. The sentence fragment of the next four lines is vertiginous in its line breaks and images, and the squinting modifier "blind"—shouldn't this adjective be an adverb?!—longingly personifies the streetlight and underscores the speaker's self-ignorance. Internal and external landscape are made one: meanwhile, this stanza's last bitten-off two-beat line and the barely rhyming "end" and "blind" undo the consoling repetitions of forms and land the speaker on his ass.

The bizarre mixture of street talk and heightened speech that follows in stanza two and three is so desperate that it seems almost droll. Where, for instance, did a word like "rebuffed" come from? Can we possibly hear this word choice, given the "flat voice" the poem's strategy established in the first stanza, as anything but parody? How can a poet who proposes to speak in a flat voice now start to quote—if brokenly, snapping the quote across line breaks—from Ecclesiastes? How can parodic gestures possibly serve the end of emotional honesty? But here they do: they deflate the heroic stratagems that continue to tempt the speaker despite his best efforts to conceal his emotional unrest. What follows is an abbreviated catalog of heroes who are losers: Sonny Liston, who may have thrown the fight of his life; Ernie Doty, a murderer. Wright's sympathies often go out to criminals, cheats—disenfranchised, dispossessed, violent men. Much has been made of this fact in James Wright by critics, and real generosity is there—but what hasn't been noted is that these figures also allow for a measure of self-contempt. In that Liston's and Doty's respective histories speak for themselves, they've damned themselves every bit as much as the speaker is damned to his illusions. Here are the same human mistakes repeating themselves, and poeticizing them doesn't change them.

The stanza that follows presents an absolute collision between the plainly said and the formally said. There's Jenny, Wright's Beatrice but a prostitute by trade and a mother by default and, by way of juxtaposition with Liston and Doty, herself in hell again—and, within the speaker's inescapable urge to maintain mastery over his emotions by maintaining a rhyme scheme, also seemingly damned to repeat her mistakes. Repetitions be damned: with the poem settled into its fixed rhyme scheme, all it can seemingly do is to reenact an unalterable past. Yet the rhyme of "damned" and "old" isn't competent enough even to be a legitimate half-rhyme, and the poem strains syntactically to pull off this bare measure of decorum. The next four lines sound both judgmental and hurt, and that hurt is muffled by its being masked by the contempt of a despairing wit: what a hideous phrase, "new baby," what an inhumane way for both Jenny and the poet to dispose of her child. "Sprightly," given the victimized condition of a prostitute, couldn't be a more cruel word choice. What accuracy does this adverb have except to reflect the delusions of the speaker?

With the next stanza, the speaker turns his animus upon himself. The poem becomes derisively casual again: the bad joke played on the speaker is that he isn't picked up by a trick but by a cop, and a good cop no less. For honesty to come to it unsummoned, a poem must chance bad manners: it cannot afford to retreat to the inattentive distances of pity. That the cop turns out to be a good one strikes the speaker as worthy enough a miracle of police conduct to make Ripley's—or the Lord's—*Believe It or Not!* And who do we as mere readers have to believe? There is so much arch verbal play here, so much false bravado, that we can't possibly trust the speaker to instruct us on how to interpret his mood shifts. Does the speaker actually believe that the Lord is even there to listen? By now a second strategy of concealment belies the speaker's difficulty in acknowledging to himself how seriously he longs for an audience. The poem began in reminiscence—the "you" in its fourth line figures as a lost love, maybe Jenny herself—but it is now emerging in its relationship to its audience as a prayer, albeit an ironic one. The speaker further conceals his self-contempt by transferring that contempt onto the reader—or to the Lord, if you will—he now openly addresses. "Don't ask me who he was," he says in a gesture of mock defiance that undermines itself by underscoring his inability to rescue the past from oblivion by recalling the cop's name. If the last two lines of this stanza come close to repeating the first two lines, this strategy of repetition is hardly a victorious one—it offers up less a brag than an admission.

The next two line breaks constitute the most subtly forceful line break and the most heart-rending refusal I know of in contemporary American poetry. We can almost hear the first line of this stanza longing to fulfill itself in some Whitmanic expression of collectivized sympathy: for a moment we might even think that collective sympathy is the strategy the speaker now requires to break out of his brooding. But that's not the case. What's needed is accuracy, and qualified faith, and that's exactly what we get: the speaker hasn't gone forward with everyone, only with "some, a few lonely some." Our empathy has bounds. Yet it exists less abstractly and more accessibly if we admit those bounds. These "few lonely some" have also fallen to death—either literal death or a daily spiritual death—and the speaker dies with them. True. As their memory of him dies, part of him dies. I don't know how to account for the resumption of a biblical rhetoric in the last four lines, but maybe by now I don't have to. The house and its "cursed . . . beauty"—and that this curse has beauty to it is finally acknowledged—clearly evokes the "whorehouse old" of the third stanza. It combines the two sides of the listener the poem has invented for itself—lover and lord—and it is mostly honest about their being one figure. In beginning in plea and ending in pure question, the last two lines—three short sentences, five leaden spondees—suggest the impossibility of a quest finalizing acceptance. Which is a quest for self-acceptance. These lines are a reminder of René Char's claim: "It is from lack of inner justice that the poet suffers most in his relations with the world."[4] The poet no longer strategizes his self-doubt out of existence. Poems obsessed with spiritual ugliness don't get any more beautiful than this.

WRITING PROMPT

Write a poem that consciously, if surreptitiously, tries to break with the ruling strategies the poem invents for itself. That's it, and it's maybe a life's work to pull this off even a few times, but it's worth a try. Permit the poem to dramatize an awareness of its own limitations: to critique itself, recoil from itself, contradict itself, whiplash in one way or another from the most tyrannical status quo of all, selfhood. Be as "personal" or as "public" in your voice as you wish, or both, but let the poem run against its own good manners: let it be, in terms of your own sense of poetic responsibility, impolite, indecorous, awkward (of course that may require you at turns to be elegant, graceful, resounding). Let its composure break down altogether if you wish—and then continue anyway.

A few things you might try: radically changing your sentence length or syntax (even just once); radically changing the sorts of information the poem admits—from objective reportage to the figurative and back, or from the observational to the intellectual and assertive and back; destabilizing your sense of audience and breaking with any address and letting any addressee morph just as you yourself morph.

The goal of this assignment is to encourage rebelling against the most powerful censurer in your writing life, your sense of your own authority. And, rather to "earn" or puzzle out an ending, to be unnerved into an inconclusiveness.

GROCERY NIGHT / *William Olsen*

I have seen nothing that hasn't already been
lost from its birth
so many times the avenues have a sheen
like a car passed through a car wash glows
from happening in the now, which isn't talking
in this city of snowmen
who lose their heads
and then their torsos
and even their nakedness.

And these same doors to needs
and to these shoppers
wheeling carts around
and almost every time the same bagger
who shall remain nameless
pushing my groceries into the back seat
as if to push his own
existence out of his hands and shut the door
speaks in a voice fatigued by its own formality
the words for just how tedious it is
to buy this night and many like it,
shoppers with sacks of perishable goodness
their heads moon above
with the borrowed light
of the streetlights and the car lights
spread across our features
carved at times as out of sheer inertia
and that light changing like the money
we try to make all day and into night
to provision our lives
while our children roll another evening away
until it snowballs
to people with nothing but weather on their minds
shaped out of this snow,
still wearing hand prints,
looking more and more like the mess
one life is not enough to face.
Landscape of demand and demand
and little lights of comprehension,
supply of saving graces,
the sacks of groceries in back
death cannot celebrate
and famine cannot touch,
as each engine turns over
like a sleeper and is gunned alive
I look up from my hands on the wheel.
There is a person or two behind each pair of lights,

families or workers gone home
merging with the bound
and back into the night,
all this glamorous stone-cold paradise
you must see to believe,
this wilderness that falls to its white knees,
streetlights lit like need
on a face—please stay on—.
A razory lace blows
across the old fear of darkness
building from gaze after gaze
this life, this wilderness,
this and every night we see ourselves alive.

Notes

1. Elaine Barry, *Robert Frost on Writing* (New Brunswick: Rutgers University Press, 1973), 155–56.

2. James Wright, *Collected Poems* (Middletown, Conn.: Wesleyan University Press, 1979), 157–58.

3. Mark Richardson, *The Ordeal of Robert Frost: The Poet and His Poetics* (Urbana: University of Illinois Press, 1997), 178.

4. René Char, *Hypnos Walking: Poems and Prose*, trans. Jackson Matthews, James Wright, et al. (New York: Random House, 1956), 49.

Writing Against Your Music

Kevin Prufer

As a student, I often heard that the music of a good poem ought to be inseparable from the poem's meaning. I had no idea, however, what that meant, though I could play like I understood it. I could talk about prosody with some fluency, nodding occasionally toward the neat fit of form and function in certain classic poems. But when it came to my own work—or when it came to discussing the work of most other writers—I was, for many years, unable to separate words from their most reductive meanings. Then I saw Stanley Kubrick's brilliant *A Clockwork Orange*, and I began to think about poetry in an entirely new way.

There is a well-known scene in that movie during which a woman is attacked by a gang of sex-hungry young men. As she is dragged across the screen, abused, and violated, a song plays in the background. It's nothing like the screeching of Hitchcock's *Psycho* shower scene, nor is it like the slightly discordant music that plays during the tense moments in John Carpenter's *Halloween*. Rather, Kubrick offers us a cheerful bit of Beethoven, played lightly on what sounds like an electric piano. In other equally disconcerting moments, he offers "Singin' in the Rain," conjuring with it images of love, of the grand movie musicals of the past, of Fred Astaire. The more I thought about it, the more I understood the power of his music to throw the visual scenes of violence and terror into a sort of stark relief. Moreover, the music seemed to accuse me, the viewer, of finding pleasure in misery, of participating in the violence, if passively, from my seat in the dark theater.

And, as I walked home that night, I began to think not about Kubrick's spooky dystopian England but about my very favorite American poet, Emily Dickinson. In particular, I found myself considering her poem #465:

> I heard a Fly buzz—when I died—
> The Stillness in the Room
> Was like the Stillness in the Air—
> Between the Heaves of Storm—

The Eyes around—had wrung them dry—
And Breaths were gathering firm
For that last Onset—when the King
Be witnessed—in the Room—

I willed my Keepsakes—Signed away
What portion of me be
Assignable—and then it was
There interposed a Fly—

With Blue—uncertain stumbling Buzz—
Between the light—and me—
And then the Windows failed—and then
I could not see to see—[1]

In the past, I'd considered the poem delightfully ambiguous. What, I wondered, does that fly represent? Is it a stand-in for Emerson's God-in-nature, a sort of representative of the transcendental romantic universe, a universe the recently deceased speaker fails entirely to understand? Or is the fly a darker symbol, suggestive of Beelzebub, the lord of the flies? Or perhaps Dickinson had more prosaic ideas; perhaps the fly is merely attracted to the dead meat of the speaker, which is to say that we receive neither God nor Satan when we die. We receive only the prospect of decay.

Of course, the strength of the poem is that it means all three, and more, simultaneously. The poem doesn't make a prescriptive argument; instead, it holds within it at least three conflicting points of view, all of them vitally important to the speaker.

Walking home from the theater, however, I thought not about the literal meaning of Dickinson's words but about the suggested meaning of her rhythm and rhyme. The poem, I knew, was written in hymn meter (also known as common meter), in lines of alternating iambic tetrameter and iambic trimeter, rhyming *xaxa*. Somewhere in the back of my mind, I figured, I was meant to recognize the origins of the poem's music in the church or, more particularly, in songs whose purpose is to praise God.

And now I saw an additional power in the poem I'd failed to notice before: that the theological ambivalence of the literal sense of the poem—is there a God at all? Dickinson seems to ask—is directly undercut by the hymnlike music of the poem. Or, put another way, Dickinson seems intent on asking us to think of her ambivalence as a kind of prayer, or to throw her doubts into the pure white light of the faith the poem's music suggests.

Since then, I've been fascinated by the often perverse meanings various rhythms create. I have even begun to play games. What, I wondered, would happen if I translated Dickinson's poem from hymn meter into a series of anapests?

> As I died a loud fly was exploring
> the old room that was still as the air
> after storm clouds pass crashing and roaring, etc.

Or what about trochees?

> Fly, oh fly, I heard you buzz—but
> Dying should be silent!
> Keepsakes I have tossed away for
> God's still absent judgment

Or as, heaven forbid, a limerick:

> A fly made a noisy first entry,
> then flew between sunlight and me.
> I thought God might save
> my dull soul from the grave.
> But, alas, he has not. I can't see!

Of course, no matter how hard I try to stay true to the poem's literal meaning, it is utterly destroyed—though sometimes to comic effect. The "meanings" of the anapests or trochees have nothing to do with the subject of Dickinson's masterpiece. Neither do they undercut it in interesting ways. They are, instead, merely inappropriate. And the limerick? It is, I think, impossible to write a serious limerick. Not matter how hard I try, it comes out winkingly sad, ironically and hiply tragic, incapable of producing real tears, except as the result of its enormous incompetence.

Or, take, instead, the sestina or the villanelle. With their constant repetition of the same words and lines, these forms seem directly suited to laying open the obsessive mind, the mind working through a problem again and again, the speaker meditating on a complex notion. But is it possible to write a narrative sestina? A villanelle that tells a story? It is, I suppose, but it isn't easy. Nevertheless, many of the best poems in the English language—Anne Bradstreet's poems to her lost grandchildren, Stevie Smith's "Not Waving but Drowning," Theodore Roethke's "My Papa's Waltz" among them—employ a sort of music that to great effect undercuts any literal reading of the words.

WRITING PROMPT

And this has led to a writing exercise that, at least for me, has produced some pretty good results: try to write a *good* poem in which the music of the poem—the rhythm, the rhyme, the sounds of the words—works in the opposite direction of the superficial meaning of the poem. If you are writing an elegy, see what happens if you couch your words in a form that, superficially, seems unrelated to it. If you are writing about a happy memory, compose it in the uncertainties of nervous slant rhyme. If you are writing an elegy, try anapests. And if, like Emily Dickinson, you are writing a poem filled with cosmic doubt at the possible absence of God, compose it in hymn meter.

THIS WAS THE MODEL TO WHICH I HELD / *Kevin Prufer*

This was the model to which I held:
a bee in its hole like a gasp
in my throat. Silence or dirge
as the petals unclasped,

dusted with blush at their folds.
This was the standard—I'd speak no word
when, after your long death, a thrill of bees
thrummed into the air, the chord

of their wings blaring flowers out.
This was my theory—I had no other—
the yard like a harlot, but you
still dead. Spring was a terror

of sensuous things—in my throat, a song
where a stinger hurt, where quiet belonged.[2]

Notes

1. Emily Dickinson, *The Complete Poems*, ed. Thomas H. Johnson (Boston: Back Bay Books, 1976), 223–24.

2. Kevin Prufer, *The Finger Bone* (Pittsburgh: Carnegie Mellon University Press, 2002), 65.

"Lucifer Matches": Epistles and Other Conversations (The Epistolary Lyric)

Jane Satterfield

As I write this week, there is almost too much to report. Close to home, the local drama that's played out to vast acclaim on HBO has left two dozen murdered on Baltimore's gritty streets. Car bombs go off daily in Baghdad; senators debate a proposed "troop surge"; the Iraqis themselves criticize the delayed security plan; still no solution—political, humanitarian—to the bloodshed in Darfur. Meanwhile, other inconvenient truths come home to roost: there's ice storms, gale storms, tornadoes, and floods—unexpected weather conditions appear across the globe. The loop of the updated banner on flat screen TVs, desktops, BlackBerry devices, and cellular phones is a snake biting its tail. The world too much with us, indeed.

In the face of headline news, the poet's sometimes seems a tiny voice, and the lyric itself may seem irrelevant, indulgent, inadequate—an idiot's tale, signifying nothing. "Poor words," wrote the anonymous journalist huddled in a cellar as Berlin fell into the hands of the Russian army, a reflection of deepest regret at the horrors her writing was made to contain.[1] And yet, day after day, as the atrocities of war swirled around the beleaguered city and its citizens, she returned to the page. Her account—chronicle and elegy—attests to the redemptive power of language: at one point, she transcribes from memory a couplet from Horace onto her building's damaged wall, an *aide-memoire* from her past's more civilized terrain. The gestures of the lyric, as Plath put it, watching her infant dance in the dark of an icy winter night, are "warm and human"; their light "Bleeding and peeling / Through the black amnesias of heaven."[2]

In his essay "The Government of the Tongue," Nobel Prize–winning poet Seamus Heaney addresses this very issue—the "great paradox of poetry and the imaginative arts in general." "Faced with the brutality of the historical onslaught," he writes, "they are practically useless." After all, as Heaney reminds readers, the "efficacy of poetry is nil—no lyric has ever stopped a tank." And yet, he continues, "in another sense it is unlimited. It is like the writing in sand in the face of which accusers and accused are left speechless and renewed." Heaney refers, of course, to a singular moment in the Gospel of John, where Christ's intervention saves an adulteress. Although the content of the invisible script is never revealed, John's account makes it clear that its impact is immediate: the crowd, dispatched by guilty conscience, is soon dispersed; the woman has narrowly escaped being stoned. The social order has been momentarily disrupted: something *has happened*—there has been a *response*. Like that compelling and mysterious script, poetry, in Heaney's view, is "arbitrary and marks time in every possible sense of that phrase. It does not say to the accusing crowd or to the helpless accused, 'Now a solution will take place,' it does not propose to be instrumental or effective. Instead, in the rift between what is going to happen and whatever we would wish to happen, poetry holds attention for a space, functions not as distraction but as pure concentration, a focus where our power to concentrate is concentrated back on ourselves."[3]

I discovered this essay in the days following the televised annunciation of the first Gulf War when the image of the Baghdad skyline in predawn light, crossed with the green-flared tracing of missiles, played and replayed in mind and on-screen. The strangeness of the moment—that narrowing of time where something happening at a distance was brought unbearably near—commanded attention. The unsettling effect reminded me of Wilfred Owen's letters from the western front, where the details of daily life—lovingly rendered—stand in stark contrast to the brutalities of war. At one moment, Owen describes the difficulties of gathering necessary equipment; in the next, he observes, "We were stranded in a certain town . . . the place was like a bit of Blighty, all hung with English greetings and Miseltoe [*sic*]."[4]

Poetic insight often arises from crises of life or craft, out of the invisible script of events that pass unnoticed at first, their influence more obvious in retrospect. At the time, I thought there was no seismic shift in my approach to craft, though retrospect might suggest otherwise: while my younger brother organized campus protest (laughable in scale to his Vietnam-era professors'), my father, an Air Force reservist, was called up that very night.

Although I can't claim to have directly addressed the politics of that moment in any particular poem, I did begin to think differently about the field of the lyric. Surely the witness of the "I" is artful, the field of the lyric magnetic—even politically charged. Addressed outward, it becomes intentional, incendiary—a kind of Dickinsonesque "letter to the World."[5]

In British poet Jo Shapcott's poetry, I discovered a similar epistolary quality. Like other members of her generation—heirs of W. H. Auden and Philip Larkin—Shapcott's work is preoccupied with the larger issues of our times, among them the effects of imperialism, media culture and violence, gender politics, and the uneasy relation between a government and its citizens. The poet's challenge, then, is to write accurately, without falling into the pitfalls of didacticism or polemic—to destabilize easy assumptions. In "Phrase Book," informal diction and fragmented languages (poetic, political, technological, the phrase book's questions and polite imperatives) jostle against each other to powerful effect:

PHRASE BOOK

I'm standing here inside my skin,
which will do for a Human Remains Pouch
for the moment. Look down there (up here).
Quickly. Slowly. This is my own front room

where I'm lost in the action, live from a war,
on screen. I am an Englishwoman, I don't understand you.
What's the matter? You are right. You are wrong.
Things are going well (badly). Am I disturbing you?

TV is showing bliss as taught to pilots:
Blend, Low silhouette, Irregular shape, Small,
Secluded. (Please write it down. Please speak slowly.)
Bliss is how it was in this very room

when I raised my body to his mouth,
when he even balanced me in the air,
or at least I thought so and yes the pilots say
yes they have caught it through the Side-Looking

Airborne Radar, and through the J–Stars.
I am expecting a gentleman (a young gentleman,

two gentlemen, some gentlemen). Please send him
(them) up at once. This is really beautiful.

Yes they have seen us, the pilots, in the Kill Box
on their screens, and played the routine for
getting us Stealthed, that is Cleansed, to you and me,
Taken Out. They know how to move into a single room

like that, to send in with Pinpoint Accuracy, a hundred Harms.
I have two cases and a cardboard box. There is another
bag there. I cannot open my case—look out,
the lock is broken. Have I done enough?

Bliss, the pilots say is for evasion
and escape. What's love in all this debris?
Just one person pounding another into dust,
into dust. I do not know the word for it yet.

Where is the British Consulate? Please explain.
What does it mean? What must I do? Where
can I find? What have I done? I have done
nothing. Let me pass please. I am an Englishwoman.[6]

The poem provides no single answer about the dilemmas of living a just life in today's rapidly changing, media-driven culture; it demonstrates, through the speaker's sense of fragmentation, the difficulties of finding an adequate response to external events and the fear that, in the present environment, the very things that make life bearable—the "bliss" of love, for instance—come to look (and feel) like "evasion / and escape." Writing about "Phrase Book" in the *Poetry Book Society Bulletin*, Shapcott noted: "Central to the poem is the way the vocabulary for the technology of warfare operates to distance us from the reality of the killing. I'm also interested in the position of the speaker: I tried to give her the toughness and imagination to be implicated in the atrocity while she watched it. I didn't want her just to stand outside events as witness and commentator, or, at worst, simply appropriate other people's pain. Unless it contained such self-questioning the poem would be empty, it seemed to me."[7] By the poem's conclusion, the speaker watching the news is powerless—a tourist whose nationality is a source of shame. The collage-like arrangement of narrative voice and detail reflects the tensions and contradictions of perception: the borders between public and private, historical and contemporary, Shapcott suggests, are more permeable than we might think. Shapcott's poem follows the movement of the mind as it seeks to apprehend; it possesses the polyvocality of letters and their urgency of address.

I've always loved the hurried eloquence of letters, their ability to cross space and time, to map distance and weather, to gather in number, to become whole cartographies of crises and confusion. First and foremost, I'm sure, I loved letters because they bridged distances. My mother, daughter of Irish immigrants to Scotland and then to England, received them regularly—thin blue aerograms stamped with the queen's image, the spidery handwritten lines full of descriptive detail, domestic as well as public: the steel mill closing, what Thatcher did or failed to do, which neighbors' sons had found work overseas, the storm clouds over Europe that week, who popped in and stayed for tea. Long distance calls were expensive, out of our reach, and until his last few years of life, my grandfather had no phone in his home. So when I crossed the Atlantic to spend a summer with my grandfather, I wrote reams of postcards home, a way of passing along the perfumes of travel—its varied bouquets. I still have them—tissue-wrapped in a scrap box I'll someday pass along to my daughter—the sole traces of a journey that might otherwise be lost in memory and time. Later, of course, I discovered letters *as* literature: in the Cicero and Seneca I learned, painstakingly, to translate; in the eighteenth-century epistles whose author's heroic couplets yoked a heady mix of didactic wisdom and savage wit; in the writers whose letters I scoured late nights in the library, searching for origins of poetry and prose, hoping to get closer to the actual sources of inspiration. But the magnetism of the letter, for me, was the power of a single voice to reach across time, part of a grand tradition of men and women—literary and ordinary—giving and getting news in both public and domestic forums.

In "Ornament and Silence," Kennedy Fraser recounts a troubled period in her life that was made bearable and comprehensible by her reading of women's letters, diaries, and biographies. "They were like mothers and sisters to me," Fraser says, "these literary women, many of them already dead; more than my own family they seemed to stretch out a hand."[8] During the instructive, generative silence of pregnancy, a time between books when I lived abroad, I became fascinated with reading women's letters. Reading Charlotte Brontë's letters to her friend Ellen Nussey or hearing a Radio 4 reading of Plath's letters to her mother, I was relieved to discover that my idols voiced concerns I shared, both the joys of domestic life ("creaky floors, leaky faucets, peeling paper and plaster and so on . . . but the house has a real, generous, warm soul to it . . . the most exciting thing to me: owning flowers and trees . . .") as well as its challenges ("I am enjoying my slender foothold in my study in the morning again. It makes all the difference in my day. I still get tired by teatime and have spells of impatience for not doing all I want in the way of study and reading. But my mornings are as peaceful as church-going—the red plush rug and all and the feeling that nothing else but writing and thinking is done there").[9] I soon saw that letter writers, often confined by domestic routine, could shape so much out of the material at hand and found great solace in the epistolary form—a testament to voice and craft.

Letters, it seems to me, create a path through silence: documentary and reflective, the rapid shifts in voice and subject allow a writer to accommodate multiple perspectives and narrative threads, to replicate and honor the simultaneity of experience. This forms the backdrop of my poem below, which draws on descriptions of poet Anna Akhmatova's daily life described in Lydia Chukovskaya's journals. During the Stalinist era, Chukovskaya witnessed the poet write, memorize, then destroy her poems. I hoped to capture what it meant to inhabit that sort of powerful erasure:

REQUIEM

In my time I have had to flee twice.
As I fled I knew what I was running from and why.
I was standing at the window of a train watching the platform
sail past me, thinking of the morning's friendly telephone call,
our own clumsily crafted lives.
Who could have guessed the content of my days, whispers,
guesses, real life omitted, just faint glimmers here & there, a hint
of it, some sign, some future which was never to be—
Residue of sleepless nights, little squares of the parquet floor—
my daughter, I felt I had to stay alive for her—
What documents was I keeping and where. . . .
Sometimes, in mid-conversation, silence, followed
with something mundane—"Would you like some tea?" "You're
very tanned," "Autumn came early this year—"

> The bookcase, the writing desk, the clock—
> chiseling out of this some beautiful and mournful ritual.[10]

Writing about reportage from postwar Germany, poet and journalist Hans Magnus Enzensberger observed, "The specialists in perception are at their best when they generalize least, when they do not censor the fantastic contradictions of the chaotic world they have entered, but leave them as they are."[11] Parenthood is its own chaotic world; any mother confronts powerful societal prescriptions. But for the artist/mother, these can become censures. I was aware, too, that the nature of my struggles might lead my writing too deeply inward, that I risked the dangers of solipsism, of falling from artfulness into mere self-expression. For me, the letter/poem provided a strategic advantage: it created a space where shifts in identity and narrative could coexist, where I honor "fantastic contradictions" and converse across time. The epistolary form provided, in critic Terry Eagleton's words, "a public compact, . . . a mirror before which the author may unite with an 'ideal ego.'"[12]

In late October 1854, Charlotte Brontë wrote from Haworth's twilit parlor to her friend and confidante Ellen Nussey: "Arthur has just been glancing over this note—He thinks I have written too freely . . . letters such as mine never ought to be kept—they are dangerous as Lucifer matches."[13] Her husband's cautious censorship—born of a fear that "a letter may fall into any hand"—is not an uncommon one.[14] As critic Terry Eagleton noted in his reflection on Samuel Richardson's *Clarissa*, that masterful and riddling sequence of communications, writing and epistolary writing especially "is a matter of record and contract which may be turned against its author, cited out of context, deployed as threat, testimony, blackmail. It is the 'iterability' of script—the fact that its materiality allows it to be reproduced in changed conditions—which makes it such an efficient instrument of oppression. The free utterance of the heart, once taken down in writing, may always be used later in evidence of the speaker."[15] Given his wife's unconventional views and her growing literary fame, it's no wonder the Irish curate desired to play the censor (and thereby shape the way Brontë as a writer would be represented—Elizabeth Gaskell, in fact, would later use letters to Nussey in her Brontë biography to foreground a more appealingly "domestic" image of the writer). As a husband with a public office, Arthur Bell was not merely subscribing to Victorian standards of emotional reserve—he stood to inherit Patrick Brontë's Haworth parsonage and with it the duty to shepherd the souls of his fellow townsmen. A letter, Bell would have clearly recognized, possesses a potentially long afterlife. Because it may circulate free of its writer/sender, the epistolary revelation has a far-reaching potential to ignite and inflame. If the poet's job, as Owen suggested at the last century's start, is to warn, then surely "Lucifer matches" are ours to send.

WRITING PROMPT

Write an epistolary lyric—your own "letter to the world," using either a direct address to a specific designee or a more general address, as if to a group (written *as if to be discovered or shared* by more than a single recipient). Either way, the approach and subject of your "letter" should be dictated by the fact that you are writing a response: to document and reflect on a particular question or experience that is unsettling or even, perhaps, difficult to resolve. Your writing should be conversational in tone, cinematic in detail; it may juxtapose eras and events as necessary; it may shuttle between the public and the private, the contemporary and the historical. You may want to consider the ways your own internal drama intersects with or forms an odd contrast to external events. Of course, you need not write about "current events": the beauty of the letter form is that it lovingly extends the field of the newsworthy. The goal, after all, is to stretch narrative skills by adopting multiple narratives, perspectives, or points-of-view: as writer Lawrence Sutin put it, "to shatter the mirror of the everyday."[16]

Norman Dubie's *Selected Poems* contains some wonderful examples of letters to specific designees (for instance, in the "Czar's Last Christmas Letter: A Barn in the Urals," the poet adopts an historical persona), and much of Frank O'Hara's opus, in fact, arises from lyric response and informal, direct address. Other possible models include Elizabeth Spires's "Good Friday. Driving Westward" (the poet considers the world's darkness and converses across space and time, meditating on Donne's work as she drives); Eleanor Wilner's "Found in the Free Library" (an imagined epistle to future generations about contemporary government's continued erosion of civil rights); John Matthias's "Persistent Elegy" (in this fine sestina, recollections of a student are juxtaposed with the news of her murder in KwaZulu, Africa, shortly before Mandela's 1994 election, by an Inkatha hit squad); and Geoffrey Hill's *Mercian Hymns* (textural poems where the historical and contemporary life/landscape of middle England are intertwined).

Notes

1. Philip Boehm, *A Woman in Berlin: Eight Weeks in the Conquered City: A Diary* (New York: Picador/Henry Holt, 2006), 15, 160.

2. Sylvia Plath, *Ariel: The Restored Edition: A Facsimile of Plath's Manuscript, Reinstating Her Original Selection and Arrangement* (London: Faber and Faber, 2007), 29.

3. Seamus Heaney, *The Government of the Tongue: Selected Prose, 1978–1987* (New York: Noonday Press, 1990), 107–8.

4. Wilfred Owen, "Letter 476: To Susan Owen," January 4, 1917, *The First World War Poetry Digital Archive*, http://www.hcu.ox.ac.uk/jtap/ (accessed March 11, 2010).

5. Emily Dickinson, "This is my letter to the World," in *The Poems of Emily Dickinson*, ed. Thomas H. Johnson (Boston: Little, Brown, 1960), 211.

6. Jo Shapcott, *Her Book: Poems 1988–1998* (London: Faber and Faber, 2000), 65.

7. Jo Shapcott, "Phrase Book (Commentary)," *Poetry Book Society Bulletin* 154 (Autumn 1992): 2–3.

8. Kennedy Fraser, *Ornament and Silence: Essays on Women's Lives* (New York: Vintage Books, 1998), 3–4.

9. Sylvia Plath, *Letters Home*, ed. Aurelia Schober Plath (New York: Bantam Books, 1975), 530.

10. Jane Satterfield, *Assignation at Vanishing Point* (Minneapolis: Elixir Press, 2003), 3.

11. Hans Enzensberger, *Civil War* (London: Granta Books in association with Penguin Books, 1994), 84.

12. Terry Eagleton, *The Rape of Clarissa: Writing, Sexuality, and Class Struggle in Samuel Richardson* (Minneapolis: University of Minnesota Press, 1982), 48.

13. Qtd. in Juliet Barker, *The Brontës: A Life in Letters* (New York: Overlook Press, 2002), 394.

14. Ibid.

15. Eagleton, *Rape of Clarissa*, 48.

16. Lawrence Sutin, *A Postcard Memoir* (St. Paul: Graywolf Press, 2000), 3.

(On Preparing for a Tribute Reading) A Few Thoughts on O'Hara's "Personal Poem"

Ralph Angel

This chapter was originally delivered as a lecture at Vermont College of Fine Arts, January 2000.

1

I'd been on the phone one morning, one day back in September, I think. A pleasant young man from a start-up magazine in San Francisco called at the arranged time to interview me. He asked smart questions. He was clearly well read. He cared about poetry, and he cared about language and its gazillion possibilities. But near the end of a perfectly amicable, even sweet, chat, he grew impatient with me. I got testy. I'd let him down.

He wanted to know about my process. I said, "I don't have one." He recalled things we'd already talked about and concluded that I was mistaken. "You must have a process," he said. "There's no such thing as process," I replied. He paused and he sighed, and he paused again. And I paused, and then I said, "Listen, if there's such a thing as process, and if I have one, I don't know what it is. And if I knew what it was, I don't think it would be very wise to tell you about it."

So, I went shopping—I live in L.A.—for groceries. Pears were in season; well, Bartlett pears were in season. I mailed a package to my sister from the post office and bought some stamps. I walked to the neighborhood public library. I still love public libraries. I paged through some magazines, the *New Yorker, Harper's, Home and Garden.* I checked out *The Disappearance,* an epistolary memoir by Geneviève Jurgensen concerning the simultaneous, freak deaths of her two very young daughters.

That same afternoon, I was down in my study listening to Gershwin and wrote a postcard to a friend in Denmark. Then the phone rang. It was someone from a local arts center inviting me to participate in a tribute reading for Frank O'Hara with three other poets. I got very excited. As requested, I rattled off the top of my head a half dozen or so poems that I said I'd love to read. Then I sat back down at my desk and signed the postcard I'd just written. The music had just stopped; everything was quiet. On a legal pad I wrote:

> Now you are crossing a wide street at night
> anxious in the traffic and rushing
> to get to the bakery
> before closing.

That was all, maybe the beginning of something—I don't know. I wrote it down because I could hear it. It's all I could hear.

Then I thought about O'Hara. I went to the bookshelf and picked out the *Collected Poems* and read for the first time in a long time the first poem I had mentioned on the phone. It's titled "Personal Poem."

> Now when I walk around at lunchtime
> I have only two charms in my pocket
> an old Roman coin Mike Kanemitsu gave me
> and a bolt-head that broke off a packing case
> when I was in Madrid the others never
> brought me too much luck though they did
> help keep me in New York against coercion
> but now I'm happy for a time and interested
>
> I walk through the luminous humidity
> passing the House of Seagram with its wet
> and its loungers and the construction to
> the left that closed the sidewalk if
> I ever get to be a construction worker
> I'd like to have a silver hat please
> and get to Moriarty's where I wait for
> LeRoi and hear who wants to be a mover and
> shaker the last five years my batting average
> is .016 that's that, and LeRoi comes in
> and tells me Miles Davis was clubbed 12
> times last night outside BIRDLAND by a cop
> a lady asks us for a nickel for a terrible
> disease but we don't give her one we

don't like terrible diseases, then
we go eat some fish and some ale it's
cool but crowded we don't like Lionel Trilling
we decide, we like Don Allen we don't like
Henry James so much we like Herman Melville
we don't want to be in the poets' walk in
San Francisco even we just want to be rich
and walk on girders in our silver hats
I wonder if one person out of the 8,000,000 is
thinking of me as I shake hands with LeRoi
and buy a strap for my wristwatch and go
back to work happy at the thought possibly so[1]

I was flabbergasted, excited, and in awe. And totally intimidated. It was genius, that poem. Syntactical and formal genius. It generated an exhilarating experience, profoundly human, inimitable—that's why I was excited. But it made me self-conscious. Its personalness, as if it were pure autobiography, self-revealing, unabashedly naked. As if it were the stuff of '90s tabloid, whatever we've been living. I didn't make poems like that. I couldn't make poems like that even if I wanted to make poems like that. And I wanted to know why I was asked to participate in such a reading. I, of all people. I mean, I hadn't really read O'Hara in years. And whatever it was I thought I knew about O'Hara back then, I couldn't remember. I felt defiant and resistant, just as I had at the end of that phone interview early in the day. I wanted to call that young man back: "You want process? Here, take it, it's yours. This was my day."

2

One great thing about Frank O'Hara's poem about the death of Billie Holiday is that it's not titled "Personal Poem." Instead, it's titled "The Day Lady Died."

It is 12:20 in New York a Friday
three days after Bastille day, yes
it is 1959 and I go get a shoeshine
because I will get off the 4:19 in Easthampton
at 7:15 and then go straight to dinner
and I don't know the people who will feed me

I walk up the muggy street beginning to sun
and have a hamburger and a malted and buy
an ugly NEW WORLD WRITING to see what the poets
in Ghana are doing these days
                                        I go on to the bank
and Miss Stillwagon (first name Linda I once heard)
doesn't even look up my balance for once in her life
and in the GOLDEN GRIFFIN I get a little Verlaine
for Patsy with drawings by Bonnard although I do
think of Hesiod, trans. Richmond Lattimore or
Brendan Behan's new play or *Le Balcon* or *Les Nègres*
of Genet, but I don't, I stick with Verlaine
after practically going to sleep with quandariness

and for Mike I just stroll into the PARK LANE
Liquor Store and ask for a bottle of Strega and
then I go back where I came from to 6th Avenue
and the tobacconist in the Ziegfeld Theatre and
casually ask for a carton of Gauloises and a carton
of Picayunes, and a NEW YORK POST with her face on it

and I am sweating a lot by now and thinking of
leaning on the john door in the 5 SPOT
while she whispered a song along the keyboard
to Mal Waldron and everyone and I stopped breathing[2]

This is not a jazz poem. This is not a jazz poem about the great jazz singer Billie Holiday. This *is* jazz, pushing its sounds and its rhythms and derailing itself into some kind of openness, persistent, ongoing, right up to its breathless, heartbreaking breathlessness.

There are no periods here, really, a few commas, a single indention, a syntax that collides with itself and runs on and on, lines that break themselves apart as they build themselves up again. Oh, there's a story here, a chronology of events, specifically detailed places, objects and things, names of people, but it is the story of what isn't the story in the end, if there is an end to this poem.

This is not the logic of the rhetorician, but it's logical. Nor is it the reality of that great canon of poetry that began in the Renaissance and led up to O'Hara and to our very day. But it is literal. It is the language of fact, literally.

And it's not about Frank O'Hara, either. There's a speaker here, a very present self going where one goes and getting things done in the greater with-or-without-you hum of the city, and the solaces of just walking around.

It is literal, and it is the language of fact, literally. Not the fact of sprawling expansive Los Angeles with its long, empty streets and drably forbidding buildings. Where its ten million inhabitants rarely encounter one another. How could we? We are each alone in our cars on the way to encountering one another.

Rather, it is language enacting the fact of messy cluttered New York City where brushing shoulders with people and their smells and their attitudes is unavoidable. Where to step out the door of one's building is to be swept into an energy much greater than oneself, always, without choice.

In L.A., we must generate our own energy. The city doesn't provide it. In fact, if we can't do that each and every day, we risk being sucked into oblivion. Could O'Hara have been a poet living in L.A.? Of course, yes. Would his poems even resemble those he left us? Of course not.

O'Hara was unfailingly, super-humanly true to the only tools a poet has to work with: one's experience and the language in which one composes. So the poems are literal, but selective. Literal and very present reality. Selective, because the language enacts one person's experience of that reality.

3

There is a deceptive casualness in Frank O'Hara's poetry—though the idea that it is casual is misguided—the way we've come to think of his poems, the way I sort of cavalierly thought of them, though I loved them, before I started reading him again. In actuality, his is a structured, disciplined language, a strategy of nonchalance that allows him to get his readers to let down their guards. And he's tenacious, the way language can be tenacious, the way imagination can only keep moving forward, like the will to live, like living and playing, like existence itself.

"Perhaps it is to avoid some great sadness" begins the poem "Sleeping on the Wing," as if the thought itself could stop anything.

> Perhaps it is to avoid some great sadness,
> as in a Restoration tragedy the hero cries "Sleep!
> O for a long sound sleep and so forget it!"
> that one flies, soaring above the shoreless city,
> veering upward from the pavement as a pigeon

does when a car honks or a door slams, the door
of dreams, life perpetuated in parti-colored loves
and beautiful lies all in different languages.

Fear drops away too, like the cement, and you
are over the Atlantic. Where is Spain? where is
who? The Civil War was fought to free the slaves,
was it? A sudden down-draught reminds you of gravity
and your position in respect to human love. But
here is where the gods are, speculating, bemused.
Once you are helpless, you are free, can you believe
that? Never to waken to the sad struggle of a face?
to travel always over some impersonal vastness,
to be out of, forever, neither in nor for!

The eyes roll asleep as if turned by the wind
and the lids flutter open slightly like a wing.
The world is an iceberg, so much is invisible!
and was and is, and yet the form, it may be sleeping
too. Those features etched in the ice of someone
loved who died, you are a sculptor dreaming of space
and speed, your hand alone could have done this.
Curiosity, the passionate hand of desire. Dead,
or sleeping? Is there speed enough? And, swooping,
you relinquish all that you have made your own,
the kingdom of your self sailing, for you must awake
and breathe your warmth in this beloved image
whether it's dead or merely disappearing,
as space is disappearing and your singularity.[3]

Is this not the mutual shaping of language and self? Consciousness in motion? The syntactical, perceptive, immediate, present performance of being oneself and living in the world. The noise of any one thing—a door slams and a pigeon veers upward. The unshakable will of gravity, like thought itself, colliding with thinking, like the mind in flight.

4

Frank O'Hara's "Personal Poem" isn't personal. It's intimate. It doesn't insist upon its importance. It is a collage in which disparate elements coexist.

Madrid and New York coexist, and the House of Seagram and Birdland. Miles Davis is there, and LeRoi and Mike Kanemitsu. Construction workers in silver hats alongside literary figures, and there's a beggar too.

It's not personal but disarmed in the face of its progressive, moving-forwardness, its persistence, its open-endedness. It is a great poem. Like all great poems, it makes us think that we too are encountering and discovering these things, or remembering things that we knew all along.

You see, I had it all wrong. I had confused the personal with the intimate. And I wanted to resist in my insecurity, in my feebleness, in my distractedness. I wanted to resist the vulnerability that intimacy requires absolutely. I wanted to resist the surrender of myself and the individuality and separateness that's at risk in each intimate encounter.

And it is not unlike that young man from San Francisco, representing that magazine, who made me feel grateful to be asked once again to be interviewed. It is not unlike how he was wrong to think that if I could articulate for him—the way we all do, the way it is fashionable now—my process, that he could get closer to and make contact with my work.

I was pissed at him. When I encountered "Personal Poem," and then went back to O'Hara, and then started reading the poems, I was pissed at myself. More than being pissed at myself, I was ashamed. I was ashamed for my need to be so present, to be that important, to not be vulnerable, to not risk everything and engage in yet another intimate encounter in my life.

Now, I could tell you about everything I went through between that phone call and reading some of Frank O'Hara's poems again and that tribute reading. Would it help you to know what I was up to, or which books I went to, or what phone calls I made? No. But it is the things we do, isn't it? Of course I went to Marjorie Perloff's book, *Frank O'Hara: Poet among Painters*. It is one of the few critical texts on O'Hara in existence. Reviewers did not understand O'Hara in his time, and the great scholars of our great English departments don't understand him now. Or, that I went back to passages in a book I read only a year or so earlier by David Lehman, *The Last Avant-Garde*. Those are two terrific books.

But did they help me prepare to stand in front of an audience and read some Frank O'Hara poems? No. They were pleasant distraction.

Did it help me to remember everything we know about Frank O'Hara? About the way he used to dash off poems at odd moments. That he often made poems in his office at work; he was a curator at the Museum of

Modern Art in New York City. That he made an entire collection of poems while on his lunch break. That he used to make poems in rooms full of people. That he often put them aside and tucked them in drawers, boxes, or jars, or in coat pockets, and forget about them forever. That some of the poems in the collection exist only because people to whom he showed them kept them or even transcribed them, as Ashbery once did in a letter to Kenneth Koch. Only because Koch still had that letter from Ashbery did the poem end up in the *Collected*. Did it help me to come to terms with O'Hara's poems? No. But what glorious distraction.

Did it help me to know that he died freakishly like Geneviève Jurgensen's children who were in a car with her husband's brother and his wife and some jerk spun in front of them going the wrong way so she had to slam on the brakes and had to somehow manage control of this car in the rain? And then her husband looked at her and said, "Thank God, you pulled it off. We're safe." And then they turned around to the three children, their own child and their two nieces in the back seat. Only to find their nieces gone because they had been ejected through a window and died instantly.

This stuff, this articulation of process, does not help us to come to terms with poetry. It is a pleasant and rich and sometimes painful distraction. It is the stuff of life. Process is a ruse. Process is a distraction. Naming process is a lie.

If I filled in the gaps and told you everything I went through to come to terms for myself with his poems, so that I could stand up in front of an audience and read a few of them and pay homage to the man who made them, it would have nothing to do with the nature of process, with how things really get done. It would have a lot to do with how we live, or how we survive, or get through the day, but it would not have anything to do with the poems.

If I went on and told you more biographical information about O'Hara, it would have nothing to do with your coming to terms, if you cared to, with his poems. It would be a pleasant distraction. It would be an easy way of saying I know what Frank O'Hara is about. I love him. I love his poems. Ahh.

If there is such a thing as process, it exists in the poem. Frank O'Hara made intimacy. That's what he made, and in intimacy there is an organic process. Because in part he did what all poets do, what great, inimitable poets like himself do—because every poem is in itself, by its very nature, about making a poem.

This poem is titled "Why I Am Not A Painter."

I am not a painter, I am a poet.
Why? I think I would rather be
a painter, but I am not. Well,

for instance, Mike Goldberg
is starting a painting. I drop in.
"Sit down and have a drink" he
says. I drink; we drink. I look
up. "You have SARDINES in it."
"Yes, it needed something there."
"Oh." I go and the days go by
and I drop in again. The painting
is going on, and I go, and the days
go by. I drop in. The painting is
finished. "Where's SARDINES?"
All that's left is just
letters, "It was too much," Mike says.

But me? One day I am thinking of
a color: orange. I write a line
about orange. Pretty soon it is a
whole page of words, not lines.
Then another page. There should be
so much more, not of orange, of
words, of how terrible orange is
and life. Days go by. It is even in
prose, I am a real poet. My poem
is finished and I haven't mentioned
orange yet. It's twelve poems, I call
it ORANGES. And one day in a gallery
I see Mike's painting, called SARDINES.[4]

BREATHING OUT / *Ralph Angel*

Now you are crossing a wide street at night
anxious in the traffic and rushing
to get to the bakery

before closing. What could be more breathtaking
than your beauty if not in my arms
at least on that side
of peril. That's
why I'm yelling at the driver of the pickup truck
I just slammed into so much did I
want to park there and
wait for you.

May I never live with love
by surviving love and loving blocks and days away
the most ancient of the dead desire earthly
our getting born again
alone without
choice

children fill the air
the spices and the rugs of the bazaar.

I buy you tulips.
They are yellow and bright.
The port is dark and glittering blue airplanes
hover there. Like clarity
itself. Like
faintly wailing sirens attached to absolutely
nothing.
Like socks and sweaters and
the blanket that slipped somehow
from your legs while I
tidied up the balcony so lost in your book
are you tonight.[5]

Notes

1. Frank O'Hara, *The Collected Poems of Frank O'Hara*, ed. Donald Allen (Berkley: University of California Press, 1995), 335–36.
2. Ibid., 325.
3. Ibid., 235–36.
4. Ibid., 261–62.
5. Ralph Angel, *Twice Removed: Poems* (Louisville: Sarabande Books, 2001), 23–24.

Hiding Your Heart's Desire

David Keplinger

One night last summer in the Umbrian city of Assisi, it came to me. What lends Italy its compelling energy, why I return year after year, is exactly what the country hides from me. The sun had begun to set. At one of those hairpin curves where small trucks (nun-driven) ride so closely the shoulder, I stopped and waited for traffic to clear. Within a grayish alcove I saw a small painting: Mary holding an infant-sized Christ. It had been painted directly onto the facade of the apartment house. There was a tarnished bronze placard the size of my hand. This painting, the plaque indicated, was completed with gratitude when prayers were answered. The fresco was dated to the seventeenth century. The bottom half was blackened from the smoke of votive candles.

Were I in Philadelphia or New York or Boston—which claim long histories—this fresco on a busy corner might be preserved under glass or removed to a museum. In Assisi, art and daily life seem not to be divided. In the first in the Giotto series at the cathedral (twenty-seven frescos depicting the life and miracles of Francis), the saint stands before a Roman facade in the square at Piazza del Commune. A poor man spreads his cloak for the twenty-four-year-old nobleman to step upon. Francis wears the fine clothes of his birthright, as yet enjoying a life of privilege.

Those nights in Assisi, I'd sit and eat or read on the steps of that facade where Francis once accepted (albeit with a baffled look) the poor man's gesture. Little has changed in the piazza since Giotto recorded the encounter, seven hundred years ago. The Augustan, classical facade has remained there two millennia. In the Italian cities, one can't go a day without encountering some relic, a stone or a tapestry or a stage, set in the background of the everyday: bus stations, restaurants, barber shops. It always startles me.

Perhaps I return to Italy because I am reminded of some vital thing all artists and performers have to learn. That which I hide from the reader inevitably strengthens our bond. In *The Cloud of Unknowing*, the anonymous fourteenth-century author calls it "hiding your heart's desire from God" during prayerful contemplation. He's using religious language, but essentially the reasoning is the same: "One reason I have for advising you to hide your heart's desire from God is because when you hide it I think he actually sees it more clearly. By hiding it you will actually achieve your purpose and see your desire fulfilled sooner than by any means you could devise to attract God's attention. . . . God is all-knowing and nothing material or spiritual can actually be concealed from him, but since he is spirit, something thrust deep into the spirit is more clearly evident to him than something alloyed with emotions."[1] What is the difference between thrusting the poem "deep into the spirit" and alloying your poems with emotions? Two things happen when we're starting out. We try to tell our biggest stories in one poem. And we feel required to articulate significance. Micromanagement of poems, our longing to imperiously control the outcome in the reader's head, is a counterproductive activity. I have found that otherwise remarkable student poems lie muffled in what actors might call "indicating" gestures.

To indicate is a failure of trust. You underestimate your audience. While referencing someone behind him, an indicating actor will conspicuously point with his thumb to the person behind him. The indicating actor wraps his arms around himself and gives a little shiver while delivering the line, "I'm cold." My acting coach, Tom Foral, said this: "The last thing a drunk wants to reveal is his drunkenness. To act drunk, act like a man trying *not to be* drunk."

WRITING PROMPT

What wisdom that still holds. I apply it in the following exercise. Give your draft to two trusted readers. These readers are to meet and decide which two lines are the best and second best in the piece. When they arrive at a decision (and it's best to find two readers with at least a little similarity in taste), they return the poem to you. Now I would like you to take the best line (as your readers ranked it) and position it, unquestioningly, at the end of the poem. Position the second best at the beginning. Cut out all remaining lines, and, from memory, rewrite the poem.

What has happened to your draft? The indicating gestures are the first to go. The poem, commonly, will now begin and end on some subtle image. There's usually a step away from predictable, linear thinking, too. Your poem now looks more like a skeleton—starting and stopping at its best.

Anything else you write, to fill the gap, will have been preceded by a very high standard. Let go of your fear that the poem will not be understood. Stop trying to tell, in one poem, the big story. Concentrate on one small fresco at a time. Write a poem like a city—that's Yeats's advice—in which metaphor and daily life cannot be differentiated. A city whose treasures might suddenly appear within the most mundane contexts. These treasures can't be mapped ahead of time. Even you can't say where they are hidden.

LETTER FROM HUERFANO MOUNTAIN, 1910 / *David Keplinger*

I know such orphans where I come from,
And you, my darling, are one. On high

Plains came magpies whose source no soul
Remembers. When they come, I think

About the dead heart of Boleyn, displayed
Inside a jar; the head of Thomas More

Preserved in spices; the funeral clothes
Of Lincoln, his blue skin underneath.

What mythic tree have they been exiled from?
Their blues and blacks resemble Neolithic

Wings, some fairies I have seen. I send this
After giving up all hope. We are old and you

Have never loved me. Even the twenty-six
Horses, where four windows hold a field,

Concur and cock their ears in my direction.
Thus I feel no loneliness. As for my body,

Vast things are passing through it one
By one, as through a narrow, opened door.[2]

Notes

1. *The Cloud of Unknowing*, ed. William Johnston (New York: Doubleday, 1973), 113.
2. David Keplinger, "Letter from Huerfano Mountain, 1910," *Zone 3* 22.2 (Fall/Winter 2007): 69.

The Poem, Its Buried Subject, and the Revisionist Reader: Behind "The Guardian Angel"

Stephen Dunn

To revisit an old poem of yours is often to come to it as an interested stranger. By degree, you're more reader than author, and like all readers you bring to the poem an aesthetic and a psychology forged by personal history and your history of reading. If twenty years have elapsed since you've written a poem about a certain kind of spiritual endurance, and in the meantime you've become, say, a communist and have turned almost exclusively to reading poems for their political significance, then you're likely that poem's revisionist. Even if you've remained roughly the same, the world around you hasn't and inevitably provides you with a slightly different angle of regard. The good reader works hard at trying to compensate for these vicissitudes, tries to give each poem a fair trial and a fair sentence, though the writer as reader of his own poem may still be clinging—perhaps even rightly so—to some old allegiances. But one thing is sure: as author, no matter how well you've blended your intentions with your discoveries, the reader always completes your poem.

At first, I found this intolerable, like someone renaming my child. And, I confess, it remains intolerable much of the time. But. So much that's instructive begins with *but*. Moreover, if I agree with Stendhal, and I do, "that speech was given to man to conceal his thoughts," then I shouldn't have been very much surprised that my poem "The Guardian Angel," or any poem, for that matter, might have an elusive subtext.[1] But I was surprised.

No, I hadn't become a communist, but twenty years did elapse before I revisited "The Guardian Angel," enough time for me to witness the poem differently. Almost instantly, there it was—the buried subject—hiding like much of the world itself, not far from the surface.

More often than not, to be wholly unaware of what's driving your poem means that you're listening to the wrong cues and therefore likely to make poor choices. You think you're writing about *that time she left me* but fail to realize that your poem might simultaneously need to be exploring the nature of loss. You're following the lesser drift. You need to revise, but as long as the deeper subject remains hidden, you're thinking only cosmetically, just shifting a few words around. Or, what you allow yourself to think of as subtlety is really just a kind of avoidance, an unconscious refusal to enter certain delicate territory. Or, even more typically these days, you're in the headlong process of composing associatively, disparate image following disparate image, but never seem to arrive at the poem's locus of concern. You're dazzling, you're on your way to postmodernist heaven, but you've yet to find a principle of selection; almost anything can be substituted for anything else. The radical entry into your subject eludes you. Your poem has taken its place among the many casualties of indulgence and unconsciousness.

But here's the paradox. Successful poems are often written with a similar unconsciousness. Buried subjects, for example, even when they are the products of inattention or avoidance, can give poems a behind-the-scenes radiance. "The Guardian Angel," I'm quite sure, is one of those poems that profited by what I didn't know about it. What follows—this retrospective foray into the making of a poem—will be a re-creation, thus a fiction, which is to say it's interested in approximating the truth. With luck, it'll live as the poem's good companion, casting some light and maybe a few shadows.

Trust the tale, not the teller, D. H. Lawrence admonishes.[7] I'm aware of such wisdom. *But*. But, on the other hand, let me say that I wish for you to trust everything I say. This is just to let you know I'm not without guile or strategy. Here, finally, is the poem:

THE GUARDIAN ANGEL

Afloat between lives and stale truths,
        he realizes
he's never truly protected one soul,

they all die anyway, and what good
        is solace,
solace is cheap. The signs are clear:

the drooping wings, the shameless thinking
    about utility
and self. It's time to stop.

The guardian angel lives for a month
    with other angels,
sings the angelic songs, is reminded

that he doesn't have a human choice.
    The angel of love
lies down with him, and loving

restores to him his pure heart.
    Yet how hard it is
to descend into sadness once more.

When the poor are evicted, he stands
    between them
and the bank, but the bank sees nothing

in its way. When the meek are overpowered
    he's there, the thin air
through which they fall. Without effect

he keeps getting in the way of insults.
    He keeps wrapping
his wings around those in the cold.

Even his lamentations are unheard,
    though now,
in for the long haul, trying to live

beyond despair, he believes, he needs
    to believe
everything he does takes root, hums

beneath the surfaces of the world.[3]

I like to talk about the composition of poems as involving a series of allegiances that we keep as long as we can but that we modify and refine as the language we employ starts to make its own demands. In "The Guardian

Angel," my initial allegiance was to creating a secular angel, an allegiance I gradually abandoned. Instead, I found myself with a disaffected guardian angel, the poem's first real discovery. I vaguely remember discarding all the language and claims (two or three stanzas worth of warm-up) that had gotten me to that discovery and beginning right away with his disaffectedness. "Afloat between lives and stale truths, / he realizes / he's never truly protected one soul." I was in a "what if" poem. What if there was such a thing as a disaffected angel? How would he act? What would he be thinking? I had two allegiances now, to the serious playfulness of executing his disaffection and to finding an imaginative logic for it. A drama was unfolding. He was, by definition, a do-gooder who now was thinking only of self. Worse, he was thinking of results, as if he could be the arbiter of what a result was. Wasn't that for Someone else to decide? I was starting to become interested in him. But only in him. I had no idea that something else might also be driving the poem.

I suppose the next lines became available to me because I was at a writers' colony. The angel seeks out his own kind, is restored by them, especially by the angel of love, who, by example, is able to remind him of generosity and its worth. Prior to these moments, my compositional possibilities were wide open. Now I had narrowed them by choosing to have him healed. He might have been an interesting renegade, confrontational and subversive, disruptive of the established order. He might have wanted a new identity, an angel's job that required less of him. I'm sure I could have written in either of those directions as well as in others. We learn, as Theodore Roethke says, by going where we go.[4]

I can't remember if, around this time, I knew that I was taking him on a rather classical religious journey—that he would lose his way before he found his way, that some kind of passage was being enacted. Certainly it was apparent to me later. What I did know at the time was that play had gotten me beyond the purely fanciful—that is, beyond the pleasures of invention, beyond, say, the poem as exercise. I had arrived at some principle of selection, something that could help me find the poem's next moments: the guardian angel would not quit; it wasn't one of his choices. Nevertheless, I recognized how difficult it would be for him "to descend into sadness once more." I only half-knew where I was going and therefore could still avoid the perils of purposefulness, could ride some uncodified energy. In retrospect, these were my new allegiances: to the poem's adjusted original impulse; to the texture, sounds, and rhythms of the language used so far; and to the unknowns of this new, governing drift.

I wasn't conscious of needing to come up with a series of tests for his newfound resolve, but that's what I found myself doing. Okay, he returns to earth and to his job. What's likely to be his experience? Certainly, if the poem were to stay in the realm of the probable, he would once again fail. But I was as much committed to the poem's rhythmical recurrences as I was to the recurrences of his ineffectuality, and may have known there couldn't be the latter without the former. I had begun to feel for him, and the rhythm had to authenticate this. Which is to say that content decisions were inseparable from decisions about syntax and flow and were just a part of the overall orchestration of effects. Earlier, perhaps, I could have let content drive the poem. But no longer. Of course, there were still various content options available to me. I could have allowed him, for example, one success. That would have set the poem on a slightly different course. In this case, what I ended up *not* selecting proved instructive. It, too, pointed the way.

The poem was leaning into its structure though hadn't yet found its true form, if form, as Denise Levertov says, is the revelation of content.[5] (At the time, I frequently used that step-down, three-line stanza to harness and discipline my discursive inclinations. Initially, it was an editing device, to help identify and abolish excess content. It would evolve into a way of thinking about the poem as architecture—that is, as something that would seek its shape, stanza by stanza, by an acute attention to its inner relationships.) Structurally, thus far, the poem had three movements: the introduction of the disaffected angel, his resurrection into new resolve, and his return to duty, which proved no more successful than before. Whatever mixture of intellection and obsession that was driving the poem was now calling for a fourth movement and thus would take me toward the often illusory world of closure. The poet's temperament and compositional tics are always involved in that mysterious world, but since they're usually the last things we can do anything about, it's better instead to be as alert as possible to the poem's overt promptings. I tried to be. But by this time my choices, to a significant degree, were being made for me. I was both creator and responder to my creation. I'm not sure if I ever consciously *chose* to have the guardian angel live with his ineffectualness.

Nor did I ever consider having him quit again, which now seems a reasonable option. It just felt right, I suppose, to have him persevere in spite of repeated failure. At the moment, I knew I had moved him from disaffection, but to what? Acceptance? Resignation? A desperate hopefulness? Some instructive thread would need to be pulled through if closure were to take the poem to what could feel like its inevitability.

Well, that's one fiction, one way to speculate about what I found myself doing. Another, which will be even less coherent and therefore, I think, closer to the truth, is that the poem was composed during many sittings and had many false starts, much extraneous language, and stanzas in various orders. Parts of it, I vaguely recall, were cargoed in from other poems, those failed poems most of us save and steal from. I revised it over a period of months, and many of the revisions were arrived at, as I said before, because of the exigencies of rhythm and the seeking of cooperative sounds, determining what weight of language a stanza could bear and other considerations that had more to do with problem solving than with genesis or willfulness. At some point, that hint of a thread, that elusive something, famously invisible when the poem isn't on the right course, appeared. The angel, "in for the long haul," could not *not* be who he was. As it turns out, it was only a semblance of the real thread, but finding the ghost of it enabled me, I think, to create an illusion of orderliness and authority. Such a thread starts to become visible the more a poem's surface felicities get in some concordance with the pulse of its undercurrents.

Now, having said this, I recognize that from the start I was the god of this universe made of words and had considerable time before book publication—cool, considered time—to assay and evaluate all of my choices, conscious and unconscious. I am responsible for everything in it and could have, had I been foolishly or even perhaps wisely willful, changed its direction, pulled the thread through to a different conclusion, made the poem happier, sadder, or the like. But my overriding allegiance was to the poem as a whole, to my fiction and its interlocking parts, and to how they held up for examination their revelations and concealments. Finally, we leave or abandon our poems because no more aesthetic decisions seem available to us that will help enact or explore our subject. At least I could think of none before "The Guardian Angel" found its way into my book *Between Angels*.

But "finally" is premature. Twenty years after the poem was written, I was visiting a colleague's class in which some of my poems were under discussion. She was, in fact, teaching *Between Angels,* and one of her students asked if I could read and comment on "The Guardian Angel." I hadn't read the poem in a while, and as I read it, it seemed clear to me what my buried subject had been, though I hadn't known it had a buried subject. Was I seeing what was truly there, or was I bringing new urgencies to an old poem that somehow permitted them to be entertained? It's true that at the time of the rereading, I had been preoccupied with the generation of poets in love with the romance of self-destruction, the generation of John Berryman and Delmore Schwartz and Randall Jarrell, to name just a few, and how so few of them made it out of their fifties. And it's true that I had begun to wonder about myself in that regard. I remember smiling as I told the class that the poem is an analogue of the poet's condition in America. The poet does his job, I said, and hardly anybody listens or cares. All his life he lives with his ineffectuality, his invisible presence, the reality that there's little evidence that he makes anything happen. But

> . . . trying to live
>
> beyond despair, he believes, he needs
> to believe
> everything he does takes root, hums
>
> beneath the surfaces of the world.

There it was, my dogged optimism, my little anthem for continuing on. This "what if" poem, this verbal construct that had found out just enough about itself to sustain the angel's journey from disaffection to endurance, was a personal poem after all. The buried subject, I was sure now, had been the poem's co-driving force and its secret glue.

But wait. Even if what I just said is persuasive, there's one more wrinkle. If the poem's hidden subject and the thread I pulled through are similar, as they now seem to have been, how can I have pulled through a thread I didn't become conscious of until years later? One answer, as I've suggested, is that the making of a poem is a constant compromise between author's intent and the discoveries that confound it, that this process itself is a kind of decision maker, has its own intelligence, and is more alert to undercurrents than I could have been. Another is that there's no answer, just more or less plausible fictions, and this entire essay constitutes one of them. Or, in fact, I did it, I pulled the secret thread down and through while thinking only of an angel's problems and how to arrange them, and that such things happen all the time and take their not unfamiliar places among the mysteries of composition.

Trust the tale.

Notes

This essay originally appeared in *Lyric Poetry Review*, no. 11 (2008): 54–62.

1. Stendhal, *The Red and the Black*, trans. C. K. Scott-Moncrieff (Kingston, Mass.: R. S. Means Company, 2004), 202.

2. D. H. Lawrence, *Studies in Classic American Literature*, ed. Ezra Greenspan, Lindeth Vasey, and John Worthen (New York: Cambridge University Press, 2003), 8.

3. Stephen Dunn, *Between Angels* (New York: W. W. Norton, 1989), 15–16.

4. Theodore Roethke, *The Collected Poems of Theodore Roethke* (Garden City, N.Y.: Anchor Press, 1975), 49.

5. Denise Levertov, *New and Selected Essays* (New York: New Directions, 1992), 73.

Bring Yourself Along

Mary Ann Samyn

Some of the best advice I've ever received came from my friend Rebecca and was not in the context of poetry but could have been. She said, "Don't forget to bring yourself along." My poems are the record of my effort. So, too, is this essay:

*

I recently made two purchases at a favorite used bookstore: *Just a Box* and *Puppet Party*, both by Goldie Taub Chernoff with pictures by Margaret Hartelius. Scholastic, no surprise, published these books in, no surprise again, 1971, a crafty time.

The books are, in a word, delightful.

Just a Box reminds us that "a box can be a horse" or a train. Just "cut on [the] dotted line; fold on [the] solid line," and there you have it, boys and girls. At the Puppet Party, "the troll and the dragon are cardboard tubes." "I have a terrible temper," growls the green troll as a nearby mouse squeaks "help!" And a stage, don't you know, can be "a blanket over a chair . . . a three-sided cardboard . . . a bush or hedge . . . [even] an apron" held high above the head.[1]

Surely there's some instruction here for poets: "everything you need is right in the house."

I'm not, or not only, thinking, though, of found material but also of the materials themselves: as forms. The cereal box says "cereal" as certainly as do its sugary or disappointingly not-so-sugary contents and not only on its label but also via its shape. We are familiar.

And then the box is a caboose or coal car, the body of an elephant or a cage for a lion. But not, it turns out, a cradle for a doll. We'll need an oatmeal canister for that. Not a canoe, either. A toothpaste box is better suited.

The sonnet is, perhaps, our most familiar poetic cage for a lion. But what's the old saying: it's the spaces that make the cage—?

All poems are formal poems, I was taught (Charles Wright). All questions, formal questions.

You've got the lion, presumably, by the tail. If not, we'll wait while you set out a treat . . .

*

My lion is named Mary Ann. She prefers the spaces but understands about the bars.

Your average circus wagon is not your average savanna. Or zoo enclosure or glitzy Vegas show where Mary Ann wears a collar of rhinestones and bells.

To write the lion, as of course you must, is to write the cage, the method of transport, the spotlight, and what's downstage. Even the savanna is not without boundaries; all poems are formal poems.

What I write is Mary Ann-ness. This is subject matter. It is also form.

Just as the ferocity of the lion dictates how wide the spaces between the bars or how near we might approach, so too the ferocity of the lion-poem dictates how wide the spaces, how near we might approach.

One lion can have many moods. Hence, not all of my poems move across the page. To say "stalk it" would be easy now, so let's not. Controlling metaphors start to get on my nerves.

*

Naturally, I'm on to motion now and the Red Gate Park of my childhood—so named because in addition to the usual array of swings and slides, there was one red gate, creaky on its hinges. And a little shelf to stand on, catch a ride. Was this fun? Yes, it was.

Among the things I did not wonder: Where did the gate come from? Had it been useful, once? The gate was not a narrative, though, yes, my mother took my hand.

Instead the gate was a motion, and emotion (happiness). It was mostly out of context, both its original and perhaps useful one and the context of my day with my mother, which of course I don't recall. This is the lyric moment pared nearly all the way down.

I consider the gate not only as a topic but (and more important) as a formal suggestion, a compositional strategy.

Remove the trappings (fence), leave it a little squeaky, paint it red.

This is a kind of assignment.

There is, of course, only one assignment (says Brenda Hillman and I believe her): write the poem that scares you. I think we know we've made progress as poets when we tell it to ourselves straight: just write the next poem. No more projects or assignments, no more hijinks, just a willingness to keep at it, to go ahead.

*

Usually my poems begin with the slightest edge of the thing. A fluttering. These are not ideas. They are instead pieces of language that take a certain length of time, shape of space. Form = time. The line. Structure = space. The page.

I generally begin with a title and a first line. Not a first idea. Not a first sentence though the line may in fact be a sentence.

White space is otherwise occupied. I can't just move it around. Neither can I "cut up" lines.

For me, an accurate line is accurate not only in what it says but in how it says. Music. Duration. There's a little click.

This all sounds mysterious, I know. But it does not feel that way. In fact, it feels quite straightforward.

"Boot" is a good word, and I just remembered it, and it will help us now. Consider it for a moment: deep in the middle with a sturdy consonant at each side to tug on. Boot boot boot. Very pleasing.

And what do we do in boots? Well, first we put them on and then we walk about. Snow or rain or high fashion: nothing can stop us in boots. One booted step at a time and we're where we want to be, quick as that.

A poem is the very same way.

A title is a first step. A first line is another. An idea or "point" is much too much. You'll never even get to the corner that way.

Think of how nice your bootprints look spread out behind you in snow. Now imagine that each print is a line in a poem. Wouldn't it be sad to rush through? It's very satisfying to put one's boot into snow. Especially snow with a bit of crust on top. And I say this as someone who isn't even particularly fond of winter. Even I can appreciate the satisfying crunch of a boot packing down snow.

Next time you write, imagine you are wearing boots. What kind will you wear? Funny, fringy, animal-looking boots? Big, serious military boots? Impractical boots with a dangerous heel? Magic boots with jet packs attached? Lots of boots are possible. When you're writing, even impossible boots become possible.

But you are not writing about boots. You are writing like boots. Step step step. A nice crunch of snow. An icy spot. Yikes!

Think about this. I am not being silly. If you think I am, then you are not being serious.

*

The best work often comes when we distract ourselves long enough for bravery to happen. I jump up a lot when I am writing. *Oh!*, I think, *is that the UPS truck? A package for me?* Or, *Here is a cat to hold.* Or, *Some soapy dishwater just might accomplish the task.* These are not postponements. They are the work of getting to the work. Perfectly acceptable. I agree with Heather Sellers: sometimes a nap is what comes next. Jumping up, for me, is not distraction, or not only. It is, rather, invitation. I work by letting more in and by maintaining emotional awareness. To look for the UPS truck is to hope. *Has someone sent me a little urgency?* To be aware of hoping is the start of writing. Very often my poems feel like the moment + the moment + the moment, etc. I record the little shifts. Bravery means I'm still willing.

*

I'm writing this essay in bits and pieces. I'm learning as I go; is there a better way? Today's bravery lesson came via the work of one of my MFA students. What is it, I asked myself, that makes me read her poems and say, *This is poetry*. Truly marked. And I return to the idea of authority. And to something I'm coming to understand as an individualized clarity.

In his essay "Strangely Abstracted Images," David Porter identifies Emily Dickinson's poetic power with her ability to use images that are "so abstract they have given up their sensuous immediacy to pure meaning." "These peculiar figures with light-catching body perform," at least some of the time, in Dickinson's poems in a way they would surely refuse to do for lesser talents.[2] And what accounts for her success? Porter cites Archibald MacLeish, who asserts that it is Dickinson's "extraordinary mastery of tone" that allows her to make generalizations and abstractions seem, in her particular voice, particular.[3]

What I have been suggesting in this essay is similar: one must find one's particularity. The boot that fits, as it were. The clarity communicates, yet is yours alone.

My student, the one with the remarkable poems, has just that sort of talent. Her strength is not abstractions made strangely tangible but juxtapositions keyed just so. This is sensibility. Just as it is challenging to teach someone to have a "good ear," my focus on honing sensibility—Mary Ann-ness—is not easily taught: step one, step two, step three. You don't want to end up with Mary Ann-ness. It can, however, be modeled. Or, as with the boots, metaphor can indicate a way.

Isn't it Gaston Bachelard who reminds us that we are the curators of our own images? He does not mean self-image, though that might be relevant, but something more like Stanley Kunitz's "key images." I'd suggest key metaphors might be worth considering, too.

And not only the metaphors that happen within poems but, more important, the ones that occur prior to, or alongside, or beneath poem-writing. The metaphors that help us gain access to the work and to the process of work.

*

For instance, I'm getting ready to be done with smallness. So if you're looking for a crawl space, I'll be carting my metaphors to the curb. You can go through them, if you want.

What I'd recommend, though, is this: look about you.

My home state, my favorite state, Michigan, has a nice motto, which, when translated, means roughly "If you seek a pleasant peninsula, look about you." I've always liked that. Very no-nonsense. Very get-over-it. Stop your whining and pay attention.

As I said, everything you need, etc. etc.

But didn't I also say that I dislike a controlling metaphor?

This is my life lesson, in case you haven't noticed.

But even my controlling metaphors, thank goodness, work metaphorically like three-dimensional Venn diagrams: lassoing me and each other momentarily, then looping high in the air, a funny oblong shape like the "oh" of your open-mouthed amazement.

*

It is difficult to isolate the writing of one poem and prove everything to you. I would like to, of course. But the poems I've already written seem so far past their process of becoming, while the poems I've yet to write seem so far from it. I will say, though, that the poems of my own that I continue to feel close to are the ones that have an accuracy, a clarity that I cannot translate or paraphrase, that I hear, when I read them aloud even now, as a little click. Line by line. They ring true.

Often people want me to say that I was trying to make a certain point or explore a particular poetic element when I was writing. *Um, no.* That's just not how it works. Not for me. Whenever I've written, especially a successful poem, what I've done is paid attention: very close attention for a limited amount of time. This is how I understand the lyric poem: bring yourself along.

*

When in doubt, turn to the dictionary, that's what I always say. So, "authority," which of course has an author in it and thus is, no surprise, something writers are after.

My preferred definition is #7 in my trusty *American Heritage*: "Grounds for a particular course of action."[4] I like thinking of a poem in these terms, which seem to get at the notion of writing as a process, a series of decisions made by a particular sensibility, a physical undertaking unique to its moment. A poem itself as grounds, which appeals to my longstanding feeling/belief that a poem is a space where an event made of language happens.

*

Which brings us back to the "Puppet Party" we were planning to have. Will you use a paper plate to make a singing frog or a bag to make an owl? "Bird and his friends are made from Folded Paper." Can you count yourself among his company? Use what you have; "there is nothing to buy." Therein lies the secret, and the ongoing assignment: tend to your metaphors, name your lion, construct a little something, love the sound a word makes, bring yourself along, be as brave and clear as you can.

A GIRL CAN IMAGINE, CAN'T SHE, A GIRL CAN DREAM

/ *Mary Ann Samyn*

Now then. This won't hurt a bit. Boys & Girls. Yes, I promise.
Verbs explain how to do it.
This page is full of words in much the same way I can't sleep some
nights between two and four.
If you think you know, then you probably don't, thank goodness, or
we couldn't be friends.
*He developed special instruments to probe and extract the bullet, after
which he applied a styptic . . .*
For information about this account, press 1; for a little push ("Go
away." "Submit."), hold the line.

Look at yourself in the mirror. Pin the parts together to look like a body. Make your final pattern.

Eyes far apart mean younger; eyes close together mean shrewder; children need only a small stitch.

O Sister Miriam of the Holy Spirit, O Sister Rose of God, am I not His Little Question-Mark?

Lively does it, fish line or strong linen thread, a large-eyed needle, and you measure and you measure.

The wonder of it is how and why if you really want to have fun with electricity as famously illustrated.

Some dolls walk and talk. I knew one who blew bubbles. One with stiff limbs and a soft cloth body.

I practice being serious. I practice love of knowledge. I practice busyness. I practice the braver way.

O honeybee, what sweet results are wrought by industry. If you doubt that I am happy, listen to me hum!

In the background, velvet. A small table for my stage. Flood lights, silence, your attentive gaze.

The hand here depicted contains a great deal of information. I don't sit still and hope and wonder.

The cupboard as it should look. Nouns in a row. I'm just as surprised as you are. Action = Reaction.

Try these activities. Don't worry. Follow directions and diagrams. You will have a great deal of fun.

Some dolls tear up. Also, the Virgin Mary. The pull of a string. A garden or alcove. *Oh my.*

So daily I aimed for something practical, something personal, something charitable, something spiritual.

Consider *Ben and the Green Corduroy Angel.* Consider this a little page of no thanks to you.

Electricity doesn't just happen. Oh no? This story was not made up. My town stood still for eight hours.

"Your whole life would be different if you had a chart with feet on it." Well, I guess that's right.

For assessment purposes, please list three visions worth working toward and three dumb questions.

The first step in the writing process is "romancing." The third is "writing." The last is "showing off."

Some dolls prefer a more pragmatic, reality-oriented practice. Some surgeons admire their own work.

Who will read my work and what is special about my writing that will make my readers glad?

If you are experiencing an emergency, by all means, proceed to your local emergency room.

If you would like to make up jump-rope rhymes using the multiplication facts, please go elsewhere.

O Sister Miriam, O Sister Rose, *how great the lions and tigers are, filling the air with sound!*

Arrows mean movement. Numbers mean help is on the way. When you press the button, it lights up.

Imagine this poem sequenced movie-style. Frame by frame by frame. Which scenes are you missing?

Make a list of eight ways to cook without electricity, nine ways to tell time, a dozen uses for eggshells.

He was dexterous. She was lovely. He was brusque. She was fervent. He was gentle. She was stormy.

Gather together, give entertainments, illustrate interesting points in history, practice, practice, practice.

Sometimes a question mark is also used inside parentheses after a date or statement to show doubt.

The answer is *transfigure*. List as many questions as you can think of for which that is the answer.[5]

Notes

1. *Just a Box* and *Puppet Party* have no pagination.

2. David Porter, "Strangely Abstracted Images," in *Emily Dickinson: A Collection of Critical Essays*, ed. Judith Farr (Upper Saddle River, N.J.: Prentice Hall, 1996), 141.

3. Ibid., 143.

4. Second college edition.

5. Mary Ann Samyn, "A Girl Can Imagine, Can't She, a Girl Can Dream." *Zone 3* 49.1 (Spring 2009): 24.

Credits
Contributors

CREDITS

Ralph Angel, "Breathing Out" from *Twice Removed: Poems* (Sarabande Books). Copyright © 2001 by Ralph Angel. First published in *American Poetry Review* (Sept./Oct. 2001). Reprinted by permission of Sarabande Books and the author.

Joelle Biele, "Family Stories" from *White Summer* (Southern Illinois University Press). Copyright © 2002 by Joelle Biele. Reprinted by permission of Southern Illinois University Press and the author.

Victoria Chang, "Seven Reasons for Divorce" from *Circle* (Southern Illinois University Press). Copyright © 2005 by Victoria Chang. Reprinted by permission of Southern Illinois University Press and the author.

Lisa D. Chávez, "In an Angry Season" from *Americas Review* 24.1, 2. Copyright © 1997 by Arte Publico Press–University of Houston. Reprinted by permission of Arte Publico Press–University of Houston and the author.

Staceyann Chin, "I Don't Want to Slam" from *Poetry Slam: The Competitive Art of Performance Poetry*, ed. Gary Mex Glazner (Manic D Press). Copyright © 2000 by Staceyann Chin. Reprinted by permission of the author.

Patricia Clark, "Riverside Ghazal" from *My Father on a Bicycle* (Michigan State University Press). First published in *Atlantic Monthly* 289 (April 2002): 4. Copyright © 2005 by Patricia Clark. Reprinted by permission of the author.

Jim Daniels, "How" from *Show and Tell: New and Collected Poems* (University of Wisconsin Press). Copyright © 2003 by the Board of Regents of the University of Wisconsin System. Reprinted by permission of The University of Wisconsin Press and the author.

Rita Dove, "The House Slave" from *The Yellow House on the Corner: Poems* (Carnegie Mellon University Press). Copyright © 1980 by Rita Dove. Reprinted by permission of the author.

Stephen Dunn, "The Guardian Angel" from *Between Angels* (W. W. Norton and Company). Copyright © 1990 by Stephen Dunn. Reprinted by permission of W. W. Norton and Company and the author.

Nancy Eimers, "Book of Invisible Things." Printed by permission of the author.

Alice Fulton, "==" from *Sensual Math: Poems* (W. W. Norton and Company). Copyright © 1994, 1995, 2001, 2005, 2006, 2007, 2008, 2009 by Alice Fulton. Reprinted by permission of W. W. Norton and Company and the author.

Alice George and Cecilia Pinto, "Thirst" from *Saints of Hysteria: A Half-Century of Collaborative American Poetry*, ed. Denise Duhamel, Maureen Seaton, and David Trinidad (Counterpoint/Soft Skull Press). Copyright © 2007 by Denise Duhamel, Maureen Seaton, and David Trinidad. Reprinted by permission of Counterpoint Press and the authors.

———, "Your Five + My Four = Nine." Printed by permission of the authors.

Louise Glück, "Pomegranate" from *The First Four Books of Poems* (Ecco Press). Copyright © 1968, 1971, 1972, 1973, 1974, 1975, 1976, 1977, 1978, 1979, 1980, 1985, 1995 by Louise Glück. Reprinted by permission of HarperCollins Publishers.

Jeff Hardin, "Always Upstream or Downstream" from *Florida Review* 32.1 (Spring 2007). Reprinted by permission of the author.

Terrance Hayes, "Sonnet" from *Hip Logic* (Penguin). Copyright © 2002 by Terrance Hayes. Reprinted by permission of the author.

Anthony Hecht, "The Transparent Man" from *The Transparent Man* (Knopf-Random House). Copyright © 1990 by Anthony Hecht. Reprinted by permission of Knopf-Random House.

A. Van Jordan, "The Flash Reverses Time" from *Quantum Lyrics: Poems* (W. W. Norton and Company). Copyright © 2007 by A. Van Jordan. Reprinted by permission of W. W. Norton and Company and the author.

Claire Kageyama-Ramakrishnan, "The Denver Lady" from *Shadow Mountain: Poems* (Four Way Books). Copyright © 2008 by Claire Kageyama-Ramakrishnan. Reprinted by permission of Four Way Books. All rights reserved.

David Keplinger, "Letter from Huerfano Mountain, 1910" from *Zone 3* 22.2 (Fall/Winter 2007): 69. Reprinted by permission of *Zone 3* and the author.

Phillis Levin, "The Stairwell" from *Temples and Fields: Poems* (University of Georgia Press). Copyright © 1988 by Phillis Levin. Reprinted by permission of University of Georgia Press and the author.

Elline Lipkin, "Epithalamion Manqué" from *The Errant Thread* (Kore Press). Copyright © 2006 by Elline Lipkin. Reprinted by permission of the author.

Shara McCallum, "Persephone Sets the Record Straight" from *The Water Between Us* (University of Pittsburgh Press). Copyright © 1999 by Shara McCallum. Reprinted by permission of the University of Pittsburgh Press.

Maria Melendez, "Untitled" from *Flexible Bones: Poems* (University of Arizona Press). Printed by permission of the author.

W. S. Merwin, "Just This" from *The Shadow of Sirius*. Originally published in the *New Yorker*. Copyright © 2008 by W. S. Merwin. Reprinted with the permission of Copper Canyon Press, www.coppercanyonpress.org.

Deirdre O'Connor, "Wake." Printed by permission of the author.

Frank O'Hara, "The Day Lady Died" from *Lunch Poems* (City Lights Books). Copyright © 1964 by Frank O'Hara. Reprinted by permission of City Lights Books.

———, "Personal Poem" from *Lunch Poems* (City Lights Books). Copyright © 1964 by Frank O'Hara. Reprinted by permission of City Lights Books.

———, "Sleeping on the Wing" from *Meditations in an Emergency* (Grove Press). Copyright © 1957 by Frank O'Hara. Reprinted by permission of Grove/Atlantic, Inc.

———, "Why I Am Not a Painter" from *The Collected Poems of Frank O'Hara*, ed. Donald Allen (Knopf-Random House). Copyright © 1971 by Maureen Granville-Smith, Administratrix of the Estate of Frank O'Hara, copyright renewed 1999 by Maureen Granville-Smith and Donald Allen. Introduction copyright © 1971 by Alfred A. Knopf, a division of Random House, Inc. Reprinted by permission of Knopf-Random House.

William Olsen, "Grocery Night." Printed by permission of the author.

Stanley Plumly, "Lapsed Meadow" from *Summer Celestial* (Ecco Press). Copyright © 1983 by Stanley Plumly. Reprinted by permission of HarperCollins Publishers.

———, "Simile" from *Old Heart* (W. W. Norton and Company). Copyright © 2007 by Stanley Plumly. Reprinted by permission of W. W. Norton and Company and the author.

Kevin Prufer, "This Was the Model to Which I Held" from *The Finger Bone* (Carnegie Mellon University Press). Copyright © 2002 by Kevin Prufer. Reprinted by permission of Carnegie Mellon University Press and the author.

Susanna Rich, "F Y I Need to Talk." Printed by permission of the author.

Tomasz Różycki, "Iterations" from *The Forgotten Keys*, trans. Mira Rosenthal (Zephyr Press). Copyright © 2007 by Mira Rosenthal. Reprinted by permission of Zephyr Press.

Tomaž Šalamun, "To Immerse the Weight," trans. Christopher Merrill from *Poetry Daily*, April 5, 2006, www.poems.com. Reprinted by permission of the author.

Metta Sáma, "The universe is moving away from us" from *Pebble Lake Review*. Reprinted in *Letters to the World: Poems from the Wom-Po Listserv*, ed. Moira Richards, Rosemary Starace, and Lesley Wheeler (Red Hen Press). Reprinted by permission of the author.

Mary Ann Samyn, "A Girl Can Imagine, Can't She, a Girl Can Dream" from *Beauty Breaks In* (New Issues Press). Originally published in *Zone 3*. Reprinted by permission of the author and New Issues Press.

Jane Satterfield, "Requiem" from *Assignation at Vanishing Point* (Elixir Press). Copyright © 2003 by Jane Satterfield. Reprinted by permission of Elixir Press.

Jo Shapcott, "Phrase Book" from *Her Book: Poems 1988–1998* (Faber and Faber). Copyright © 2000 by Jo Shapcott. Reprinted by permission of Faber and Faber.

Jim Simmerman, "Low-ku," reprinted from *Prairie Schooner* 75.3 (Fall 2001), by permission of the University of Nebraska Press. Copyright 2001 by the University of Nebraska Press.

Angela Sorby, "Asphalt" from *Distance Learning* (New Issues Press). Copyright © 1998 by Angela Sorby. Reprinted by permission of New Issues Press and the author.

Marcia Southwick, "Winter Gulls" from *The Night Won't Save Anyone* (University of Georgia Press). Copyright © 1980 by the University of Georgia Press. Reprinted by permission of the University of Georgia Press.

Philip St. Clair, "Water" from *Zone 3* 2.2 (Spring 1987). Copyright © 1987 by Philip St. Clair. Reprinted by permission of the author.

May Swenson, "Bleeding" from *Iconographs* (Scribner). Copyright © 1970 by Scribner. Reprinted by permission of The Literary Estate of May Swenson. All rights reserved.

Michael Theune, "The Value of Man." Printed by permission of the author.

Diane Thiel, "Memento Mori in Middle School" from *Echolocations* (Story Line Press). Copyright © 2000 by Diane Thiel. Reprinted by permission of the author.

Tomas Tranströmer, "Along the Radius," translated by Robin Fulton, from *The Great Enigma: New Collected Poems*, copyright © 2006 by Tomas Tranströmer. Translation copyright © 2006 by Robin Fulton. Reprinted by permission of New Directions Publishing Corp.

Michael Waters, "Beloved" from *Poetry International* 13 (2009). Copyright © 2009 by Michael Waters. Reprinted by permission of the author.

James Wright, "Speak" from *Collected Poems* (Wesleyan University Press). Copyright © 1971 by James Wright. Reprinted by permission of Wesleyan University Press.

CONTRIBUTORS

Ralph Angel is the author of four books of poetry—*Exceptions and Melancholies: Poems 1986–2006* (2007 PEN USA Poetry Award), *Twice Removed: Poems*, *Neither World* (1995 James Laughlin Award of The Academy of American Poets), and *Anxious Latitudes*—as well as a translation of the Federico García Lorca collection, *Poema del cante jondo / Poem of the Deep Song*. His poems have appeared in scores of magazines and anthologies, both here and abroad, and recent literary awards include a gift from the Elgin Cox Trust, a Pushcart Prize, a Gertrude Stein Award, the Willis Barnstone Poetry Translation Prize, a Fulbright Foundation fellowship, and the Bess Hokin Award of the Modern Poetry Association. Angel is Edith R. White Distinguished Professor of English and Creative Writing at the University of Redlands and a member of the MFA Program in Writing faculty at Vermont College of Fine Arts.

Joelle Biele is the author of *White Summer*, winner of the Crab Orchard Series in Poetry First Book Award, and the editor of *Elizabeth Bishop and* The New Yorker: *The Complete Correspondence*. A Fulbright scholar, she has received awards from the Poetry Society of America and the Maryland State Arts Council. She has taught American literature and creative writing at Goucher College, the University of Maryland, Jagiellonian University, Poland, and the University of Oldenburg, Germany.

Victoria Chang's second book of poetry, *Salvinia Molesta*, was published in 2008 as part of the *VQR* Poetry Series by the University of Georgia Press. Her first book of poetry, *Circle*, won the Crab Orchard Series in Poetry First Book Award and was published in 2005. It won the Association of Asian American Studies Book Award and was a finalist for the 2005 PEN Center USA Literary Award for Poetry and for the Foreword Magazine Book of the Year Award. Her poems have appeared in or are forthcoming in journals such as *Paris Review*, *Nation*, *Poetry*, *New Republic*, *Threepenny Review*, *Kenyon Review*, *Virginia Quarterly Review*, *Slate*, *Pleiades*, *Ploughshares*, *TriQuarterly*, and *Best American Poetry 2005*. She is the editor of the anthology *Asian American Poetry: The Next Generation*.

Lisa D. Chávez is the author of the poetry collections *In an Angry Season* and *Destruction Bay*. Her poems have appeared in such anthologies as *Floricanto Si! A Collection of Latina Poetry*, *The Floating Borderlands: 25 Years of U.S. Hispanic Literature*, and *American Poetry: The Next Generation*. She teaches in the creative writing program at the University of New Mexico.

Patricia Clark is an award-winning poet who is both a professor in the Department of Writing and the poet-in-residence at Grand Valley State University in Allendale, Michigan. Author of *My Father on a Bicycle* and *North of Wondering*, her poetry has also appeared in magazines such as *Atlantic Monthly*, *Poetry*, *Slate*, *Strand*, *New England Review*, *North American Review*, *Pennsylvania Review*, *Black Warrior Review*, and *Seattle Review*. She is the recipient of a Creative Artist Grant from ArtServe Michigan for 2003. She is also the coeditor of *Worlds in Our Words: An Anthology of Contemporary American Women Writers*. A new full-length book of poems, *She Walks into the Sea*, came out in 2009, as did a chapbook, *Given the Trees*.

Stephen Dunn has written fourteen collections of poetry and has won the Pulitzer Prize for Poetry for his 2001 collection, *Different Hours*. He has taught at Wichita State University, the University of Washington, Columbia University, the University of Michigan, Princeton University, and the Richard Stockton College of New Jersey. Dunn now spends time at homes in Ocean City, New Jersey, and Frostburg, Maryland.

Nancy Eimers is the author of three collections of poetry: *A Grammar to Waking*, *No Moon* (winner of the 1997 Verna Emery Prize), and *Destroying Angel*. She has been the recipient of a Nation "Discovery" Award, two National Endowment for the Arts Creative Writing Fellowships, and a Whiting Writer's Award. She teaches creative writing at Western Michigan University and at Vermont College.

Blas Falconer is the author of *A Question of Gravity and Light*. He directs the creative writing program at Austin Peay State University and is the poetry editor for *Zone 3: A Literary Journal* and Zone 3 Press.

Alice George lives in Evanston, Illinois, and teaches as a visiting poet in area schools and libraries and as an instructor at the University of Chicago's Graham School. She served as an editor of *RHINO* for ten years and is now on the advisory board of that award-wining magazine. Her poetry and prose have appeared in such magazines as *Diagram*, *Bellingham Review*, *Sentence*, *Denver*

Quarterly, Another Chicago Magazine, Quarter after Eight, New Orleans Review, American Literary Review, and *Spoon River Poetry Review.* A seven-time recipient of Ragdale Foundation Fellowships, George was awarded an Illinois Arts Council Fellowship for Poetry in 2005.

Jeff Hardin teaches at Columbia State Community College in Columbia, Tennessee. He is the author of two chapbooks and one collection, *Fall Sanctuary,* which received the 2004 Nicholas Roerich Prize from Story Line Press. His poems have appeared in *Southern Review, Gettysburg Review, Ploughshares, New Republic, Florida Review, Mid-American Review, Smartish Pace, West Branch, Measure,* and others.

A. Van Jordan is the author of *Quantum Lyrics, Rise,* and *M-A-C-N-O-L-I-A.* Among other awards, Jordan has received the Whiting Award, the Anisfield-Wolf Book Award, the PEN/Oakland Josephine Miles Award, and the Pushcart Prize. He teaches at the University of Michigan.

Claire Kageyama-Ramakrishnan is the author of *Shadow Mountain,* winner of the 2006 Four Way Books Intro Prize. She is a full-time instructor at Houston Community College, Central Campus. Her second book, *Bear, Diamonds and Crane,* will be published in 2011. She lives in Houston with her husband, Raj, and their three cats.

David Keplinger is the author of three collections of poetry, most recently *The Prayers of Others,* which won the 2006 Colorado Book Award, and *The Clearing,* which was short-listed for the 2005 Colorado Book Award and the Akhmatova Award for Excellence in Writing. His first collection, *The Rose Inside,* won the 1999 T. S. Eliot Prize. Keplinger has received grants and fellowships from the National Endowment for the Arts, the Pennsylvania Council on the Arts, the SOROS Foundation, the Academy of American Poets, and the Katey Lehman Foundation. He directs the MFA program in creative writing at American University.

Phillis Levin is the author of four volumes of poetry: *Temples and Fields* (winner of the Poetry Society of America's Norma Farber First Book Award), *The Afterimage, Mercury,* and *May Day.* She is the editor of *The Penguin Book of the Sonnet: 500 Years of a Classic Tradition in English.* Her poems have appeared in numerous literary publications, such as the *New Yorker, Paris Review, Poetry, New Republic,* and *Atlantic.* Levin's honors include an Ingram Merrill Grant, a Fulbright Scholar Award, the Amy Lowell Poetry Travelling Scholarship, and fellowships from the Guggenheim Foundation and the National Endowment for the Arts. She is a professor of English and the poet-in-residence at Hofstra University and also teaches in the graduate creative writing program at New York University.

Elline Lipkin's first book of poems, *The Errant Thread,* won the Kore Press First Book Award and was published in 2006. Her poems have appeared in the journals *Crab Orchard Review, Margie, North American Review,* and *Texas Review* and in the anthology *The Poets' Grimm: 20th Century Poems from Grimm Fairy Tales.* From 2004 to 2006 she was a postdoctoral scholar with the Beatrice Bain Research Group on Gender at the University of California at Berkeley. She is currently a research scholar with the Center for the Study of Women at UCLA where her work focuses on girls' studies and contemporary American women's poetry. Her book *Girls' Studies* was published in 2009.

Beth Martinelli has taught writing and literature at several colleges and universities, including Slippery Rock University and Saint Vincent College. Her poems have appeared in such journals as *Threepenny Review, Bellingham Review,* and *Pleiades.* Her chapbook, *To Darkness,* was published in 2007.

Shara McCallum has published two books of poems, *Song of Thieves* and *The Water Between Us* (winner of the 1998 Agnes Lynch Starrett Poetry Prize). Her poems and personal essays have appeared in literary journals in the United States and abroad and have been reprinted in over twenty anthologies of American, African American, Caribbean, and world poetry. Originally from Jamaica, McCallum directs the Stadler Center for Poetry and teaches at Bucknell University. She lives in Pennsylvania with her family.

Maria Melendez teaches creative writing and literature courses at Utah State University. Her first book-length collection of poetry, *How Long She'll Last in This World,* was awarded Honorable Mention at the 2007 International Latino Book Awards and was named a finalist for the 2007 PEN USA Literary Awards. Her next collection, *Flexible Bones: Poems,* is forthcoming in 2010.

Helena Mesa is the author of *Horse Dance Underwater.* She lives in Ann Arbor, Michigan, and teaches at Albion College.

Deirdre O'Connor is director of the Bucknell University Writing Center and associate director of the Bucknell Seminar for Younger Poets. Her first book, *Before the Blue Hour,* received the 2001 Cleveland State Poetry Prize. She has completed a second book manuscript, "Notes on Disappearance."

William Olsen is the author of four collections of poetry: *The Hand of God and a Few Bright Flowers, Vision of a Storm Cloud, Trouble Lights,* and *Avenue of Vanishing.* He is the recipient of a Guggenheim Fellowship, a National Endowment for the Arts Creative Writing Fellowship, a Nation/Discovery Award, the Texas Institute of Arts Award, a Breadloaf Fellowship, and poetry awards from *Poetry Northwest* and *Crazyhorse.* He was recently named editor of New Issues Press. He teaches creative writing and literature at Western Michigan University and at Vermont College.

Cecilia Pinto's fiction and poetry have been published in a number of journals and magazines including *RHINO, Fence,* and *Quarter after Eight.* Her short story "Monster" won *Esquire Magazine*'s 2000 short fiction contest, and her haiku took first place in Permafrost's annual contest in 2002. Her work is anthologized in *The City Visible: Chicago Poetry for the New Century.* Her collaborative work with Alice George appears in the anthology *Saints of Hysteria: A Half-Century of Collaborative American Poetry.* She teaches in Chicago.

Stanley Plumly's work has been honored with the Delmore Schwartz Memorial Award and nominations for the National Book Critics Circle Award, the William Carlos Williams Award, and the Academy of American Poets' Lenore Marshall Poetry Prize. *Now That My Father Lies Down Beside Me: New and Selected Poems, 1970–2000* received an Academy Award from the American Academy of Arts and Letters in 2001. *Old Heart* was nominated for the National Book Award in Poetry and received the Los Angeles Times Book Prize and the Paterson Poetry Prize. *Posthumous Keats: A Personal Biography* is his most recent work. He is currently a Distinguished University Professor and professor of English at the University of Maryland.

Kevin Prufer's most recent books are *National Anthem* and *Fallen from a Chariot.* With Wayne Miller, he is also editor of the anthology *New European Poets* and *Pleiades: A Journal of New Writing.* His work has won three Pushcart Prizes and appeared in *Best American Poetry, American Poetry Review, Georgia Review, Virginia Quarterly Review,* and elsewhere. His next book, *Little Paper Sacrifice,* will be published in 2011.

Susanna Rich is author of *Television Daddy* and *The Drive Home,* the 2008 Featured Poet of *Darkling Literary Magazine,* a Fulbright Fellow in Creative

Writing, and baseball poet for the documentary *Cobb Field*. She tours in the staged, one-woman, audience-interactive poetry experience *Television Daddy* and appears in *Shakespeare's *itches* (opening in 2010). Professor of English and Distinguished Teacher at Kean University in New Jersey, Rich teaches such courses as Emily Dickinson, William Blake, Writing Poetry, Poetry and the Poetic Experience, and 20th Century American Women Poets. Please visit her at www.susannarich.com.

Mira Rosenthal is the translator of *The Forgotten Keys* by Polish poet Tomasz Różycki. She is now working on his most recent volume, *Colonies*, for which she received the PEN Translation Fund Award and a National Endowment for the Arts fellowship. Her translations have appeared in numerous journals and anthologies, most recently *A Public Space*, *AGNI Online*, *Literary Review*, and *Poetry Daily*. Her own poetry has appeared in such journals as *American Poetry Review*, *Ploughshares*, *Notre Dame Review*, and *Beloit Poetry Journal*, among others. She is the recipient of a Fulbright Fellowship and has been a resident at the MacDowell Colony and the Banff Centre.

Metta Sáma is a textual and visual artist. Her poems, reviews, and scholarly articles have been published under her legal name (Lydia Melvin) and her adopted name. Originally from Chattanooga, Tennessee, she is composing a lyric–narrative–song cycle–"biomyth"–journalism piece about the places that rendered magnolias, moons, and dampened bridges objective correlatives.

Mary Ann Samyn's books of poetry include *Inside the Yellow Dress*, *Purr*, and *Beauty Breaks In*. Her poems have appeared in *Field*, *Denver Quarterly*, *Colorado Review*, *Court Green*, *Meridian*, *Pleiades*, and elsewhere. She teaches in the MFA program at West Virginia University where she is an associate professor of English and, currently, Bolton Professor of Teaching and Mentoring.

Jane Satterfield, a 2007 National Endowment for the Arts Fellow in Literature, is the author of two collections of poetry: *Shepherdess with an Automatic* and *Assignation at Vanishing Point*. She is a recipient of three Individual Artist Awards in poetry from the Maryland State Arts Council, and her poems have been anthologized in *Sweeping Beauty: Contemporary Women Poets on Housework* and *White Ink: Poets on Mothers and Mothering*. Her prose has been awarded the Gold Medal for the Essay from the Pirate's Alley Faulkner Society, the John Guyon Award in Literary Nonfiction, the *Florida Review*'s Editors' Prize, and the Heekin Foundation's Cuchulain Fellowship for the Essay. *Daughters of Empire: A Memoir of a Year in Britain and Beyond* was published in 2009.

Angela Sorby is the author of *Distance Learning* (poems), *Schoolroom Poets* (criticism), and *Bird Skin Coat* (poems). She teaches at Marquette University.

Michael Theune is the editor of *Structure and Surprise: Engaging Poetic Turns.* His poems, essays, and reviews have appeared in numerous journals, including, most recently, *Alaska Quarterly Review, Pindeldyboz,* and *Pleiades.* He teaches English at Illinois Wesleyan University.

Diane Thiel is the author of eight books of poetry, nonfiction, and creative writing pedagogy: *Echolocations* (Nicholas Roerich Prize), *Resistance Fantasies, The White Horse: A Colombian Journey, Writing Your Rhythm, Crossroads: Creative Writing Exercises in Four Genres, Open Roads: Exercises in Writing Poetry, Winding Roads: Exercises in Writing Creative Nonfiction,* and *Cleft in the Wall* (chapbook). Thiel's translation of Alexis Stamatis's poetic novel *American Fugue* (a translation that received a National Endowment for the Arts International Literature Award) appeared in 2008. Her work is found in many journals, including *Poetry, Hudson Review, Sewanee Review,* and *Best American Poetry 1999*; is reprinted in over forty major anthologies, including *Twentieth Century American Poetry* and *Contemporary American Poetry*; and has been translated widely. A recipient of numerous awards, including the Robert Frost and Robinson Jeffers Awards, and a Fulbright Scholar, she is associate professor at the University of New Mexico. For more information, please visit www.dianethiel.net.

Michael Waters has published eight books of poems, including *Darling Vulgarity* (finalist for the Los Angeles Times Book Prize) and *Parthenopi: New and Selected Poems* (finalist for the Paterson Poetry Prize), and has edited several volumes, including *Contemporary American Poetry.* He has been the recipient of fellowships from the National Endowment for the Arts and the Fulbright Foundation, Individual Artist Awards from the Maryland State Arts Council, and four Pushcart Prizes. He teaches at Monmouth University and in the Drew University MFA Program and lives in Ocean, New Jersey.